ADVENTURES OF A
BASEBALL FAN

Baseball Diamonds are This Girl's Best Friend

CANDY L. VANDYKE

authorHOUSE®

Candy L Vandyke
June 2011

AuthorHouse™
1663 Liberty Drive
Bloomington, IN 47403
www.authorhouse.com
Phone: 1-800-839-8640

First published by AuthorHouse 8/26/2010

ISBN: 978-1-4520-2335-9 (e)
ISBN: 978-1-4520-2333-5 (sc)
ISBN: 978-1-4520-2334-2 (hc)

Library of Congress Control Number: 2010912571

Printed in the United States of America

This book is printed on acid-free paper.

This wonderful experience would not have been possible without the help and support of so many people. Some took care of things on the home front when I was gone; others shuttled me to and from airports, traveled with me, or kept me company through phone calls when I traveled alone. Then there was the kindness of strangers and those who kept me in their prayer while I was on my adventures. I am deeply grateful to all of you.

I am especially thankful for my sister Cindy for going above and beyond in every category. It was also her creative thinking that came up with the subtitle for this book.

CONTENTS

HOW IT ALL BEGAN

Growing up, I was never a big baseball fan. Sure, there were softball games in school and with the neighbor kids, but I never attended a baseball game or even watched the sport on TV. My family watched football and car racing. When I got older, I chose the New York Mets as my team, mostly because I grew up in upstate New York and they weren't the Yankees. I have always been drawn to the underdog, and the Mets seemed to me to be the opposite of the big-name, big-budget Yankees. I could name few of the players, but I was pleased when the Mets did well. I remember hearing a great deal about the 1986 World Series, although I didn't watch it until almost two decades later. I had been married the year before, and there was plenty going on in my life. Watching baseball wasn't a priority. At the time I was happy the Mets won. My new mother-in-law was a huge Yankees fan. I was so impressed that she knew all the players and watched as many games as she could. I still wasn't that big a fan of the game, but I would sit and watch a game with her on occasion.

In 1992 the Mets' Double-A farm team, the B-Mets, moved to Binghamton, New York, not too far from where we lived. We always meant to get to a game but never did. My husband and I split up in 1998. A friend of mine from church would get B-Mets tickets on occasion, so we would go games together sometimes. I got to know a few of the players. Every once in a while as I was flipping through channels, I would see a game on and recognize some of the players I had seen in Binghamton. I saw Jose

1

Reyes, David Wright, Ty Wigginton, Mike Jacobs, Lasting Milledge, Carlos Gomez, Mike Pelfrey, Nick Evans, Daniel Murphy, Joe Smith, and Bobby Parnell play in Binghamton, to mention a few. I found myself becoming more and more of a fan of the game and of the New York Mets.

Another friend of mine, Eric, was also a big fan of baseball. He and I would go to see the B-Mets whenever we had the opportunity. It was at one of those games in 2002 that he suggested I might like to go to a major-league game. I hadn't really thought about it before. Why not? Eric's idea was all the encouragement I needed. We made plans to go to see my first big-league game. Eric had gone to college in Boston and was a big Red Sox fan, and I had never been to Boston, so that was where we decided to go.

We decided to spend a couple of days in the Boston area to see some of the sights. We stayed at a hotel in Danvers, Massachusetts, on Route 1. I remember it so well, because it was one of those places where, when you ask someone how to get somewhere they say "you can't get there from here."

The first day there we bought a little propane grill and a large pot so we could cook out some clams and lobsters. We found a nice park near a quarry while we were wandering around Salem and had a little cookout. Or we tried to, anyway. It was a cool day for June, and the wind eventually won out. We ended up cooking the lobsters on the balcony of the hotel.

The next day we tried to find a beach so that I could stick my toe in the ocean. We ended up going all the way to New Hampshire because most of the beaches near our hotel were private. On the way back we happened upon a small fair. We decided to stop to ride the Ferris wheel and play some carnival games.

The last two nights of our trip we stayed in downtown Boston. We found a place to park the car and planned on taking the T, as the subway in Boston is known, for getting around town. We went to the waterfront, the aquarium, and Quincy Market on the first afternoon. Eric had asked me to bring something a little dressy along. The night before the game, I found out why. He had made surprise reservations at the Top of the Hub restaurant, on the fifty-second floor of the Prudential Building. Our reservations were for 8:00 PM. We got ready and took the T to our destination. As we arrived at our table, we were greeted by the beautiful sight of lights coming on around the city. Before long, a full moon peaked over the harbor. It was breathtaking! That night it became clear to me why people love Boston.

The game was the next day, but not until the evening. In the morning we decided to go out on a whale watch, which was a lot of fun. We weren't having too much luck seeing whales, so they kept us out a little longer than was scheduled. The delay made us a little nervous because we needed to go back to the hotel before the game to change into our fan garb. I had purchased a t-shirt at Quincy Market just for the occasion.

It was a close one, but we made it to the park in time for my first major-league baseball game on Tuesday, June 25, 2002, at Fenway Park in Boston. As we walked toward the stadium in a crowd of people, there was so much anticipation and excitement all around. Everywhere I looked, people showed their support for their team and favorite players with all kinds of shirts and hats. I was a bit envious of the true fandom on display. Little did I know I would become just like them! I didn't know what to expect so I just watched, listened, and followed Eric.

We had grandstand seats. When we ordered tickets, we couldn't get seats right next to each other, so we got seats in two different rows but very close together. One was in the second to the last row and the other one in the last row of the grandstand. The seating was the original wooden chairs. We started out sitting next to each other in the last row, and fortunately no one came to kick us out of the seats. Sitting in the last row made it easier to get out, as we could climb over the back of the seat and sneak out through the railings into the standing-room area behind us, rather than bother the entire row to let us pass by. As the game went on and more beer was consumed by the guys standing near the railing, sneaking out that way became more challenging. But we dealt with it.

The Red Sox were playing the Cleveland Indians. I knew very little about either team, but Eric had been following baseball for years and had been to both team's games before. He had a good knowledge of the game and the players, so I felt comfortable asking him questions, which I did—a lot!

There was something about the Red Sox players that intrigued me right away. The players were a diverse group, yet their teamwork was extremely apparent. They really seemed to enjoy themselves. The park itself was awesome. Our seats were on the first base side facing the Green Monster, which was totally cool! 2002 was Fenway's ninetieth anniversary, and there was a large sign in the center of the Green Monster to celebrate that fact. Boston, being a sports town, just had a feeling of celebration in the air. I was overwhelmed trying to take it all in. Fenway Park had a life of its own. It felt like we were so close to the field, even in row seventeen. I was awestruck, to say the least. From our seats, the famous CITGO sign on top of a nearby building was visible and was especially beautiful when lit up after nightfall.

The game was not off to a very good start for the Red Sox. The Indians scored three runs in the first inning when Jim Thome, a name I became all too familiar with over the next several years, hit a home run with two on— one of which had been a leadoff walk. I reminded myself I was at *Fenway* even so, and I was so excited to be there. The score didn't matter that much to me. After all, it was early in the game.

I got to see some of the players who would become my favorites: Johnny Damon, Nomar Garciaparra, and Jason Varitek to mention a few. Garciaparra hit a high fly ball that I was sure would prove to be the first Red Sox home run, but it wasn't deep enough. Then the place got crazy loud. I wasn't sure what was going on. I looked at Eric quizzically. It turned out that Manny Ramirez, who had been on the disabled list with a thumb injury, was coming up to bat. The place went wild. I had never experienced anything like it. Manny lined out to end the bottom of the first, but it didn't matter. I was in awe!

Cleveland scored another run in the second inning to make it Indians 4, Red Sox 0. But it was early in the game. In the bottom of the second I saw a few more of my favorites for the first time, including Shea Hillenbrand, Trot Nixon, and Tony Clark (who drive in the first run) *Here we go*, I thought. A walk loaded the bases. I could hardly contain myself! Damon came to the plate and I was sure it was going to be a big play. He only hit a single, but a run scored. We had hope. The rally was short-lived, but the lead was cut in half.

There were only a couple of more hits the rest of the game, and no more runs scored. The home team lost 4–2, but I had fallen in love with Fenway Park, the Boston Red Sox, and the game of baseball. One of the things that I thought was really neat was the singing of the song "Sweet

Caroline" in the middle of the eighth inning, and how the whole crowd got into singing along. I thought it was consistent with the team spirit so present in Boston.

After the game we took the T back to the hotel. We went down the stairs into the subway station, got our tokens, and made our way to the platform. Eric knew I wasn't fond of crowds, so he stayed close. The subway was running extra cars on game nights and departed every few minutes, so it didn't take long before we got on. It was beyond crowded. I was hugging a pole in the very front of a car and Eric was standing on the steps. He kept an eye on me and kept asking if I was alright. I was less than thrilled, but refused to let the crowded T ride ruin my magical baseball night—a three hours and thirteen minutes game at *Fenway*! We were packed in like sardines, with a significant percentage of more than 34,000 people trying to get home on the T at the same time. We were so close that I could tell you how much change the gentleman behind me had in his pocket! Eric told me later that night that my face was getting redder and redder as the subway car moved. It took me a long time before I could explain to him why. That train ride sure was a culture shock for a country girl like me.

At the end of that 2002 season, I heard about the Red Sox hiring a new general manager, the eleventh GM since the position was established in 1933. The new GM was Theo Epstein. He was the youngest general manager in major league history at twenty-eight years old. He grew up only a mile from Fenway Park and had been a fan of the Red Sox all his life. What a dream come true for him. As time went on, Theo would make dreams come true for the team and fans as well.

NEW YORK, NEW YORK 2003

I couldn't wait to get to more major-league games. The logical next step was to visit the home of my favorite team, the New York Mets. As fate would have it, the Mets were Eric's second favorite team, so he was up for another road trip. As soon as tickets went on sale, we booked seats and made our plans.

My second live major-league baseball experience came almost exactly ten months after my first. On April 27, 2003, we traveled to New York City's Shea Stadium for a Saturday afternoon game against the Arizona Diamondbacks. We were planning to drive down see the game and drive back afterward, as it was only a three-and-a-half-hour trip each way. We left a little early that morning because Eric had planned to show me the Unisphere in Flushing Meadows Park, but it was raining so we didn't stick around the park for long.

We parked in the stadium lot and then walked around so I could take some pictures. The park looked so big from the outside! The images of players on the outside of the stadium made out of lights were particularly neat. We decided to go into the stadium despite the rain. We had brought our rain gear, which came in handy even though our seats were under the overhang. As fond as I was of Shea Stadium, it really didn't have many special features—except the apple that pops up after Mets home runs. I did like that. Shea seemed so big compared to Fenway, which at the time was my only point of reference.

After waiting for the rain to stop for about three hours they finally announced that the game was postponed. I wasn't sure what that meant until they announced we could exchange our tickets for admission the next day, when they would play the make-up game and a regularly scheduled game. Oh boy, two games for the price of one!

We debated whether to drive home and back in the morning but decided it was prudent to just stay in New York for the night. We found a hotel and got something to eat at a local diner. I had never spent time anywhere near New York City, so it was an added bonus to get to stay the night in Queens.

I didn't understand the significance of the pitching matchups at the time, but I was in for a real treat. In the first game it was Tom Glavine for the Mets against Brandon Webb for the Diamondbacks. In 2007, Tom Glavine got his 295th career win against the Yankees, and I was there!

Glavine wasn't exactly at his best against the Diamondbacks. He walked the leadoff hitter. I had already seen how bad leadoff walks were the previous year in Boston. The free pass did result in the first run for Arizona. After the top of the first, there were no other hits by either team until the bottom of the fourth when Ty Wigginton, a former B-Met, hit a single with one out. We were only down by one, so a rally could easily tie it or even give the Mets the lead! Well, the excitement was short-lived. A double play ended the inning. At least I was getting to see players who would join the ranks of my favorites: Mike Piazza, Cliff Floyd, Mo Vaughn, and Ty Wigginton, to mention a few.

Glavine came back to the mound for the top of the fifth. The first batter hit an infield single and took second base on a Glavine throwing error. Not good! The second batter made it safely to first on another Mets throwing error. Well then. Brandon Webb came up next with one out and hit a sacrifice to advance the runners. A double scored two more Arizona runs. Now we were down by three, and running out of chances to catch up.

In the seventh inning, the first Arizona batter hit a solo home run. Ugh! The Mets were down by four. Next came a double, and then a single advanced the runner to third. Still no outs and two men on! I did not like the way the game was going at all. I didn't yet fully understand the intricacies of the game, pitching changes, etc. I felt rather hopeless at that point. Again, Webb hit a sacrifice, moving the trailing runner into scoring position. That was one out.

Maybe we could stop them. Nope. A single drove in two more runs! Finally, a Mets pitching change. We got out of the inning without any further damage.

In the bottom of the seventh we got a glimmer of hope when Mike Piazza singled, but his efforts were wasted. In the top of the eighth, Tony Clark, whom I had seen play in Boston the previous year, came in to play first base. That move paid off in the bottom of the inning. Clark hit a home run! The apple popped up in celebration! The score was now 6–1 Arizona, which ended up being the final score. The game took just about two and a half hours. I'd learned more about baseball and still had another game to see that very afternoon, so I wasn't too bummed.

In the second game of that doubleheader, I got to see the "Big Unit," Randy Johnson, pitch for Arizona. Even from our seats in the left field stands, he looked really tall. The Mets scored first in the bottom of the second inning. Alas, Arizona came back to score two in the top of the third. Humph! The Mets tied it up in the bottom of the third. Randy Johnson drove in the go-ahead run in the top of the fourth, with a little help from a throwing error that allowed the runner to score. Ugh! Both pitchers settled in and only gave up a few scattered hits over the next few innings.

The fan giveaway that day was a Mets cap. I was so pleased to have such a treasured memento of my beloved Mets. Our seats were the first row in the upper deck in left field. April baseball can be a bit chilly. Eric pulled me onto his lap to share our warmth. At one particularly disappointing moment, I leaned forward and covered my face with my hands. My hat toppled down behind the sign in front of our seats. I was embarrassed for letting such a silly thing happen, but I was also sad to have lost my treasured gift. After a couple of minutes, Eric took a plastic bag that had been blowing around the stands, ripped it into strips, tied the strips together, tied his pocket knife to the improvised rope, and lowered the rig to retrieve my hat. He had rescued my hat! He was definitely my hero that day, and yes, I have that hat to this day.

In the top of the seventh the Diamondbacks scored another run, and I learned what a balk was. A pinch hitter came up and drove in another Diamondback run. A real disappointment came in the top of the ninth when closer Armando Benitez took the mound for New York, only to walk the first batter. Eric was all too familiar with Armando's antics. A subsequent double put runners in scoring position with one out. A sacrifice fly led to one more run. A home run scored two more runs, making the score Diamondbacks 7, Mets 2. Ty Wigginton was able to produce one more run for the Mets, making the final score 7–3 in favor of the visitors.

Even though the Mets lost both games that day, I was happy to spend some time in the home stadium of my team and to see two games in one day with over 36,000 of my fellow fans. I realized there was nothing like seeing baseball in person. Thus the madness began.

Early in April we had made plans to go to another game as well. Yankee Stadium was a little closer to home than Shea, so we could certainly make a day trip there as well. On May 26, which was Memorial Day that year, a day we both had off, the Yankees were playing the Red Sox. The choice was clear.

It was early in the season, but the Yankees–Red Sox rivalry was already dialed up. I hadn't realized how big a rivalry it was until that Memorial Day game. The visit to Yankee Stadium was my second visit to New York City, which was a source of additional excitement for me.

It was a fairly nice day, overcast and with a cold breeze. We parked in a small lot down the street from the park and walked over. The stadium was so big, and I was surprised about how close it was to everything. Having only been to two other stadiums, I wasn't sure what to expect. We went in and found our seats, which were in the very top section, not too far from the last row of seats. The stadium looked even bigger from that vantage point. The seats were behind home plate, a little to the third base side. Did I mention we were very high up? The stands were steep up there. The white façade around the top of the stadium was definitely unique, and the dramatic interlocked "NY" logo painted behind home plate really stood out as well.

This pitching matchup was a good one. The Rocket, Roger Clemens, for the Yankees against knuckleballer Tim Wakefield for Boston. I had no idea what a knuckleball was, but I was looking forward to finding out.

Manny Ramirez got things started in the second inning, helped by Kevin Millar and Shea Hillenbrand. I liked how Millar played. His big heart would become very apparent the following year. For now, the team I was rooting for had a lead and I was excited. It was early in the game, so Eric warned me not to get too excited. Superstition is a big thing in baseball, and not just with the players. I was learning not to get too excited or gloat, because that would jinx the team. There was so much to know, but I was determined to learn as much as I could.

I was becoming familiar with some of the players on the Boston team and had my favorites. One of those favorites was Nomar Garciaparra, who was the shortstop for the Red Sox at the time. I so enjoyed watching him prepare for his at-bats. His ritual was almost robotic, full of glove tightening and toe tapping exactly the same every time he came to the plate.

In the second inning Todd Walker singled, Garciaparra singled, and Ramirez was intentionally walked. I didn't understand why a pitcher would put someone on base on purpose at the time. Trot Nixon drew a walk to bring home a second run. This was the first time I had seen a run walked in, and it was by Roger Clemens! Millar hit a sacrifice fly, which allowed Garciaparra to score. *Two more runs for the good guys,* I said to myself very carefully.

Wakefield had already struck out three by the third inning, facing only three batters in that inning. I was impressed! He also became another one of my favorite players. Watching him pitch just amazed me.

In the top of the fourth, Bill Mueller hit a single, and Doug Mirabelli hit a single behind him. Both runners advanced on a Johnny Damon sacrifice. Yes, Damon played for the Red Sox at that time. Walker grounded out but it was enough for Mueller to score and Mirabelli to make it to third. Mirabelli then scored on a Clemens wild pitch. The Red Sox were ahead 5–0. Being fairly new to the game, I got really excited, much to Eric's chagrin.

I was quickly disheartened when the Yankees scored three runs in the bottom of the inning with the help of a one-out walk and a throwing error. Nothing good can come from a walk! That was when Eric admonished me with a stern "You can never count the Yankees out; ever!"

Fortunately, the Red Sox scored three more runs in the sixth, helped partly by a Yankee throwing error. The Yankees scored only one more run, coming in the seventh when the Red Sox pitcher walked the lead-off batter (leadoff walks are never good!). There were only two more hits the rest of the way, both by Red Sox. The final score was Red Sox 8, Yankees 4.

I was very happy to finally see one of "my" teams win a game, especially in their main rival's "house," in front of over 55,000 fans. I also learned that Red Sox-Yankees games typically ran longer than most. This contest was three and a half hours long.

WHERE TO NEXT?

On the drive home, we couldn't help but talk about what our next adventure was going to be. We came up with the idea to combine baseball and camping, two of our favorite things, and planned a camping trip for June. The plan was to spend a weekend in Philadelphia, catch a game, followed by a week camping in Delaware, and then wrap it up with a game in Baltimore. Research was done, tickets were bought, and reservations were made. I was psyched!

A month later, we were heading for Philadelphia on a Friday night to see the Red Sox play the Philadelphia Phillies. This was going to be my first interleague game. Mind you, I was still learning which teams were in which league and division, so interleague play was an added wrinkle. I knew there was a difference in the leagues in style of play, but I understood little else about the divide between AL and NL.

It was a three and a half hour drive, so we left work early with plans to check in to the hotel and then go to the game. Unfortunately on our way there, it started storming big time. At times we could hardly see the road, and traffic was moving very slowly. The hour was getting later and later.

We debated whether to even try to get to the hotel or go straight to Veterans Stadium, the home of the Phillies at that time. We were hoping that we would pass through the storm and the game could still be played. Eric's boss (I also worked at the same company part time) called to tell us the game was postponed. We weren't sure how to respond, because he was always teasing us, but then we heard confirmation on the radio. The storm had thwarted us. We knew they would play that game at some point, so the tickets would still get us into a game.

Once we got to the hotel, we ruminated on what to do with the rest of our time in Philly. Eric had an idea: the postponed game was the first of a three-game series so why not see if we could get tickets for the Saturday game? We could, and I got to see my first interleague game the next day.

We got to the stadium, parked the car, and headed inside. The Vet was a big, somewhat generic-looking stadium, just like you would expect a multi-purpose park to look like. It was an overcast day in the mid sixties. What better to do on such a day than watch a baseball game, especially when the Red Sox were playing?

The seating capacity was over 62,000, and the stadium felt very large, even compared to both Shea and Yankee stadiums. Our seats were fairly close to the field in the first level that went all the way around the stadium. But we were situated way down the first-base line, which isn't my favorite vantage point. We both agreed that we would rather be higher up and closer to home plate than looking in from the outfield. But we were still ready to watch a baseball game!

As it turned out, we would get to see a pitcher who in my mind was one of the greatest ever, Pedro Martinez. He had been with Boston since 1998, so Eric was very familiar with him and liked him very much.

In the top of the first, Nomar Garciaparra a hit single off Randy Wolf but his teammates couldn't bring him around. In the bottom of the first, Jim Thome got the only hit for the Phillies but was stranded. I had seen Thome hit a three-run home run in Boston at my very first game when he was with the Indians. He definitely made me nervous.

Both pitchers were looking really good. But in the bottom of the second, the first batter proceeded to hit a home run off Pedro. Oops! Okay, it was only the second inning so we had time. I told myself to calm down. I was learning that one run could make or break the game. Martinez settled in and got the next three batters out, which helped to calm me.

In the top of the third, Todd Walker hit a home run to tie the game. Wahoo! That was the last hit for the next three innings. In the top of the sixth, Walker did it again! He hit another home run, and I felt like I could breathe a little bit.

Martinez pitched through seven with the lead still intact. In the eighth, Mike Timlin came in to pitch for Boston. With two outs, Thome hit a home run to tie the game. My concerns about Thome were justified! No fingernails were safe now.

That game became my first experience with extra innings. In the top of the twelfth inning, Garciaparra hit a single. Yeah! We were getting it going! Kevin Millar hit a triple and Garciaparra scored. The Red Sox had taken the lead again!

In the bottom of the twelfth, the first batter struck out, the second batter flied out ... one more out and we would be home free! Jim Thome came to the plate and yep, he hit another home run to tie the game again. On to the thirteenth! Can you say disbelief?

In the top of the thirteenth, Johnny Damon hit a single with two outs and then stole second! Walker hit a double, and Damon scored to regain the lead for Boston. Garciaparra hit a single and Walker scored to give us the biggest lead of the game, 5–3! There was hope! Just three more outs and the game was ours! Oh how I wanted to see the Red Sox win like they did against the Yankees!

In the top of the thirteenth inning a walk to the leadoff batter! Uh oh—nothing good could come from that! A fly out advanced the runner to second. A double scored a run, bringing the lead down to one. My heart was in my throat! We still had the lead, I told myself, with only two outs to go. What were the chances they would score two runs? A pinch hitter and a pitching change just made me more nervous. My nerves were justified when Todd Pratt hit a homer. Two runs and the Phillies had won just like that. The leadoff walk came back to bite us—go figure! Game over! I was stunned at how fast it happened. The Phillies won 6–5 in just under five hours in front of over 35,000 fans, but what a game it was! It took me a while to get over the shock. We made our way back to the hotel and grabbed some dinner.

After that, I was ready for a relaxing week of camping and beach fun. On Sunday, we headed to Cape Henlopen, Delaware, site of a state park with a very nice ocean beach. We got to our site, set things up, and settled in for a week of camping.

We spent the first day on the beach. At one point in late morning we actually saw dolphins "playing" in the water. I am particularly fond of dolphins, so that was an unexpected treat. The dolphins seemed to be around for quite a while. Eric didn't have his glasses on so he didn't see them. Pretending not to believe me, he teased me about seeing dolphins whether we were on a beach or not. We spent time jumping through the waves and had a blast. Being on the beach and in the ocean is one of my favorite things to do.

We cooked most of our meals either on the portable grill or a camp stove. We had lobster, bluefish, and clams. During the week we went deep-sea fishing, which was a first for me. We also wandered around the park, drove to Wildwood to spend the day on the boardwalk and took the ferry back, another fantastic experience. There were dolphins that swam right along with the ferry. We spent another day on the beach and by Friday we were ready to pack it up and sleep somewhere other than on the ground.

We headed to Baltimore to see the Phillies play the Orioles. I was starting to become familiar with and develop a fondness for the Phillies, even though they are division rivals of my favorite non–Red Sox team, the Mets. We arrived at the park only after getting lost but still in time to see the game start. I have become a pretty good map reader, even though online mapping programs are usually all one needs. Once in a while there are glitches, and this was one of them. I hadn't before seen a case where an interstate and a state highway with the same number intersect. In this case I believe it was I-6 and state route 6. I promptly got us lost. Once we found our way we pretty much parked the car in the first lot we saw that wasn't full and sprinted to Camden Yards to make sure we saw the first pitch.

Camden Yards is a very unique ballpark, famous for its variety of food. There was a wide alleyway behind the right field seats where many of the food vendors are located. I really liked the clock atop the scoreboard with birds on either side of it. The warehouses beyond right field were very different. I was so impressed with the differences between the stadiums.

Our seats were down the first baseline beyond first base in the second section from the field. Not our favorite vantage point, but it was a warm, sunny day and what better place to be than at a baseball game in person? It's also great to watch a game on TV, but on TV you only get to see what the cameras point at. When you are there, you can see the interaction between the players and even between fans. Live baseball is just fantastic!

Having just seen the Phillies the weekend before, the players were still pretty fresh in my mind. In the top of the first, Jim Thome did what we had seen him do a few times already: hit a home run. This time it was okay with me. In the top of the second, the Phillies added another run to extend their lead on back-to-back doubles. I wasn't overly invested in either team but was more familiar with the Phillies, so I was happy that they were winning. I was focusing on learning more about the game. Fortunately, Eric was extremely patient and answered all my questions.

Despite a hit in each inning, the Orioles weren't able to score. In the top of the third the Phillies added two more runs. The Orioles got another hit in the third but it again came to nothing. I was beginning to wonder if this game was going to be a blowout. In the top of the fourth, Ricky Ledee, who came to play for the Mets in 2006, hit a home run to score two more runs after, you guessed it, a one-out walk. I was learning more about the game, seeing more players, and loving it!

In the bottom of the fourth, Baltimore scored their first run. That seemed to be the turning point for Baltimore. The fifth was the first Philadelphia scoreless innings. The Orioles scored two more runs, making for more of a game. It was an eye-opener to see how quickly the momentum of a game can shift. It helped that the Orioles had another baseball great, B. J. Ryan, pitch the sixth, posting another scoreless inning. Baltimore scored two more runs in the bottom of the sixth. The Phillies got one of the runs right back, to maintain a three-run lead. The Phils scored another run in the eighth, set up by Thome. He was a player I was really getting to know and fear, especially when he played against the team I was rooting for.

There were only a few more hits. The final score was Phillies 9, Orioles 5 in just under three hours, in front of a sellout crowd of 49,500. It wasn't the most exciting game I had seen, but it was a good learning experience, and the team I wanted to win won. So all was well.

The next morning we headed home. When we got home we were still on a baseball high from our trip. After we unloaded the car we decided to see if we could get another trip planned. Pittsburgh wasn't too far away, and they were playing the Houston Astros at home on July 5. We both had July 4 off, so Pittsburgh was our next target, a chance to see another ballpark and a couple more teams. We got tickets, found a hotel, and mapped out our trip to Pittsburgh. The following weekend we would be off to a game again!

In the Northeast, from spring to fall, it is not uncommon to encounter road construction. However, I had never seen the likes of what we encountered in Pittsburgh. We kept running into detour after detour. We finally got to the hotel and could only hope that getting to the ballpark wouldn't be as much of a hassle. But it was.

That game was only the second night game I had been to, so I was looking forward to seeing how the city looked from the ballpark. I wasn't disappointed. The skyline across the river was very nice, and the blue lights outlining the pedestrian ramps were a unique touch. I regretted not bringing my camera with me. The stadium was fairly generic in structure but the low wall in the outfield offered a very nice view of the river and the bridges crossing it.

We had really good seats for that game, fairly far up in the second section from the field, almost directly behind home plate. Even though it had been a bit of a hassle getting there, it was warm and clear, a perfect night to sit back and enjoy a baseball game.

I wasn't familiar with any of the players on either team so I wasn't sure who I would be rooting for. I was just excited to be seeing another park, two more teams, and another baseball game in person. There is nothing like being in the ballpark watching a game. I was still deciding if I preferred day games or night games.

Jeff Suppan was pitching for Pittsburgh, a pitcher I would see pitching for Boston in a couple of months in the makeup game from June's rainout in Philadelphia. Houston took a two-run lead in the top of the first. If it weren't for a fielder's choice, which Eric had to explain to me, that allowed Biggio to get tagged out at home, the lead would have been 3–0 Astros after the very first half-inning. I was seeing Houston's famous Killer B's, and I thought it was pretty cool. In the bottom of the inning, the Pirates made some noise of their own, scoring three runs. At that point I decided to root for Houston. I didn't realize it yet, but I was getting to see some truly great players.

Both pitchers settled in. Suppan only gave up two hits in the next couple of innings. He did his part at bat in the bottom of the fourth, hitting the second double of the inning to add another run. This prompted a pitching change for Houston. The score of Pittsburgh 4, Houston 2 held until the top of the ninth, which was when Geoff Blum, one of the Killer B's, hit a home run. But it wasn't enough, and Pittsburgh won 4–3 in front of a small crowd of about 22,000 in about three hours. We half-jokingly wondered if the detours kept the fans away.

We began the detour-laden trek back to the hotel. All told it was a nice drive to Pittsburgh. It was just getting around once we got there that was such a pain. We took back roads and enjoyed some beautiful countryside and small towns in route. We like to stop at non-chain restaurants when we travel, and were pleased to find a couple such places on our route.

TWO TWO TWO

When we got back home, we headed right for the computer to see what else we could plan for that summer. Cleveland wasn't too far and Eric had the idea of maybe seeing two games in one weekend. We grabbed the atlas from the car to see what ballparks were close enough to Cleveland to make it happen. Maybe Detroit? We checked to see if Detroit was home any of the same weekends as Cleveland.

We already had plans to visit a friend of Eric's in Chicago in August and had gotten tickets to see the White Sox, mostly because the Cubs weren't home that weekend. The Phillies–Red Sox makeup game was rescheduled for Labor Day weekend, so we had to work around those dates.

Both the Indians and Tigers were home the second weekend in August, so that was the plan. We got tickets, mapped out our route, and planned our trip. This would be a whirlwind trip. Two more ballparks, four more teams, and more new players for me!

We headed out early on Saturday and headed straight for Jacobs Field, which later became Progressive Field. We knew it would be a long day but we were excited to be headed to a game. We had taken going to a game to a new level: two games in two parks in two states in two days. Call me crazy, but I was loving it!

On the drive out we talked about the teams we had seen and the ones we were about to see. Eric had been to Jacobs Field before so he filled me in on all kinds of stuff. Jacobs Field was built in 1994 and was a really neat place. I love the way it teases you as you pass it on the highway. Once we got inside, I was very impressed with the scoreboard and the Home Run Porch in left field. They also had the team name painted behind home plate, which was done at most of the ballparks with the exception of Fenway and Camden Yards. I was expecting the place to fill up on a warm, mostly sunny Saturday afternoon but it really didn't. The crowd was fairly small, with only about 26,000 in attendance. The Indians were playing the Los Angeles Angels of Anaheim (then known as the Anaheim Angels), who I think had more name changes than any other team just since I have been following the game. I liked it when they were the Anaheim Angels the best but I am really not sure why.

At that time the Indians had Coco Crisp, who would eventually play for Boston after Johnny Damon went to the Yankees in 2006. Cleveland's lineup also featured Milton Bradley, whom I would eventually see play for the Angels, Dodgers, and Texas Rangers. The names stuck with me because to me, until then, they were a cereal and a board game manufacturer!

Both pitchers did a great job with a combined total of five hits, all singles, until the sixth inning. The game was going fast. Our seats were just below the upper deck, so we could see the skyline very well and enjoyed the view between innings.

In the bottom of the sixth inning, the game picked up a bit when Crisp started it off with a double and then scored the first run of the game. I was relieved to see some action, even though I think we were rooting for the Angels. Maybe that was just me. The next score was in the bottom of the seventh. What started as a single for the Indians ended with a runner on third because of an error. The runner then scored on a wild pitch. To me it looked like the Indians were going to walk away with the game.

Then, in the ninth, Danys Baez came in to pitch for Cleveland. Baez had been the starting pitcher in 2002 when the Indians beat the Red Sox, so I was sure they had it locked up. Not so. The Angels hit a single. The runner then took second in fielder's indifference, which Eric had to explain to me. The Angels ended up tying the game after a double plated one run and a combination of a wild pitch and passed ball brought home the man on second. Eric had to explain the difference between wild pitch and a passed ball to me. I was seeing my second extra inning game. So much for this game going fast. I was surprised!

The score remained tied until the bottom of the thirteenth, when Johnny Peralta started a rally that led to the winning run. The Indians won 3–2. The thirteen-inning game took just about three and a half hours. I was really learning a lot about the strategy of the game. I learned why a pitcher would intentionally walk a batter! With so much to learn from each game, I was looking forward to each and every one we could get to.

After the game we headed for Detroit in preparation for the next game the following afternoon. It was only a two and a half hour drive, so we planned on getting there in time for a late dinner. We got to the hotel and headed out to get some dinner. There was some construction on the street that the hotel was on, so we decided to head out on foot to find a place to eat. The only place we found was a take-out pizza place, so we got a pizza and took it back to the hotel. It had been a long day but we were pleased with our quest to see two games in two cities in two days.

The next morning we had breakfast and headed downtown to the stadium. We had to go right past old Tiger Stadium, so we found a place to park and took a stroll around the team's former home. It was so sad to see what the stadium looked like after a few years of disuse. I wished I had had an opportunity to see a game there. Tiger Stadium held so much history, but was just sitting there falling apart. The old park was built the same year as Fenway. There were empty lots and boarded-up buildings all around. The businesses that were around had bars on the windows. One place we stopped at for a snack had bulletproof glass protecting the cashier. I hadn't seen anything like that in my life.

We headed on downtown and found a parking spot. We ended up a ways away from the field but did find a free parking spot. It was a day game. and a nice day to boot, so the walk was not an issue. There was a presumably homeless man there that said he would watch the car if we bought a toothpick flag for a dollar. So we did, and he and the car were still there when we came back.

Comerica Park was so neat! On the outside there are tigers holding baseballs in their mouths adorning the top of the stadium. There are tiger statues at the entrances also. The facility was very family friendly, with a great deal of things to entertain kids and adults alike. There was even a small Ferris wheel with baseball-shaped cages. The concourse was filled with all kinds of activities. There was a fountain in the outfield with cars on top that was just amazing. It made me think of my stepdad, who passed away in 1993. He was a car guy and he would have liked to see that. In right field was the Pepsi Porch and just beyond it was a tall building with a several-story-high ocean scene painted on it, complete with whales. It was fantastic! There were also tigers on each side of the scoreboard facing inward. Comerica was something to see for sure.

We had good seats one level up on the first base side behind the visitor's dugout. I wasn't familiar with any of the players on the Tigers or the Minnesota Twins. Little did I know I was seeing one player in particular that I would come to be extremely fond of, Doug Mientkiewicz, who was part of the Red Sox team when they won the Series in 2004 and then played for the Mets in 2005. I found it odd that so few fans were there for a Sunday afternoon game. The attendance turned out to be less than 20,000 that day.

It was an exciting first inning. Mientkiewicz reached on a bunt to load the bases. Okay then! I am a Minnesota Vikings football fan, so I was leaning toward rooting for the Twins but didn't really know enough about either team to be invested. The next batter hit a double to score two, all with no outs! I really liked what I was seeing. Next came an intentional walk which I had come to understand was a sign of respect. A single followed to score two more, before the leadoff batter, up for the second time in the inning, grounded out to end Minnesota's at-bat. That was the first time I had seen all nine batters up to bat in one inning.

In the top of the second inning the Tigers' right fielder and coach were ejected by the home plate umpire. I didn't see what happened to start it off, but they were both tossed out of the game.

The Twins' early runs went unanswered until the bottom of the fifth, when the Tigers got a two-run home run to cut the lead in half. The Tigers added one more on another home run in the sixth, making it 4–3 Twins, which ended up being the final score. The Twins won in a little over two hours. We were okay with the shorter game, and I was okay with the outcome.

21

We went back to the hotel, got some dinner, and turned in fairly early in preparation for the day-long drive home in the morning. We headed home after surviving two games in two days! We talked all the way home about our next trip and other potential trips for the future, knowing our next trip was only a couple of weeks away!

FARTHER WEST

I could hardly contain my excitement over the next couple of weeks. I was watching more games on TV but it just wasn't the same. Watching at home was helping me get more familiar with the players though. At the time I didn't know for sure what kind of party we were going to in Chicago. I spent much of my time trying to figure out what I needed to pack, more to distract myself than anything.

We both took Friday off work and planned to leave after work on Thursday, drive as far as we could, and then drive the rest of the way Friday. After work on Thursday we got on the road but hit some pretty heavy thunderstorms, which produced some amazing lightning shows. But it was getting harder to see in the rain, it was after 11 PM, and we were beyond Cleveland, which was halfway. So we started to look for a place to stay. We stopped at the first place with a vacancy.

It was a small place and looked like it would be inexpensive. After we checked in Eric was a little nervous about the place. There were people milling around outside, so Eric stayed close and wouldn't even let me go to the car by myself. It was not a place I would have stayed if I were traveling alone, but it served the purpose for that night.

We got underway early the next morning and made it to the Chicago area by early afternoon. We had some time to kill so we drove to Wrigley Field for some sightseeing. It was such a thrill! We would have preferred to see the Cubs on our trip to Chicago, but they weren't playing at home that weekend, so we settled for tickets to the White Sox. They were playing the Texas Rangers so it would be another stadium and two more teams.

We stopped in at one of the watering holes near Wrigley, and I could hardly take my eyes off the park. There sat the second oldest stadium in the majors right before my eyes. The pictures on the walls of the bar were from yesteryear, and I was amazed by each one.

It was time to head to Eric's friend's house and get ready for the game. The game was at 7:00 PM, and the mapping program said the White Sox stadium was only forty-five minutes away, so we figured we would leave around 5:30 PM and have plenty of time. Wrong! We were clearly unfamiliar with Chicago traffic. Stuck in traffic on the highway, we were getting frustrated and concerned about missing the first pitch. At Eric's request, I dug out the atlas and found another route, which we told ourselves was faster because we were at least moving. We got there and found a parking place on a side road without meters and made a mad dash to the stadium. Needless to say, our host for the weekend had every reason to tell us "I told you so" and laugh, which he did … all weekend.

We didn't see much of anything on the outside of the stadium on that trip, because we were almost running to get to our seats. The game was underway before we even got to our seats. We had decent seats in the club section on the third base side. The only problem with our seats was that the people around us were more interested in talking on their cell phones or chatting about anything other than the game. It was very distracting, especially because it was hard enough to get into the game after arriving late. I don't even remember what inning we got there. Looking back, I got to see some really big names that night: Frank Thomas, whom I also saw play for Toronto; Alex Rodriguez, whom I also saw play for the Yankees; Rafael Palmeiro, whom I also saw play for Baltimore; Mark Teixeira, whom I also saw play for Atlanta before he went to the Angels and then to the Yankees; and Sandy Alomar Jr. to mention a few.

One of the neat features of Cellular One Park (the home of the White Sox) are the pinwheels above the scoreboard that spin and light up when a home run is hit by a White Sox player, something we got to see a few times that night.

The thing I remember most about the actual game was that Jose Valentin drove in four of the seven Chicago runs on two homers: one in the second after two walks for three runs and a solo shot in the eighth. Frank Thomas hit a solo home run in the third, and Carl Everett also hit a solo home run in the eighth. Alex Rodriguez drove in the only Texas run in the fifth.

The game only took about two and a half hours to play. Most of the 36,000 fans had left before the eighth inning, which I thought was odd. It was a warm, clear night so we decided to move to different seats and stay for the fireworks after the game. Elvis impersonators parachuted into the park, which I thought was pretty funny to watch.

The evening didn't go as we had hoped, but this baseball game was a bonus and not the entire purpose of the trip, so we still had the visit and party at Eric's friend's house to look forward to. We headed back to their house. The trip back didn't seem to be as bad as the trip into town, but it could just be that we had a better idea of what to expect.

On Saturday we helped our friends celebrate their marriage at a backyard reception, which was a wonderful time. We met a lot of really nice people that night and had great fun. On Sunday we headed back home knowing that in just a couple more weeks we were going back to Philadelphia to see the Red Sox makeup game. Earlier in August, we had made plans to go to Cincinnati to see the Expos at the end of September, so there were still more games to look forward to that season.

Eric had been cutting the box score out of the paper for the games we had been to, so over the next weeks I busied myself by creating a spreadsheet to track the players I had seen and who they played for. Of course the box score only gives the first initial of a player, so I asked Eric to help me, before I figured out how to look players up on the Internet. It was fun to sit and run through the list with him. He got about 90 percent of them first try, which amazed me! I also started a chart of the stadiums and teams I had seen. I think deep down I had already hatched a plan to see all the teams and stadiums, but I didn't realize it yet.

MAKEUP GAME IN PHILADELPHIA

When Labor Day weekend came, it was time to head to Philadelphia for the makeup game. We decided to go down on Friday and make a weekend of it. On Saturday we took a walk around downtown. Also we took a horse-drawn carriage historical tour, and did some sight-seeing. On our way back to the hotel we stopped at this little sub shop for an official Philly cheese steak sub. The sandwiches were incredible and huge!

On Sunday we walked around the waterfront and found a wonderful place to have dinner, but I didn't have the proper clothes for anything fancy. So we went shopping for something for me to wear. Eric came prepared and had a suit with him.

I don't particularly like to shop, so this was more of a search-and-destroy mission. There was a Dress Barn in a strip mall not far away, so that was where we went. Eric stood outside having a smoke while I went in to start my search. By the time he came in, I was in line ready to check out. I had found a dress, tried it on, and was done. Next was the shoe store right next door. He realized he hadn't brought any dress socks (so much for his being prepared!) so he went to pick them out while I tried on shoes. We were done about the same time. We even had enough time left to go for a swim in the hotel pool before we had to get ready for our dinner reservations.

We had dinner at the restaurant aboard the *Moshulu*, touted as one of the world's grandest tall ships, that night, which was absolutely wonderful!

We stopped on the deck and took in the view of the city lights reflecting on the water before we were seated at our table.

The next day was the makeup game, an excellent way to end our weekend. We made our way to the stadium preparing ourselves for the game. Our seats for this game were closer to home plate along the first base line, on the same level as before. It was a huge crowd of over 61,000 fans, way over capacity even for Veterans Stadium. That was the largest crowd I have ever watched a baseball game with!

I was really excited about this game. Having seen both the Red Sox and Phillies a couple of times that year, I was familiar with the players. Brett Myers was pitching for Philly and Jeff Suppan was pitching for Boston, which was of some concern to me. The game started out with a little promise. The Red Sox drew three walks, but a double play and a groundout cancelled out the free passes. Hmm—usually walking the leadoff guy, not to mention two others in one inning, leads to something. But not that time.

Now it was Jeff Suppan's chance and I was nervous. He gave up a couple of singles then got the next two men out, giving us hope that he could get out of the first inning unscathed. Nope. He walked the dreaded Jim Thome (apparently not intentionally, which I would certainly have understood) so the bases were loaded with two out. I was on the edge of my seat with my hands over my face. A single to score two runs. Ugh! I have seen enough games to know that whichever team scores first seems to win more often. I don't have actual stats on that, but that was what I felt at the game in Philly.

Jason Varitek had a hit in the second inning but didn't score. I so enjoy watching him call the pitches on defense. His mind must be like a computer! I was slumping in my seat after the Phillies scored two more runs on a home run in the bottom of the second. The Red Sox were down by four! We needed some big plays, and soon.

The third inning brought up the top of the order again. I had to force myself to remember anything can happen. I had to keep rooting. Johnny Damon started off the inning with a walk, and then stole second. Todd Walker singled Damon to third. Okay, here we go. Damon scored on a groundout and Walker advanced to second, Red Sox 1, Phillies 4. I was getting excited. David Ortiz singled and advanced Walker to third. Kevin

Millar singled, Walker scored, and Ortiz advanced to second. The score was 4–2. Trot Nixon hit a double, Ortiz scored, and Millar advanced to third. 4–3! Bill Mueller grounded out, Millar scored, and Nixon advanced to third. Game tied! That was it for the third inning, but it was enough to get me really excited! We exchanged high fives with the Red Sox fans all around us.

In the top of the fourth, the Red Sox took the lead when Damon singled, Ortiz walked, Millar walked, and Nixon singled in the go-ahead run before Ortiz was thrown out trying to score. Okay, we were ahead!

Then in the bottom of the fourth the Phillies retaliated with the help of a walk to the second batter. *You have got to be kidding me! You know what happens when you walk guys,* I was yelling at Suppan in my head. A single and both runners advanced on a throwing error. Oh man! Another single and two scored to put the Phils ahead by one. Ugh!

There was only one more hit by each team until the eighth inning. I wasn't feeling much hope. And to top things off there was some substitution going on, something I was still getting a grasp on. The lineup changes included a pitching change for Philadelphia. Dave McCarty pinch-hit for Walker and drew a walk. Damian Jackson pinch-ran for McCarthy. The changes were making my head spin but I told myself, whatever it takes to win the game! Garciaparra singled to advance Jackson. Ortiz doubled in two runs to retake the lead and ended up on third after a throwing error! I took a deep breath and prayed the Sox could hold on for six more outs.

In the bottom of the eighth, Mike Timlin took the mound for Boston. From watching on TV, I had learned to trust Mike Timlin for the most part. That day he gave up a home run to the first batter he faced, Ricky Ledee (who also I saw play for the Giants, the Angels, and the Mets) to tie the game *again!*

Alan Embree, another pitcher I had seen enough to trust, relieved Timlin after he had loaded the bases with two walks, one of which was intentional, and hit another batter. Oh my, who was coming to the plate but Jim Thome? I didn't want to watch. Thome hit a single and the Phillies took the lead by two. I couldn't believe it!

Byung-Hyun Kim took the mound for Boston and Doug Mirabelli took over behind the plate. The Red Sox got out of the inning, but needed a big ninth. Eric was not encouraging. I didn't want the weekend to end with a loss!

There was another pitching change for Philadelphia. First up was Mirabelli, he walked. Okay, good start. Let's go Red Sox! Damon lined out to a loud collective sigh from the crowd, which had a lot of Red Sox fans in it despite being in Philadelphia. Damian Jackson singled—two on. Wild pitch—runners advanced! I don't think anyone dared to breathe. Garciaparra was intentionally walked to load the bases. Oh my! I was just pacing in my seat. Bases loaded with one out in the top of the ninth ... could we possibly pull it out? Even then there was the bottom of the inning to get through. Agh! I didn't want to think about that. A single scored one run. Bases still loaded with only one out and we were only down by one.

There was yet another pitching change for Philadelphia. Millar walked and in came the tying run on a walk! Wow. That was the first time I had seen that and thought to myself, *that pitcher must feel pretty crappy.* Then Trot Nixon was up to bat, and he hit a grand slam! I jumped to my feet and screamed with joy, along with about half the people in the stands. Six runs scored in the ninth. A double play ended the top of the inning. Just three more outs and we could go home extremely happy.

Kim gave up a double with two outs to dash our hope of a quick inning and keep us on the edge of our seats. But he finished off the ninth inning by striking out the next batter, phew! The Red Sox won 13–9 in a little over four (very stressful) hours. This was a very long nine-inning game.

WEST AGAIN

The last game we had tickets for in 2003 was in Cincinnati, the Reds against the Expos. Seeing the Expos was important to me because this was the last year before the Montreal club moved to Washington and became the Nationals. We were supposed to leave for Cincy right after work on Friday, find a hotel along the route, and drive the rest of the way Saturday morning in time to see the 1:00 PM game.

As fate would have it, Eric was late. I couldn't get a hold of him so I had to make a decision. I waited for an hour and then headed out—alone. That trip was the first time I went to a game alone. I wasn't about to give up a chance to see the Expos and see a new ballpark. It was also the inaugural year for Cincinnati's Great American Ballpark. We had really good seats so I had more reasons to go than to skip the solo trip. It was almost an eleven-hour drive, so once I made up my mind to go, I reviewed the directions and got underway.

I was about three and a half hours into the trip when I heard from Eric. He was disappointed that I had left without him but he wished me luck. I was in the process of finding a rest stop. A road sign said there was one coming up, but it was closed for renovation. Eric and I try to stick to rest stops while traveling to save time and avoid getting off at an exit to search for a restroom. I guess I was getting a little anxious, because I was going too fast according to the nice officer who pulled me over. He gave me a ticket and told me where the nearest restroom was at the next exit.

After that I made it to the other side of Cleveland and found a hotel just off the highway around 11:30 PM. I got some rest and headed out early the next morning, going straight to the park, which was only a little over four hours' drive from my hotel.

It was my first time in Cincinnati, and I was impressed with how clean the city was. I found a parking spot in a small lot under an overpass and walked to the park. It was close to game time, so I quickly took in the sights inside Great American Ballpark and headed for my seat. At the time, this was close as I had been to the field, sitting in the lower level just beyond first base. The park itself was fairly generic, but just beyond right field was the Ohio River and the state of Kentucky beyond. From the upper deck it's a beautiful view. One neat thing about the park was an area in the right field corner that resembled a riverboat, complete with smoke stacks that would actually go off when the Reds hit a home run. I didn't have enough time to walk around the park and take exterior photos. I had started taking my camera into the parks, so I was able to get some pictures from the inside.

There weren't too many players I had even heard of on either team. I was missing Eric because he had been following baseball a lot longer and knew way more about the game and the many players than I did. I was learning and would do the best I could on my own. After all, it was a nice day and I was at a baseball game in a new park with a fairly big crowd of about 31,200 of my closest friends.

In the top of the first inning I saw two players whom I would get to know fairly well. One was Orlando Cabrera, whom I would eventually see play for the Red Sox, Angels, White Sox, and Athletics. The other was Vladimir Guerrero, who I would also see play for the Angels. I had no idea who I would be rooting for. It was going to be an interesting game with no one to talk to.

Livan Hernandez, who came to play for the Mets for part of the 2009 season, was pitching for Montreal. He got the first two batters out. Then he gave up a single, and then a home run to Sean Casey, who played for Boston in 2008. The Reds took a two-run lead. That score held until the bottom of the eighth inning with only four more hits between both teams. It was good to see the home team hit a home run, because seeing the smoke stacks fire was really neat. Eric called during the game to see how I was making out. It was good to hear his voice but I was a little upset at how the weekend had turned out and at having to make the trip alone.

Livan Hernandez was still pitching for the Expos in the bottom of the eighth. Casey hit a single, followed by another Reds home run making it 4–0. More cool smoke stack action.

The Expos tried to rally in the top of the ninth, using pinch runners and everything. They actually scored two runs but a win wasn't to be. The game lasted only two hours and eleven minutes, which gave me a good head start on heading home.

I made it back to New York, about three hours from home, before I found a place to sleep at almost midnight. I drove the rest of the way home Sunday. I had successfully taken in my first solo game. That would be the first of many trips I would make by myself.

I updated the ledger of the players I had seen. I kept the box score and play-by-play of each game. I had all of my tickets. I was also taking pictures, and I decided it would be cool to scan the pictures and tickets to make a memory quilt of my experiences. I was becoming a fanatic.

I watched as many games as I could through the playoffs, only to feel a major sadness after the season ended. I had seen eleven games at ten new parks, and fourteen new teams, meaning I had seen one shy of half the teams already. That became the next target—seeing them all. The plans for 2004 were underway!

EVEN MORE IN 2004

Tickets went on sale in February. We checked out the tentative schedules and made plans, looking for matchups with teams I hadn't seen. It was prudent to stay within a day's drive from home. That meant revisiting the places we had already been, but that turned out to be a good thing. I could get more pictures at those stadiums.

The first trip we planned was to go back to Fenway. With the disappointing end to the 2003 American League Championship Series, the Sox needed our support, or at least that was what we told ourselves. I had become an official Red Sox Nation member. Part of my membership was two free tickets. It just so happened that my free tickets were for Sunday, May 9 game against the Royals. So we made our plans to head back to Boston.

Boston was close enough to drive up to a game, but a little too far to drive up and back in one day, as it was about five and a half hours each way. Throw in an average three hours for the game plus the extra hour ahead of the game and at least an hour after the game to get through traffic, and that would make for a really long day. For this trip Eric decided to get in touch with one of his college roommates who still lived in the Boston area to see if we could catch up with him on Saturday. He and his family invited us to stay with them Saturday night and then head into the city on Sunday, and we took them up on the offer.

Part of the process of planning one of these trips was determining what else we wanted to do in the area we were visiting, so we could locate the hotel accordingly and maximize our time. On that particular trip, we had the added bonus of Eric getting to see an old friend he hadn't seen in years (and me making a new friend). We had a lovely time and spent many hours catching up, shopping for, and then preparing a wonderful dinner on Saturday night.

On Sunday morning we headed toward Boston under overcast skies. By the time we got into Boston, a steady light rain was falling. We found a place to park and headed for any roof we could find so we wouldn't get drenched. In the Prudential building there is a shopping mall and a large food court. We wandered around there for a while before heading to the game. According to our preference to stay clear of chain restaurants while traveling, we had lunch someplace we both remembered as funky.

It was getting time to head to the game. Fortunately, the rain had stopped. I was excited about starting the season off at Fenway. It was an afternoon game. Even though it was a bit cool for May, about forty-eight degrees under overcast skies, we were watching baseball at Fenway, so we were excited.

We were lucky, finding a place to park on Commonwealth Avenue. It being Sunday, we didn't have to feed the meter. We were so excited that we got out of the car and got about a half block away before I realized I hadn't grabbed the tickets. I was very glad I remembered them before we got to the gate. Eric assured me he would have been less than happy with me if that had happened as well.

I wasn't sure where we were in relation to Fenway Park so I just followed along. Before long we were amongst a large crowd of fans. I wore the Red Sox t-shirt I had bought a couple of years earlier at Quincy Market and Eric had on his Pedro Martinez jersey. I wanted to get to Fenway a little bit early to do a little shopping to add to my fan gear.

Soon we could see the top of the Green Monster. We went into a Red Sox shop across the street from the park. I couldn't decide what I wanted, so I didn't get anything. I was amazed at all the choices but picking the perfect item would be a task for another time. That day was about the game, my second visit to the place where my fan adventures had begun. At that game, our seats were in the outfield grandstand, looking in almost straight down the first base line. This was a different and less favorite vantage point for me.

As usual it was just about a sellout crowd at Fenway, with over 34,500 fans coming out to see the game. This was my first time to see the Kansas City Royals, and to be honest I didn't expect them to give us too much trouble.

I recognized most of the Red Sox players, but this was the first time I saw Derek Lowe. He had been with Boston since 1997, so Eric was familiar with him and expressed some concern. I really envied Eric's knowledge of the game and was doing my best to absorb all I could. In the offseason I had started to keep track of the trades and read up on some of the player histories in an effort to keep up. It was all I could do to follow the players from the Mets and Red Sox.

The game started off slow. There was only one hit in the first inning, by Mike Sweeney for the Royals with two outs. Kansas City pitching sat the Red Sox down one-two-three in the bottom of the first. Lowe returned the favor in the top of the second.

This game was proving more interesting than I had originally expected. In the bottom of the second inning, Kevin Millar got a hit with two outs. Okay, let's score first! Bill Mueller made it happen by cracking, and I mean you could really hear the crack of the bat, one over the wall in left field. There we go, ahead by two.

The lead didn't last long. Lowe walked the first batter in the third, who then advanced on an error by our beloved shortstop Pokey Reese; the error meant two men were on base. Oh boy, here we go. Walks, ugh! Lowe settled down and struck out the next batter. But I had a bad feeling. Then came a double, and the score was tied. We got a couple of hits in the bottom of the third inning but no runs. The score stayed tied, with only one more hit per team until the top of the sixth.

That's when D-Lowe, as I have since come to affectionately know him, fell apart. He gave up a single and walked two to load the bases. Eric was beside himself, squirming in his seat with frustration. A single scored the go-ahead run and the bases were still loaded! That was it for Lowe, who was replaced by Mark Malaska. Malaska was in his third year in the majors and second with Boston. Carlos Beltran, whom I came to know better when joined the Mets in 2005 after finishing 2004 with Houston, was up next for the Royals. He hit a double to bring three runs in. Ugh! With the Red Sox behind 6–2, I hardly knew what to think. I had heard it said that any team can win any game at any time, but I would not have thought it possible that day if I hadn't been watching it with my own eyes.

We had a couple of chances in the bottom of the sixth but they came to nothing. Bronson Arroyo came in to pitch for Boston. He had played for Pittsburgh for four years and was in his second season with Boston. He had a young look about him but played with a great deal of heart, which would become very apparent later in the 2004 season and postseason. He sat the Royals down one-two-three. I was not really sure what happened next, but the Royals' catcher was ejected by the home plate umpire. I hoped the dispute might disrupt their rhythm.

Pokey Reese started off the bottom of the seventh with a walk and made it all the way to third on a wild pitch, but they just couldn't get him home. Next on the mound for Boston was rookie Lenny DiNardo. I admit I don't know much about the strategy of the game but down by four in the eighth and a rookie pitcher? All in all, I don't think he did too bad as he only gave up a single, a sacrifice fly to advance the runner, and a double to score *another* run. Oh dear.

In the bottom of the eighth, David Ortiz (or Big Papi, as he would soon be known) struck out swinging. My head was in my hands. Then Manny Ramirez, with a mere flick of the wrist, hit a home run! Wahoo! That was so exciting to see!

Unfortunately, we were still down by four. But there was some hope. In the top of the ninth, veteran Mike Timlin came in. I felt some sense of relief. He struck out the first two batters swinging, so I felt he was "on" that day. But then he gave up a home run to the backup catcher who was only in the game because of the ejection.

Being down by five going to the bottom of the ninth didn't leave me with a very good feeling. I had seen the Red Sox get six runs in the ninth inning in Philly the previous fall, but I had seen enough to know that kind of rally was not normal.

Here goes. Bill Mueller flied out. Dave McCarty grounded out. This could be a bland end to a dismal game. Wait, Pokey Reese drew a walk, maybe not so bland. Pokey stole second, or so I thought. Eric corrected me that it was fielder's indifference, but all I knew was that he was on second base. Damon was the next batter. I knew that it wouldn't take much of a hit for Reese to score, so my fingers were crossed on both hands. There it was! A single off Damon's bat scored Pokey! Back to down by four. Damon made it to second, indifference again. Then all hopes were dashed when Mark Bellhorn struck out to end the game. I became fond of Bellhorn, but unfortunately strikeouts were a problem for him most of his first of two seasons in Boston. Kansas City won 8–4 in just under three and a half hours.

It was a quiet ride home after a disappointing game, but we had been in Boston and it was only the first game of what would turn out to be a big baseball season. As was becoming our pattern, we did discuss where we would go next. The plan to see every team play in person was underway. It was more my goal then Eric's, but he seemed perfectly happy to tag along. This was fine by me as we enjoyed each other's company and traveled very well together.

RE-RUNS

Later that week we found ourselves in front of the computer looking at schedules to plan where our next game would be. In a little over a month the Marlins would be in New York playing the Mets. A Saturday midday game was an easy one, because it was most certainly a day trip.

What else could be planned? Did we dare to go back to Pittsburgh later in June to see the Mariners? There was Philly, Baltimore, the other New York team, Detroit, and maybe even a return Cincinnati or Cleveland. We are so fortunate in the Northeast to have so many stadiums within a half-day's drive. We had so much fun plotting and planning for each season.

We saw that the Red Sox were going to be in Detroit, in August so tickets were ordered. I don't remember exactly how many games we ordered tickets for that week, but we planned a few of what ended up being eleven games for that season. When tickets arrived in the mail I wasn't even allowed to open the envelope until Eric was there, because he didn't want me to let all the baseball smell out.

Saturday June 5 arrived. We had tickets for the game between the Marlins and Mets at Shea Stadium. I was so excited I could hardly stay in bed that morning. I wanted to get up and go! I don't think we planned on leaving until 8:00 AM to get us there around noon for the 1:20 PM game, but I was raring to go by 6:30 AM. Eric, even less of a morning person than I am, was not as raring to go as I was. So I was the one who started off driving on that trip, which wasn't normally the case. We usually planned to stop for breakfast and take a little break every couple of hours to stretch and use the restrooms (not to mention the traffic factor) so we gave ourselves at least an extra hour or so. I also had started to wander around the stadiums—especially ones that I hadn't seen before—to get some more pictures in order to preserve the memories.

The trip down was fairly uneventful and traffic was not too bad. It was a cool day for June and overcast, but we were headed to a baseball game, so all was well. All I really knew about the Florida Marlins was that they had beaten the Yankees to win the World Series the prior year. I had no idea I was about to see a player who would become one of my absolute favorites, Mike Lowell. In 2009, Mike Lowell became the only third baseman in major league baseball history to have ten straight seasons with twenty-five or more doubles. Oh, and he came to play for the Red Sox in 2006 as a salary dump in the trade that brought the Sox pitcher Josh Beckett. What a wonderful thing that turned out to be for the Red Sox!

It was good to be back at Shea Stadium. It was comfortable to return to a place where we had already spent so much time. Pitching for the Mets was Matt Ginter, who had been with the Braves for years and was in his second season with the Mets. I was getting used to the idea that players move around a lot. In the first inning, Ginter faced seven batters allowing two runs. I was ready for a long game.

The Mets got one hit in the bottom of the first on a Todd Zeile bunt, but that was all, no scoring. One thing I found interesting about Todd Zeile was his ability to play different positions. He even pitched a couple of times while with Colorado and the Mets.

It was an easy top of the second. The bottom of the inning started off with a walk. Okay, let's see what we can do with that. Two more singles to load the bases! Good, good. A sacrifice fly and the Mets scored! We took advantage of that walk just fine. That was it for the inning, but we had gotten back one of the runs.

In the top of the third Ginter still looked sharp, going three up and three down just like that. Each side only got one hit in each of the next two and a half innings. The only thing of real interest was when the Marlins pinch-hit for their pitcher with another starting pitcher, Dontrelle Willis.

That was odd. But Willis got a single, the only Marlins hit in the inning, so I guess it was a good move.

In the bottom of the fifth inning, Mike Piazza hit a solo home run. Way to go! The apple popped up, and oh, do I love to see that apple pop up! The bottom of the sixth proved to be an exciting inning. Ginter continued to impress me. Ty Wigginton hit a single to get things started and scored on a double to regain the lead. The runner made it to third on the throw. Yeah! Another single scored another run. Yahoo, Mets ahead by two! Two stolen bases followed, one on a throwing error. Another single scored another run. The Mets were ahead by three runs.

The lead didn't last long, as the top of the seventh proved to be just as exciting for the Marlins. In a sequence very similar to the previous inning, a single then advanced to second on a throwing error. Oh man! We were giving back what we just managed to take from them. A single advanced the lead runner to third. I watched and learned more about the strategy of the game. The Marlins brought in a pinch-hitter. The Mets counter with a pitching change. Oh wait, the Marlins pinch-hit for the pinch hitter with Damion Easley, who later played for the Mets in 2007. Easley turned out to be a great move for the Marlins, as he proceeded to hit a solo home run to tie the game *again*.

There were a couple of pitching changes. The Mets loaded the bases in the bottom of the seventh inning but couldn't do anything with it.

David Weathers pitched the eighth for the Mets. A single erased by a double play. Phew! A single and a walk, uh oh! Another single, and one run scored. Then both runners each took an extra base on the throw. The Marlins still had two men in scoring position with two outs. What a relief it was when the next batter grounded out.

The Mets' next three batters went down in order. Ugh! In the top of the ninth, John Franco came in to pitch for the Mets. A groundout was followed by a triple! Dan Wheeler came in to relieve Franco for the Mets and gave up a double. Another run scored. 7–5! Wheeler got the final out to stop the pain. I just sat there shaking my head.

Armando Benitez came in for the Marlins. He was the closer for the Mets for several years through 2004, and we had seen him give up three runs against the Diamondbacks the previous year. So we were actually pleased to see him as closer for the opponent. Mike Piazza hit a solo home run to bring the score within one, but that was it. The final score was Marlins 7, Mets 6. It took only a little over three hours, but it sure felt like a long game for the very small crowd of just under 25,000 people.

We were heading back that evening, so we decided to drive for a while then stop for dinner to break up the drive. I am usually the one to scout out food. I saw a place that looked promising, and we stopped for dinner just out of the city. After dinner I took over the driving and managed to stay awake to drive all the rest of the way while Eric slept. I even stopped for gas, and he never even stirred. Oh, to be able to sleep so soundly!

Just two weeks later, on June 19, we were back on the road to Pittsburgh to see the Mariners for the first time. We both felt that there was something about PNC Park that was neat, but last time we were there it was such a hassle actually getting to the park that I don't think either of us really properly settled into the game.

I was in for a real treat at that game. It was going to get to see Ichiro Suzuki, only the second player in the history of the game to win rookie of the year and most valuable player in the same year, which he did in 2001. The first was outfielder Fred Lynn of the Red Sox in 1974. I was also excited to see another new team, the Mariners.

In games where neither team was one of my favorites I took the opportunity to get familiar with more players. There have been many players that I had seen play on other teams who have eventually come to play for one of my teams.

On the drive we took the same scenic route that we had taken the previous year and looked for some of the neat sights we had found the last time. It was a cooler day, and overcast, but still a nice six-hour drive. In keeping with our Pittsburgh luck, we hit a detour, exiting the highway one exit before the one we wanted because of construction. We were once again trying to find our way through the detours to get to our destination. We finally had to call the hotel to find out how to get there. The good news was that the entrance to the highway going the other way was open, and that was a matter of feet beyond the hotel. The real trick would be finding our way back to the hotel after the game. Fortunately, the front desk clerk was very helpful and we made it with very little difficulty.

We went down to the stadium early to take a walk around and get some pictures. We walked across the Sixth Street Bridge over the Allegheny River to get some pictures from that angle. There was also a detour sign hanging near the walkway along the river. We couldn't resist taking our pictures with that sign, as it pretty much sums up our driving experiences in Pittsburgh.

This trip was a much more relaxed experience than the first time we were at PNC Park, and we agreed that the stadium had more appeal than we both had remembered. I still felt it was somewhat generic, but it had little bits of charm throughout. The bridge in the background and the river along one side were definite pluses for me.

The game started with Sean Burnett on the mound for the Pirates. He retired the first three batters, including Ichiro Suzuki. Joel Pineiro was pitching for Seattle. I saw him again in April 2006 when the Mariners visited Boston and again in August 2007 on the Cardinals when they played the Cubs at Wrigley. He returned Burnett's favor and sat the Pirates down one-two-three. That went on for the first three innings.

Eric and I looked at each other, and I was sure he was thinking the same thing I was. Hmm ... no hits for either team; it was going to be a quick game.

In the top of the fourth there was one hit but no score. The top of the fifth started off with a walk to Scott Spiezio, a name I remembered from seeing him play for the Angels in Cleveland the August before. I remembered him to be a good player. Spiezio took second on a wild pitch and scored on a single. The batter advanced to second on the throw. Another single led to another run, making it Seattle 2, Pittsburgh 0.

The bottom of the fifth was another quick half-inning for Pineiro. He faced four with just one hit, a single by Jason Bay. Bay was another player who became a favorite of mine when came to play for Boston in 2008 through 2009 and for the Mets in 2010.

The Pirates made another pitching change. The new hurler ended up loading the bases when he intentionally walked John Olerud. Olerud was another player I came to know and like because of his time with the Red Sox in 2005. In the fifth and longest inning of the game another single scored two more Mariner runs.

The next several innings were brief, with only one hit until the bottom of the eighth. The Pirates finally scored on a solo home run by Bay. The Mariners went on to score one more run making the final Seattle 5, Pittsburgh 1, in one of the shortest nine-inning games I would ever attend, lasting just two hours and eighteen minutes.

We stayed in our seats for a little bit as the small crowd of just over 24,000 exited so we could admire the view of the lights on the bridge and enjoy the blue lights on the ramps for a few more minutes.

Our drive home was fairly uneventful except for the talk of what would be next. Our next adventure was only a couple of weeks away. We were going back to Philadelphia to see the new stadium, Citizens Bank Park, and watch the Braves play the Phillies. We stopped at a little sub place to get a bite to eat and keep going, thinking it would be fairly quick. Boy, were we wrong. It took forever. They weren't bad subs, but by the time we got our order we were very anxious to get back underway.

The game in Philadelphia was a Friday night contest, so we decided to take the day off and go down and do some sightseeing before the game. We went to the hotel that we had prepaid for online, located just across the river in New Jersey. But when we got there the check-in clerk said we had to pay there. I explained we had already paid and showed him the confirmation and he still insisted we pay before he would give us keys. I was ticked off, but rather than waste time trying to find another place to stay, I gave in and paid the man. I intended to contest the double payment as soon as I returned home, which was exactly what I did.

We headed back to Philadelphia to do some sightseeing. We parked in a garage and walked around town for a while until it started to sprinkle. We headed back toward the car but had to make a mad dash as it began to rain harder and harder. We were soaked by the time we got to the car. We decided to go back to the hotel to dry off and clean up before the game.

I was fond of the Phillies, and I found I could root for them against most other teams except, of course, the Mets and Red Sox. So it wasn't a stretch to root for them over the Braves. I was again going to get to see some players for the first time who became dear to me. One in particular I was later amazed by, Julio Franco. I was thrilled to see Franco play for the Mets part of the year in 2007! Eric and I often chat about silly things. Once we were talking about if we could talk to any player, who would it be? My answer was Julio Franco, because he played wherever he could and I believe he played longer than any other player in the game. I imagine he must have seen and been through some really interesting things. Eric actually thought that was a pretty good answer.

We arrived at the stadium and found a parking spot. We took our usual walk around the outside of the stadium to take some pictures. We found a place to sit and wait for the gates to open. After the rain it became a beautiful clear day in the mid-eighties. We were about to see a baseball game, so all was right with the world. It was a new stadium, and I couldn't wait to get inside to see what it was like.

Once we got inside, I saw that it was definitely different than the Vet. It was smaller, and it was obviously a baseball-only park. I really liked the Liberty Bell out in center field that lit up and swung back and forth on a Phillies home run. I was enjoying the unique touches in each of the different parks. That game I was hoping for a couple of home runs from the Phillies to see the bell in action.

The place was packed beyond capacity, with over 44,000 in attendance. The game started slowly, with only one hit by Chipper Jones in the top of the second. In the bottom of the second the Phillies did a little better and managed to get a run.

In the top of the third the Braves retaliated with a home run by Rafael Furcal with two men on to take a 3–1 lead. Phillies manager Larry Bowa was ejected for arguing the call. I had seen enough games to know that something like that can really spark a team. Sometimes I think the manager gets ejected for just that reason.

In the bottom of the fourth the Phillies threatened, getting two men on, but couldn't score. The top of the fifth was almost exactly the same as the Braves' third inning: another home run by Rafael Furcal with two men on. Needless to say, this was not how I wanted the game to go.

In the bottom of the fifth a little ray of hope arrived. It started off with a walk and ended with two runs in for Philadelphia. Okay, 6–2.

Despite a two-out walk the Phillies managed to get through the sixth inning without allowing any runs. The Braves threatened again in the top of the seventh after a one-out Furcal single and a two-out walk to J. D. Drew, who I became a fan of when he came to play in Boston in 2007 after Trot Nixon went to Cleveland. The Braves' seventh inning ended without any scoring.

The Phillies threatened in the seventh with a hit batsman but all they managed was a two-out single before a Braves pitching change and the final out ended the inning. I had seen this Braves pitcher play for the Reds the previous year, and he had given up three hits and two runs then. So if he stayed in to pitch, I felt a little bit of hope for Philadelphia.

Roberto Hernandez pitched a quick one-two-three top of the eighth. The bottom of the inning started with a couple of quick outs. Well guys, did we give up? Then Ledee drew a walk, followed a single. Okay, that was more like it. Two on, and Mike Lieberthal was on deck. He knew exactly what to do. He hit a home run to bring the Phillies within one. I got to see the bell ring! It was a very neat thing. The Braves immediately yanked Reitsma and brought in John Smoltz. Eric and I looked at each other and admitted that Smoltz made us nervous. Smoltz got the final out for the inning. We were hoping his day was over.

Tim Worrell pitched a gem of a ninth against just three batters, one of whom was Adam LaRoche, who I did see play for the Red Sox during his short stint there in 2009.

Okay, bottom of the ninth, Smoltz back on the mound, darn it! The Phillies were down by one. Rollins struck out. Double darn it! The second batter was Chase Utley. Crack! A solo home run tied the game, and the bell rang again. Time for another extra inning game in Philadelphia!

The top of the tenth was a real treat. Billy Wagner came in to pitch for Philadelphia. At the time I didn't know who he was but came to have a fondness for him, especially the years he played for the Mets in 2006 thru 2008 and even more so after his surgery when he finished the season with the Red Sox in 2009. He gave up two singles but also struck out two to get out of the inning without further damage. Personally I was hoping to see the bell ring one more time but that wasn't to be. With a different pitcher on the mound, a long single with two men scored a runner to win the game for Philadelphia! They did it—they beat the Braves. I was very happy.

All in all, it was a good game. The right team won, in my eyes anyway, and we got to see extra innings, all in less than three and a half hours. My feelings for the Braves are similar to my feelings for the Yankees. My third favorite team was anyone beating either of them. Sorry, but someone has to be at the bottom of my favorites list.

A week later, we were set for another run to Cincinnati. I had made the trip last year but Eric hadn't been with me. We planned to do a little camping and give him another chance to get there.

The St. Louis Cardinals were playing at the Cincinnati Reds, so it was another new team for me, and a new stadium for Eric. It was a Saturday night game, so we were going to take Friday off and camp for two nights then drive back on Sunday. We got together Thursday night to load all the gear in the car, so we would be ready first thing Friday morning. It was a long drive, so we wanted to get there on Friday and have Saturday to recoup before seeing the game. We figured with the two of us to drive, we could tear down Sunday morning and still get home at a decent time Sunday night.

You know what they say about best-laid plans. As it turned out Eric had something come up after he left on Thursday night. I couldn't reach him when he didn't show up on Friday morning at the time we had set to leave. I was not very happy with him. He finally did show up to find I was on the computer booking a hotel last minute because I thought I might end up going alone *again*, and I was not interested in camping alone. We unloaded the camping stuff, and off we went. It wasn't the best start to a trip we had ever had, but we managed to pull it together and have a good time.

I had liked Great American Ballpark and was excited for Eric to see it. It was neat for me too, as the first visit was a day game and this was a night game. I hadn't yet decided whether I liked night or day games better, but considered the possibility that it might depend on the park.

We got to the hotel and got something to eat at a nearby diner. As was our custom, we settled into our room and found *SportsCenter* or a game on TV to watch.

We got to the ballpark early the next day to do some sightseeing and actually walked across the bridge that spans the Ohio River, winding up standing on the Kentucky side. The bridge gave us some great views of the park, and I was able to take some neat pictures, plus I had never been in Kentucky before. Visiting every state will be a quest for another time, though!

We headed toward the park and walked around downtown looking for a place to eat. We found a spot, went in, and took a seat at the bar feeling that was our best chance of getting served because the place was really packed. It wasn't a very friendly place, and we got ignored by most of the staff. We finally got menus and ordered food. After we were served, there was no chance of refills or anything else, so we paid the bill and away we went.

The stadium was very close to other buildings along its northern side, so we went to the top of a parking garage to see if we could get some better pictures of the field. On the top of the stadium we found Joe Nuxhall's famous signoff "rounding third and heading for home" inscribed. Nuxhall was in the majors at age fifteen, the youngest player ever to play in the big leagues. He played all but a season and a half of his twenty-two years in the majors with the Reds. He had a sixty-two-year affiliation with the Reds franchise. I felt the inscription was a wonderful tribute to Nuxhall's long contribution to the team. Joe Nuxhall died on November 15, 2007. I also learned that from 1954 to 1959, Cincinnati was called the Red Legs. What was it with baseball and the color red?

We got to our seats, which were one level up from our seats from the year before but still very good. Eric often says, "If they are inside the park, they are good seats." I was again in for a treat, about to see some players whom I would become more familiar with as they came to play for either the Mets or Red Sox. I would also see the player some have called the best hitter in the game, Albert Pujols. This was another game where I wasn't sure which team I would be rooting for.

It was a nice evening, temperature in the mid–seventies. The game was better attended than my last visit to Cincy, with just over 36,000 fans. Perhaps more people wanted to see the Cardinals than the Expos, or maybe it was just easier for the Cardinals fans to get there than it was for the Expos fans. Either way, it was getting close to game time and the stadium was filling up. I was hoping for the home team to hit a home run so we could see the stacks go off. Those touches are what make each park special in my mind.

The matchup was Cory Lidle for the Reds against Jason Marquis for the Cardinals. In his half of the first, Lidle faced three and struck out two, including Albert Pujols. Jason Marquis had a similar first inning, allowing a single but erasing it with a double play. Next inning Lidle gave up a single but no runs. Marquis had some trouble and loaded the bases, but was able to get out of the second inning without allowing a run. I was starting to root for the Reds.

Lidle was still holding his own, giving up just a single in the third inning, but Marquis continued to have some trouble. He gave up a single, and that runner ended up on third after stealing second and making a throwing error. Sean Casey, whom I really liked when he came to play for Boston in 2008—he always seemed to be smiling—drove in the first run of the game. The Reds were up by one.

In the bottom of the fifth inning, the first Reds batter hit a home run. Cool—the smoke stacks went off! The Reds went up by two. Wily Mo Pena, who came to play for Boston in 2006, got in on the action with two outs and one on, hitting the second Reds home run of the inning. More cool smoke stack action, and the Reds were up 4–0. I was happy with the score and enjoying the sights.

In the top of the seventh inning, the Cards showed they weren't going to go quietly. A couple of singles and a couple of doubles and the Cardinals scored three runs to draw within one of the Reds. Hmm, this game could turn into a good one after all.

In the top of the eighth, Albert Pujols hit a home run—tie game. Fortunately, that was it for that inning. In the bottom of the eighth, Julian Tavarez, who came to play in Boston in 2006 through part of 2008, was pitching for St. Louis. He gave up a home run to Adam Dunn with two on. Three runs! More smoke stack action! I was so liking it!

The Cardinals were able to get one more run in the ninth, making the final score Reds 7, Cards 5. I rooted for the right team that time.

We headed back to the hotel to get a good night's sleep after a long and somewhat emotional day, in preparation for the drive home in the morning.

On the way home we decided to eat someplace different. I was driving, so it was easy to just pick a place. We tried the Quaker Steak & Lube. I had seen Quaker Steaks on the road many times but had no idea what they were. It was fine food and a different kind of atmosphere. We ate and got back on our way, discussing what was next.

MIDWEEK DAY GAME

Earlier that year, in mid-April to be specific, we had planned to play hooky on a Thursday in August to see a weekday game at Yankee Stadium. We hadn't seen Oakland yet, and the A's were scheduled to play the Yankees on August 5. We figured a day game would be easier to get tickets for and probably less crowded. This proved to be a game I would never forget.

We left for the city about the time we would have been going into work, excited not to be going off to the office but to a baseball game. I truly felt like a kid skipping school! I am not sure what I thought I was getting away with, but that was how I felt.

We got into the city in good time and found a parking lot not too far from the stadium. We walked toward the stadium and window-shopped at the little shops across the street from the field. I wore my Mets shirt, and Eric wore a Red Sox shirt. As we were walking down the street, people yelled from their cars that we were on the wrong side of town. Eric just chuckled, but I wasn't sure what to think. We went into Yankee Stadium and found our seats, which were way up in the highest section. We were actually just a few rows down from the absolute top row in the stadium. Yankee Stadium was a big stadium, so that was pretty high up. We grabbed our refreshments and settled in to watch the game. I was surprised that there were that many people there. There were over 52,000 people there. The stadium wasn't completely filled but pretty close.

The pitching matchup was supposed to be a really good one. Kevin Brown was starting for the Yankees against Barry Zito for the Athletics. We of course were rooting for Oakland. It was bad enough that we were wearing opposing team garb, but rooting for the other team was really pushing it. We had popcorn thrown at us. A man walking to his seat behind us gave Eric a tongue-lashing about his Boston shirt and proceeded to spill beer on him. I think it was the same man who kept yelling stuff at us about how we'd had to come to Yankee Stadium to see a real team play. It was interesting, but the worst was yet to come.

The game started out fairly calm, with both pitchers doing really well. In the bottom of the second inning, there was no score and only one hit so far, which was for Oakland to start the second. In the Yankees' half of the second the trouble began. I am not sure as to what happened but there was an error on the Oakland outfielder and Alex Rodriguez was safe at first. Jorge Posada flied out. I have come to like Posada, tempered by the fact he is a Yankee.

Next up was Hideki Matsui, who hit a single which Eric blamed me for. He reminded me about by my comment that I liked Matsui when he first came to the United States to play baseball. There was something about the way he tried to downplay his fame because he didn't want it to interfere with the rest of the team that I liked. Eric said that I couldn't have it both ways. In his mind liking Matsui was as bad as routing for the Yankees so whenever we watched the Yankees and Matsui played Eric made me eat my words.

Next up was Ruben Sierra, who hit a double to score A-Rod. Uh oh. I had already learned that you don't give the Yankees an edge. Next up was another player I came to really respect, John Olerud, who played his last season with the Red Sox. In my mind he was an amazing first baseman. He was responsible for the next two runs when he hit a double. The Yankees were up 3–0 after the second inning. It was going to be a very long game.

That score held, with only a couple of hits until the bottom of the fifth, when Bernie Williams hit a single and Derek Jeter hit a double to bring Williams home. Now the score was 4–0 Yankees. Zito was pitching well, and that was something to cheer about. But Oakland couldn't manage more than one single in any inning.

In the bottom of the seventh, with Zito still on the mound, Derek Jeter flied out. Yeah! We were cheering. Next up was Gary Sheffield, who hit a single. Then A-Rod hit a single. Damn! Then Posada was up. He made the second out, phew. But then Matsui hit a single to score another run! Okay, that was it for Zito. The A's reliever struck out Sierra to end the inning.

In the top of the ninth, Paul Quantrill relieved Kevin Brown. That was the A's big chance. Endy Chavez drew a walk. I really liked Chavez, especially when he came to play for the Mets from 2006 through 2008. Chavez advanced on an error by A-Rod, which in itself was worth cheering about. Another Yankee error and Chaves scored. Yeah! It wasn't a shutout at least! The final score was Yankees 5, Oakland 1.

We waited a little bit before heading back to the car, mostly to avoid the crowd as much as possible. When we got back to the car we found one of the stickers that was on the bumper of on my car, a Red Sox sticker, had been moved to the windshield and profanity written all over it in black marker. I was really ticked off! It wasn't bad enough that we had stuff thrown at us, beer spilled on us, and things yelled at us! I can take bantering back and forth with the best of them, but this was crossing the line. I was fuming. It wasn't the cost of the sticker but the total disregard for others that really burned me. I would never do that to anyone else. I was really pissed off! I was sure I would not be going back to Yankee Stadium ever again! In all the places I have been, this was the rudest treatment I have ever received. I paid to park, paid for the ticket, paid for the food and beverages just like everyone else. What gives someone the right to treat me like that? It was really rude. That was all I can say: rude!

THE REAL PEDRO

Two days later we were going to see the Red Sox in Detroit. It looked like we would be seeing Pedro Martinez pitch, so Eric shared stories of the Pedro of old to calm me down on the ride home from New York City. We had seen Martinez pitch in Philadelphia the previous June in the thirteen-inning game we attended, where he pitched seven innings and gave up four hits and one home run. So when Eric told me what a great pitcher Pedro was, I had no doubt about it. I soon became so excited about our next adventure that I started to cool off about the other stuff we had just experienced.

Right after work on Friday night we headed out on our next adventure. On Friday we got well into Ohio and found a hotel. On Saturday we drove the rest of the way to Detroit and checked into our hotel there. We decided to get some sightseeing in, so we drove to the stadium and found a spot to park on the street almost right in front of the park, which was so cool. That was the second time we had found free parking in Detroit. It was around lunch time, so we started out toward downtown to find a place to eat. I was in charge of selecting our eateries, so I kept an eye out as we walked around. We walked for a few blocks when the surroundings all of a sudden grew desolate. It was really sad. It seemed like there were just a few blocks of nice clean city surrounded by rundown and boarded-up places. We didn't venture too far away from the stadium as a result.

In our wanderings we found the Detroit Brewing Company, a pub-like place with a fairly extensive menu. So we went in for lunch. The place was so neat. It had the brew tanks right there behind the bar. The food was really good, and they had a good variety of beer. After we enjoyed a nice lunch and the atmosphere, we headed back toward the ballpark. There was already a line at the gate. The fan giveaway that day was an Ivan "Pudge" Rodriguez bobblehead, and we wanted to make sure we got ours. We got to chatting with a family behind us about the merits of the old stadium versus the new stadium. Comerica Park is more state-of-the-art and has great things for kids to do, including a miniature Ferris wheel with baseball-shaped cars. And yes, we took a ride ourselves. As I mentioned before, the cars atop the outfield wall and fountain were a wonderful touch too. But I like going to ballparks for the game itself, and sometimes I think too much of the other stuff detracts from that. That was just my opinion.

We had great seats again, this time on the third base line nineteen rows up from the field, almost even with home plate. I had borrowed a friend's digital camera so I could get some great pictures from those seats. The people around us were very friendly also. We chatted with the one to my left a fair amount about where we were from and about the Red Sox. He was a Tigers fan. Now there are many teams I would root against if they were playing the Tigers. I have nothing against the Tigers at all, except that day they were playing against the Red Sox and Pedro Martinez was on the mound, so of course I was going to be rooting against them. The Detroit fan understood and was fine with that way of thinking. After all, one team has to lose.

Jeremy Bonderman was pitching for Detroit, so it certainly wasn't going to be a gimme game. The game started, and I was beside myself—I wanted a picture of everything, but Eric reminded me that if I focused on the pictures I would miss so much of the game. He was right, which was usually the case. But don't tell him I said that. I did get a few really great pictures of David Ortiz and Johnny Damon before I turned the camera off. Damon hit a single, Kevin Youkilis advanced him on a groundout, Kevin Millar walked, and then Ortiz grounded out to allow Damon to score and advanced Millar to third before Jason Varitek struck out for the third out. Red Sox lead by one after the top of the first. Yeah!

I am always impressed with the Red Sox Nation at every Red Sox game I go to. There are times that they seem to outnumber the home team fans by a great deal. This seemed to be the case in Detroit.

In the bottom of the first inning, Martinez struck out the first three batters in order. My jaw just dropped. Was this the Pedro of old that Eric spoke of? I was awestruck.

With two outs in the top of the second inning, Bill Mueller hit a single and was driven in by a double by Dave Roberts to put us ahead by two. Cool.

The bottom of the second inning was much like the first. Martinez struck out the first two and the third batter grounded out. Okay—he made it look so easy.

In the third inning we got two men on base but we didn't score. We were still up 2–0.

In the bottom of the inning Martinez faced four batters, gave up a single, and struck out two more. He had seven strikeouts in just three innings! The sellout crowd of over 42,000 were definitely enjoying it.

In the fourth inning Orlando Cabrera hit a single, stole second, and took third when Mueller grounded out. Dave Roberts hit a sacrifice fly to bring Cabrera home. The place went nuts, my-self included. There were certainly a lot of Red Sox fans in the stands that day.

In the Detroit half of the fourth, Martinez was still looking very good. He gave up a couple of singles and a run did score, in part because of a throwing error by Mueller. But Martinez had struck out two more for *nine* strikeouts so far!

The top of the fifth was a quick one for Boston, three batters, three outs. The bottom of the inning was the roughest patch Martinez had had yet that game and I started to get a little nervous. A single, and then a two-out walk, uh oh. Another single scored the second Tigers run. This was the first inning Martinez didn't have at least one strike out, and he walked a batter. Was it to go downhill from there?

John Ennis took the mound for Detroit in the sixth inning and handled the Red Sox, three up, three outs. Uh oh!

Martinez got through the sixth facing six more batters. He hit the next batter, who ended up on second on a wild pitch. Carlos Pena walked with two outs, but a pop-up ended the inning. Phew! I was starting to get hopeful that we would hold on to the lead and win.

In the top of the seventh Dave Roberts walked. He took second on a balk. Damon walked. It was time for a new Tigers pitcher. Youkilis hit a single, and our speedy Roberts scored. Damon made it to third. Millar singled, Damon scored, and Youkilis made it to second. Two more runs! Yeah! Another pitching change for Detroit, and Gabe Kapler came in to pinch-run for Millar. Ortiz hit a single, and Youkilis scored. Ortiz was out at second trying for a double, but Kapler scored on the throw. I could hardly believe it, four more runs that inning!

Martinez came back in and faced only three in the seventh, striking out two. The other lined out. Martinez struck out a total of *eleven* that day and I was so very impressed!

Mike Timlin pitched the bottom of the eighth. The Tigers scored their third run. Keith Foulke was the Red Sox closer at the time. He gave up a solo home run. Final score Boston 7, Tigers 4. As always I was happy that Boston won, but more than that I was thrilled to have seen Pedro Martinez pitch so very well from such wonderful seats. One thing that struck me was that so many people left after the seventh inning. They missed some really good baseball!

Because the game only took a little over two and a half hours, we decided to hang around outside the ballpark and visited some of the tents that were set up with displays, games, and giveaways. I remember getting a small souvenir bat from one tent and a Detroit Tigers pencil from another. It was a very good game, and we didn't want to leave even when it ended. We finally surrendered and headed back to the hotel to get some rest before the trek home the following day.

A GIANT LEAP

The very next weekend, we had tickets to see the Giants in Philly on August 14, 2004. I was still excited about the last game, not to mention looking forward to seeing another team I hadn't seen yet and Barry Bonds. He was on the quest for his 700th home run, which he did hit at AT&T Park a month later. I had hopes of seeing him hit a home run, maybe *the* home run.

As luck would have it Eric was unavailable again, so I headed off to Philly by myself, very disappointed. I wasn't going to miss seeing the Giants and Barry.

I arrived at the ballpark early and took a walk around Citizens Bank Park to get myself over the disappointment of no Eric. On my way into the park I heard talk that Barry Bonds was not in the lineup, which didn't cheer me up any. It was a little bit cool and looked like it might rain, which contributed to my glum feeling. I decided I would just go in, get something to eat, and find my seat. My seat was in the outfield, which wasn't my favorite perspective, but it was at least under a roof. I was again looking down the first baseline toward home plate.

Soon others filled in the seats around me. The older couple who sat a few seats to my left chatted a bit and seemed very nice. In some ways it was hard to feel too lonely at a ballpark.

A gentleman brought a radio and was listening to the game on it. Eric and I tried that from time to time, but I never got the hang of it. I shared with them that I had come alone in hopes of seeing Barry and was disappointed that he wasn't in the lineup. The game got underway in front of a sellout crowd of over 43,700 fans that I am sure were there for the same reason I was: to see Barry Bonds hit a home run.

Eric Milton was pitching for Philadelphia. He faced four batters in the first and was off to a good start. I was intending to root for the Phillies but found myself at odds with myself about it. Looking back, I believe this was probably the culmination of all the disappointments of the day.

Noah Lowry took the mound for San Francisco and started off the same way as Milton. In the top of the second, Milton gave up a two-out, two-run home run to give the Giants the lead. In the third inning, the first San Francisco batter hit a solo home run off Milton to extend the Giants' lead. A triple followed by a single scored yet another run. The Giants were up 5–0.

Had I driven all this way alone for no Barry and the game was blowout too? And then it started to rain—not very hard, but the people at the ends of the rows were getting wet, so everyone shifted in.

The Phillies started to rally in the bottom of the third scoring, two runs. Okay, this could be a good game after all. In the bottom of the fourth, Lowry still on the mound, the Phillies scored two more runs, making it a one-run game! In the bottom of the fifth, the Phillies continued the rally with a two-run home run to take the lead.

In the top of the sixth the Giants tied the game on a one-out home run. Yeah, I was really paying attention at that point. The batter hit a single, and then the manager used a pinch hitter who then drew a walk. The Phillies made some moves in the outfield and made a pitching change before the inning ended. There was only one more hit and a couple more defensive moves until the eighth inning. I was chatting with the group to my left.

In the top of the eighth there was another pitching change for Philadelphia. I was focusing on the game again when the gentleman next to me with the radio was reaching around his wife and started tapping me on the shoulder. "He's coming," he started saying. I am sure I had a very quizzical look on my face until I heard the announcement that Barry Bonds had stepped into the on-deck circle! Yeah! I was going to get to see him after all!

CANDY L. VANDYKE

The batter hit a home run, and the Giants took the lead. I was shocked, as I had been distracted by the announcement about Barry Bonds in the on-deck circle. Bonds was intentionally walked, which I guess was historic in its own right. I saw Barry Bonds get intentionally walked in Philadelphia. Many people left after that, which still amazed me.

The Phillies got a couple more hits, and several more defensive moves were made, but the final score was Giants 7, Phillies 6 in just over three hours. It wasn't the way I had hoped the game would turn out, but at least I got to see Barry Bonds for one at-bat. Maybe I would get to see him (if he was still playing for the Giants) when I made the trip to San Francisco, I told myself.

I drove back recapping the day, the good and the bad. I concluded that at least Philadelphia was an easy drive and I did get to see Barry Bonds.

BIRDS OF A DIFFERENT COLOR

In early June we had gotten tickets for a game in Baltimore the following weekend to see Toronto. This game was the best of possible scenarios as it was a late afternoon start time, which meant time to explore before and after the game. Baltimore was too far to drive down and back in one day, so we would have plenty of time to see the sights.

Things went as planned and the trip down was uneventful. We wandered around town and the stadium some. We went in to the stadium and headed down the walkway between the warehouse and the stadium. On the wall of the warehouse was a plaque where a ball hit by Ken Griffey, Jr. had landed during the 1993 home run derby. I remembered my first time at Camden Yards, when I had wondered if a ball ever hit the warehouse—I had my affirmative answer.

It was a nice day, albeit a bit cloudy. We made our way in and to our seats to get settled in before the game. As much as I was enjoying getting to all the stadiums and seeing the games I finally admitted to myself that I enjoy the games much more when it was a team I really liked and knew more about. But there is still nothing like being at a ball game, no matter what. During the singing of "The Star Spangled Banner," the fans emphasize the "O" in "Oh say can you see," which I thought was really neat.

Daniel Cabrera was on the mound for Baltimore. He didn't get off to a very good start, as he walked the first batter and then hit the second. I wasn't sure which team I would be rooting for, as they are both in the same division as the Red Sox, and therefore the enemy. A fly out, a sacrifice fly by Carlos Delgado, another player I came to know and like when he played for the Mets from 2006 through 2009, and the first Blue Jay run scored. Once again, a lead-off walk produced a run. Great! Toronto scored a run without even getting a hit. I found myself hoping the game would get better from there.

In the bottom of the first inning the Orioles threatened with a couple of singles, but they weren't able to score. In the top of second inning, two singles followed by a double scored two more Toronto runs. A single drove in a third. Carlos Delgado hit a home run to drive in two more for the Blue Jays. With the score 6–0 after two innings, it was going to be a long game for the Orioles fans.

Dave Bush pitched a perfect inning in the bottom of the second. His counterpart, Cabrera, gave up two more runs before being taken out of the game in third inning, behind by eight. We were a bit disappointed in the runaway game so we decide to go get some food.

By the time we got back to our seats, it was the bottom of the fourth and the score was 9–0. Bush pitched another perfect inning in the bottom of the fourth. In the top of the fifth, Williams gave up a hit in only the second inning that Toronto didn't score. In the bottom of the inning, the Orioles managed to score two runs on a solo home run and a series of singles. I found myself rooting for the underdog without really making a conscious decision to do so.

Rafael Palmeiro started off the bottom of the sixth inning with a double. Great! Here we go! Javy Lopez followed it up with a single, another run. Toronto got that run right back in the seventh. With only one more run for Baltimore in the bottom of the ninth the final score was Blue Jays 10, Orioles 4. It really wasn't the most exciting game I had ever seen, but I was pleased to have seen the Blue Jays.

THE DOUBLEHEADER THAT WASN'T

We headed back the next day looking forward to the coming doubleheader at Yankee Stadium against the then Devil Rays, as Tampa Bay was still called, in a couple of weeks. I know I said I wasn't going to go back to that place, but it was one of the closet stadiums to home and I could see more new teams there.

We decided to head to the stadium early to get a decent parking spot. We went to get a bite to eat and then walked around a little bit. When we went to go into the stadium a couple of hours before the game, we were told that the Devil Rays weren't there yet. We thought we might as well go in and wait. We went in, found our seats, and enjoyed just spending time together. We were sitting in the lower part of the upper deck, so the view was very nice. It was an overcast day and cool, not a bad day to be outside at all. It wasn't long after we got there that the announcement came that the game would be delayed, as Tampa hadn't even left the airport in Florida yet because of the hurricane. They said we could leave the stadium and come back in, which wasn't usually allowed, but we decided to stay. We were discussing heading to the concourse for some snacks when the announcement was made that anyone staying would get free hot dogs. That made our decision for us.

We figured it would be a while so Eric had the wonderful idea of going to see Monument Park. I was excited because we had missed out on Monument Park on previous visits.

We waited in line. When we got to walk through I was amazed. It was definitely something to see. Even my eyes welled up with all the wonderful history there. That was one of the most special parts of the day for me.

I believe it was after 5:00 PM when they made the announcement that Tampa was on their way and that only one game would be played, at 7:00 PM. We continued to reminisce about our rainout at Shea at the second game we ever went to, and about other games we had enjoyed. We went for more refreshment and they gave us more free hot dogs! It must have been a very long day for the concession workers.

I was in for a real treat. Orlando Hernandez was pitching for the Yankees. He would eventually play for the Mets late in 2006. He was touted to be one of the best in the game. After waiting all day, I was excited to finally see the game get underway.

Hernandez gave up a single and hit a batter with a pitch, but neither runner scored. The Tampa pitcher walked both Alex Rodriguez and Hideki Matsui, but neither of them scored either.

In the top of the second, Hernandez gave up a homer to Jorge Cantu to put the Yankees behind by one. Wahoo! That score held until the bottom of the third when Derek Jeter hit a single, A-Rod hit a double, and Gary Sheffield grounded out, scoring Jeter to tie the game. We weren't surprised but still disappointed.

In the bottom of the fourth Tampa pitching had more trouble. Jorge Posada hit a single and then took second on a throwing error by the pitcher. Bernie Williams hit a single, moving Posada to third. Those darn Yankees were on a tear! Miguel Cairo hit a sacrifice fly, and Posada scored to take the lead. Kenny Lofton hit a single and advanced Williams. Jeter walked to load the bases, and then A-Rod doubled *again* to score three more runs.

The Yankees were up by four runs, and Hernandez had another three up, three down inning in the top of the fifth. It was going to be a frustrating game!

The stands were pretty empty, even though the box score said there were over 44,400 in attendance. We decided to see if we could work our way down closer to the field. By the bottom of the fifth inning, we were able to find empty seats right behind home plate, maybe four or five rows up. These seats were the closest I had sat to the field at that point and wow, it was great.

They had already made the announcement that our tickets would be good for a future game, so we made sure we tucked them away safely. At one point, Eric reached under his seat for the binoculars or something. He came up with two more tickets in his hand. I could tell by the look on his face that he was as surprised as I was. They were tickets for the seats we were in and they were expensive! No one came back to claim them, so we decided not to let them go to waste. The tickets would become four tickets to two different games the following year.

In the top of the sixth Tampa scored another run to make it 5–2 Yankees. The next few innings had a couple of hits but no further scoring happened until the bottom of the eighth. We were just enjoying the view from the awesome seats.

In the bottom of the eighth the Yankees started off with a single by Olerud and another single by Williams. They were up by three and only needed to get three more outs. Why they pinch-ran Bubba Crosby and brought in Ruben Sierra to hit for Kenny Lofton, I didn't understand. That prompted another Tampa pitching change. Sierra hit a single, and Crosby scored. Jeter hit a sacrifice fly and Williams scored. The moves paid off.

The Devil Rays got the runs right back in top of the ninth on a two-run homer, but it wasn't enough. Yankees won 7–4. I felt bad for the Devil Rays, as they played really well after the extremely hard time they had even getting to New York.

PERCOLATING

A couple of weeks later we had tickets for a Saturday night game at Shea against the Cubs. We decided to go down early Saturday and spend the day at the beach in NJ before the game, stay over, and drive home on Sunday. I was still a member of the Red Sox Nation and had entered a drawing for a chance to purchase tickets to a playoff game. I found out the morning we were leaving that I had been chosen to purchase tickets. After being selected, actually purchasing playoff ticket involved waiting your turn in a virtual waiting room. After spending some time waiting we decided to take the computer with the hope that the hotel would have Internet access so we could make another attempt when we got there. We didn't want to waste the whole day at home trying to get tickets.

When we got there, the hotel didn't have Internet access, but the staff directed us to a place that did. We got online, and after waiting almost to the time limit we had set for ourselves, we finally got the opportunity to buy tickets. We made our choice, bought the tickets, and headed off to the beach pretty happy with ourselves. One of the things I had wanted to do was see a playoff game. I also thought it would be cool to see a spring training game, a World Series game, and maybe even two games in two different stadiums in the same day. But that day the possibility of seeing a playoff game at Fenway was excitement enough.

We had a nice day at the beach, cooking clams on the small portable grill we had brought. We thought it might be nice to tailgate at the ballpark before the game so we bought some shrimp and scallops for that purpose. After such an enjoyable day on the beach we were ready to head to the game the next day. We managed to find a great parking spot next to a sidewalk to allow extra room for the chairs and the grill. We had a very nice little tailgate party and many people who walked by commented on the fact that we were cooking seafood.

The Mets were out of the pennant race but the Cubs still had hope. They were a game and a half ahead of San Francisco in the National League wild card race. Our intention was to root for the Cubs. We had really decent seats to the game. We were in the first row behind the season- ticket-holder seats, the lowest orange seats.

An usher came over to see our tickets and we began chatting with him. He made small talk and we all agreed it was a nice evening for a ball game in September at seventy-three degrees.

Aaron Heilman was pitching for New York, and Mark Prior was pitching for Chicago, which sounded like a good matchup to me. In the first inning Heilman walked Derrek Lee and Moises Alou but wriggled out of trouble by striking out Sammy Sosa. Prior on the other hand took care of the Mets in order. I wanted to be happy but it just didn't feel right.

In the second inning Nomar Garciaparra (always good to see one of my favorite players even when they aren't with one of my teams anymore) hit a single, and then Todd Walker, who had also played for Boston the previous year, hit a home run. Well then. Two hits scored two runs in the second. I was finding it hard to root against the Mets, but Eric had less of a problem with it. I understood the logistics of the playoff race, but still, I was watching the Mets. Rooting for the other team just felt wrong to me. I kept fairly quiet, but inside I was rooting for the Mets, period. Each team got a hit in their third time up, but no runs scored.

The stands were about half empty, with about 34,000 people in attendance. After the third inning the usher that we had been chatting with told us we could move down into the orange seats, because he knew the regulars. If they weren't there by then, they weren't coming. That was really cool.

I was really getting into taking pictures at the game, so I borrowed a friend's digital camera to see if I wanted to invest in one. I had the camera in my hand when they came by tossing t-shirts into the crowd. One came right to me, but I couldn't make the catch with the camera in one hand. Eric has never let me forget it!

Both pitchers were dead on until the bottom of the fifth inning. The Mets got three men on but didn't score. Even so, it was a hopeful inning. The score was still Cubs 2, Mets 0.

Despite the score I started to get a strong feeling that the Mets were going to come back. I asked Eric if he could say "extra innings." He looked at me and was very confused because the Mets were behind. I just smiled and said "Wait and see."

Mark Prior was still in and put the Mets out in order again in the seventh. Eric was now chuckling at my comments, but I really couldn't shake the feeling I had. I just shrugged my shoulders.

In the top of the eighth, Mike Stanton gave up a single to Mark Prior, which prompted the Mets to bring in Bartolome Fortunato. He walked the next two batters to load the bases. Eric was out-and-out laughing at me by this point! Heath Bell took the mound for New York and walked in a run before getting out of the inning. It was Cubs 3, Mets 0. Eric just looked at me, grinning. Next inning each team got a hit but no runs.

In the bottom of the ninth I was quiet. Eric asked me if I was still feeling extra innings. I didn't waver. I said yes. He just about hurt himself laughing so hard.

There was a pitching change for the Cubs. Todd Zeile pinch-hit for Bell and struck out. The new pitcher walked the next two batters, which drove him out of the game. A fly out advanced the lead runner to third. Eric looked over at me with a smirk on his face only to find I was smirking too.

Then it happened. Victor Diaz hit a home run to tie the game. Eric just looked at me in total disbelief! I couldn't help but smile a told-you-so smile. I took my hand and lifted Eric's jaw which had dropped in disbelief. The next batter struck out and voilà, extra innings.

In the middle of the tenth inning, I said "Uh oh." Eric told me to stop percolating in a scolding tone. He could see by the smile on my face it was not good news for the Cubs, so he had to ask. All I said was "Can you say 'walk-off'?" He shook his head and admonished me again to stop. Three hits and four pitching changes later, it was still tied in the bottom of the eleventh.

Kent Mercker came in to pitch for Chicago, and Michael Barrett came in to catch. Craig Brazell came up to bat. Crack! Home run. Mets win with a walk-off home run. Eric just sat there in astonishment, almost afraid to look at me! I was so happy the Mets won, giddy really. But I was a little sad that the Cubs had just broken their winning streak. Shortly after that they fell out of the race all together. I know it really didn't have anything to do with me, but Eric blamed me and enjoyed telling anyone who would listen, especially after he moved to a western suburb of Chicago, how I cost the Cubs the pennant in 2004. All in all, I thought it was a good weekend.

WHICH SCENARIO?

We followed the rest of the regular season closely to see if it worked out in our favor to get to attend the playoff game in Boston we had gotten tickets for. The tickets we had were for home game three.

We were somewhat confused as to what "home game three" meant. So when the day we thought was the day of our game came, we took the day off and went to Boston. It turned out we were wrong. I was not really sure why, but apparently many other people made the same mistake as well. We had booked a hotel and spent the money on gas to get there so we decided it would be fun to go back to the hotel and watch the game there.

We made our way back to the hotel listening to the game on the radio. Next door to the hotel was a sports bar, so we went over there to get something to eat and watch the game. The place was crowded, but they got us in. It was obvious by the collective cheers and sighs that most everyone there was watching the game. After we ate we went back to the hotel to watch the rest of the game because there was a line waiting for a table.

The game was tied until the bottom of the tenth, when David Ortiz hit a two-run home run. The Red Sox won. They had swept the Angels, and we were at least in Boston when it happened!

On Saturday we decided to make the best of things and do some sightseeing before we headed back. We walked around town and enjoyed the atmosphere of celebration. We had lunch at Legal Seafood and headed back home.

We all know how the rest of the season went. But after game three of the series against the Yankees we were fearful that the Red Sox had fallen apart again. Partway through game four, Eric got so upset he threw his hat and went home. I didn't see or talk to him again until the Sox won the World Series. I watched every minute of every game. After game four of the Yankee series, I just knew it was the year, sort of like how I felt at the Mets-Cubs game. Eric called me after the final game to share the moment and so we could congratulate each other. I was disappointed that he wasn't around to watch the games with me but I was really happy the Red Sox finally had won the World Series again.

I watched the trades that off-season closely and dreamt of where I would go the following season.

THE CURSE: NOT ALIVE IN 2005

I n February, tickets for the Hall of Fame Game in Cooperstown went on sale. That year the Red Sox were playing Detroit in the annual exhibition game, so we decided to see if we could get tickets. The night before, Eric said he wouldn't be able to go, so I said I would go by myself to see if I could get us tickets. He had done it one other time and advised me to get there early, because there would be way more people than tickets.

I left early as planned. When I got there, the line was already to the end of the block so I knew my chances were slim to none. But because I had made the trip, I decided to wait it out a while anyway. It was cold, but there were a lot of people in close proximity. That helped make it tolerable. I was chatting with those near me and having a nice time.

My cell phone rang. At the time I had "Take Me Out To The Ball Game" as my ring tone, which drew everyone's attention. All of a sudden someone started to sing and we all joined in and sang it through a couple of times. I thought that was so cool!

Some time later, someone yelled out if the person with the ring tone was still there, and I yelled out yes. They asked me to play it again. I did and we sang again. I didn't end up with tickets but still had a fun day. I cranked the heat all the way home so I could thaw out.

In March we started making plans for the year. We got tickets for Boston in April and made plans to see a few games over Memorial Day weekend in May which meant three new stadiums for me. It was challenging to make sure the teams were all home at the same time. The logistics of it all were interesting. I had to map out the trip and allow enough time to get to the next stadium, in addition to finding hotels near the stadium and giving us some lead time toward the next game. Our goal was to get to Jacobs Field in Cleveland, Wrigley Field and U.S. Cellular Field in Chicago, Miller Park in Milwaukee, and the Hubert H. Humphrey Metrodome in Minneapolis all in five days. This would prove to be good practice for what was to come.

We got tickets to a game in Boston on Monday, April 18. We chose this date mostly because it was an 11 AM game and originally we thought we could make a weekend of it and then drive back Monday after the game. It turned out Eric wasn't able to go, so I decided I would be best to drive up and back in the same day.

The Red Sox were playing the Blue Jays, and unbeknownst to me it was Patriots Day which is the day of the running of the Boston Marathon. I had no idea what that would mean for my trip. I left at 3:30 AM in order to get there, find parking, and take a walk around Fenway which I so enjoyed. Traffic was a little bit heavier because of the marathon but things were pretty much on schedule. Eric called during the drive to make sure I was doing okay with the Massachusetts Turnpike, which I was. It was a nice day and my seat was in the right field grandstands. I was going to see Curt Schilling pitch for the first time. I parked in the first parking lot I saw and headed toward Fenway.

It was early in the season the year after winning it all, so it wasn't surprising that there were a ton of people milling around. I went in, bought myself a hot dog, and found my seat. I tried the Monster Dog. It took me most of the game to eat it because it was so big, but it was very good.

The first game of the season is always exciting for me. This one was even more so because I was getting to see the 2004 World Champion Boston Red Sox! That still gave me chills to say. There was a very touching pregame ceremony, and the game began. I was so excited to be seeing Curt Schilling pitching for Boston especially after the way the last season ended and his role in that victory. I had not seen him pitch in person but had become familiar with him from the prior year. I couldn't help but feel badly for Eric, who was missing out on seeing Schilling pitch. I refused to let that stuff take over my thoughts and just focused on settling in for the game and eating that Monster Dog. Yummy!

In the first inning Schilling only faced four batters. The only one to get a hit, a single, was Shea Hillenbrand, who played for Boston in 2002 and 2003. The other three struck out. That was truly a beautiful thing.

Dave Bush was pitching for Toronto. I had seen him beat the Orioles the previous August, so I knew it wasn't going to be an easy game, but I still had faith in Schilling. Bush looked pretty good until he walked Manny Ramirez, the third batter. David Ortiz hit a single, which advanced Ramirez to third. The Sox offense was looking like they did the previous fall, and I was so excited, as was most everyone else in the place. Then Kevin Millar hit a single to bring Ramirez in for the first run! It was only one run and it was only the bottom of the first inning but it was already a great game!

In the second inning Schilling gave us a little drama. He gave up a single to the first batter. He struck out the next and the next flied out. But then a single landed a man on third. Uh oh! Schilling walked the next batter to load the bases. Bill Mueller didn't help when he dropped a foul ball which would have ended the inning! Ugh! Schilling came through and struck out the next batter to finally end the inning. It was okay to breathe again.

The boys came back in the bottom of the second to score four more runs including a three-run homer by Ramirez. Okay, we were up 5–0. That was more like it.

The Blue Jays did get a run in the third inning. In the bottom of the third inning, Bush walked Millar and gave up a double to Renteria before he was replaced by Brandon League, who intentionally walked Mueller to load the bases. It was rare that anyone loaded the bases with Boston players and get out of it without giving up at least a run. League was no exception. Mark Bellhorn hit a ground-rule double to drive in two more runs. Then Johnny Damon hit a single to drive in two more. 9–1, wahoo!

The top of the fourth inning was another difficult inning for Schilling, but the healthy lead was comforting. Toronto was helped by an error by Ramirez on a fly ball, landing the runner safely on second! A single, a run scored, and still only one out. A double put men on second and third, still with only one out. A sacrifice fly scored another run. Hillenbrand hit a single, putting another man on third. Ugh—it felt like the inning that wouldn't end. Another walk loaded the bases! Ugh! Finally, Schilling got the second strikeout of the inning to end it, but two runs crossed, making the score Blue Jays 3, Red Sox 9.

After a one-two-three bottom of the fourth inning, the Blue Jays were at it again. Toronto scored two more runs making it 9–5 Red Sox. Still I was having a great time on a beautiful sunny day with 35,000 other fans.

In the sixth inning, John Halama came in to pitch for Boston and had a quick inning. In the Red Sox turn at bat, Nixon hit a single then Ramirez hit his second home run of the game, the first inside-the-park home run I had ever witnessed in person! Two more runs! The place went absolutely wild. I was amazed at how fast Manny could actually move when he needed to. The score was 11–5. Ortiz struck out, which was something that drove me nuts about him. At the time, it seemed like he either hit a home run or struck out. It was frustrating to watch, as I am sure it was for him to play through. I really like him, though. He seems to be such a good person and shows his love of the game. Millar hit a double, but they were unable to get him home, as Jason Varitek struck out.

Matt Mantei came in to pitch for Boston in the seventh, and Jay Payton came into play left field, replacing Ramirez. The Blue Jays were not going to go down easily. They were getting hits and playing very good baseball. Even a six-run lead was only a little bit comforting.

Toronto capitalized on a single to score another run with a couple of pinch-hitters despite a couple of Red Sox pitching changes. Mueller greeted the next Toronto pitcher with a double. Damon hit a single. Nixon hit a sacrifice fly to score Mueller and land Damon on third. We got the run back. Payton grounded out to end the inning, but the lead was back to six.

In the top of the ninth, Blaine Neal took the mound for Boston. That was the first and only time I saw him pitch. I had no idea what to expect. Vernon Wells greeted him with a single. Eric Hinske followed suit with another single, moving Wells to third. Hmm. Alex Rios struck out on three pitches—okay, good! Orlando Hudson hit a single to center field. As we all know, Johnny Damon doesn't have a great arm, so Wells scored easily. Darn it! One out and two on! But then the pinch hitter grounded into a double play to end the inning and the game! Wahoo! The final score was Red Sox 12, Blue Jays 7 after one very exciting three and a half hour game.

I headed out of the stadium with everyone high-fiving around me. I was making my way back to the car when all of a sudden a row of cops jumped up right in front of me with their arms out to stop the crowd. A car pulled out of the parking lot under Fenway. Who was in the car but Curt Schilling. He was smiling and waving to the crowd! I heard on the radio later that he was going to meet his wife, Shonda, at the finish line of the marathon. Mike Timlin's wife, Dawn, and Stacey Lucchino (wife of Red Sox executive Larry Lucchino) also ran in the marathon. That was so cool! That was the closest I had been to a major league baseball player. It was so neat, even though it happened so fast.

I got back to the car only to find the streets were blocked off along the route that I was familiar with to get out of the city. Uh oh! I did my best to remember the times that Eric and I had been there and tried to find any street that sounded familiar. I was able to slowly make my way back to the Mass Pike after a couple of hours in very slow-moving traffic. It felt good to be able to travel more then 10 miles an hour. This was one of the longest baseball days for me, as I didn't get home until after 10:30 PM that night. It was worth it. Driving to that great game gave me the confidence to take on many more solo baseball adventures in the future.

Early in May we decided to take another trip to Baltimore to see the Red Sox in late September and ordered tickets for that game with the intention of maybe getting some beach time in as well.

FIVE GAMES, FIVE DAYS

I t was getting close to our Memorial Day weekend five-games-in-five-days trip. I hadn't seen the Brewers play yet, but I would as soon as we hit Milwaukee. The Rockies were going to be at the Cubs that weekend, so that was another team I had yet to see as well. We decided to see the Chicago teams back-to-back so we could spend some time with a friend of Eric who lives in the western suburbs of Chicago. He offered to let us stay with him, so we got tickets for him and his wife to go with us to the Cubs game.

The logistics would go like this: we would leave work by noon on Friday and head to Cleveland for a night game, stay outside of Cleveland Friday night, get up and drive to Milwaukee for a night game Saturday night, stay in Milwaukee Saturday night, get up Sunday morning and head to Chicago for a 1:00 PM game at Wrigley, stay at Eric's friend's Sunday night, on Monday go to a midday game at U.S. Cellular, and then head toward Minneapolis for a night game on Tuesday before heading back. We decided to book a hotel in Milwaukee and we would stay with Eric's friend on Sunday night, but the rest of it was going to be open-ended so we could drive until we got tired. To top things off, we bought tickets for the following Saturday to see the Giants at Shea because Eric had missed them in Philadelphia the year before. It was to be a very busy week!

Friday came and we were both able to skip work entirely. We headed out around 9:00 AM. We made it to Ohio around 2:00 PM, which gave us

75

plenty of time to take in some of the sights before the game. We had both been to Jacobs Field before, but we really hadn't had the time to look around Cleveland until that visit.

I had a second cousin, Norman, who I was very fond of and visited weekly. He was in a nursing home. He was a baseball fan and a very big Red Sox fan. We often talked about the game and, of course, the Red Sox. He liked to travel but was unable to do it any more. I had the idea of taking extra pictures and collecting more details of the trip in my journal to send to him so he could feel like he was there with us. Taking pictures of the road signs along the way gave me something else to do while riding in the car. I knew how much Norman would enjoy it.

We started out down by Lake Erie and then walked around town for a while. I took pictures of the freighter *William G. Mather* that was docked on the lakefront to include in my letter to Norman. We found a place and grabbed a little dinner then headed to the stadium. The Oakland Athletics were in town to play the Indians. Jacobs Field was only about ten years old, and one of the first of the retro stadiums. It was a nice place and the people are friendly. I particularly liked the scoreboard with the three tall light stacks behind it and, of course, the team name painted behind home plate.

Both Oakland and Cleveland had been on a losing streak but it promised to be an interesting game. Barry Zito was pitching for Oakland again. Cliff Lee was pitching for Cleveland. The sky was cloudy and it just felt like rain, so we figured there would be a rain delay. In fact. there were two. After the second rain delay, so many people had left that we were able to find seats down closer to the field.

It was one of those games where I wasn't sure who I was going to root for. The game started with a single and two walks, loading the bases before the first out. After the first out came on a strikeout, there was a really cool double play. Keith Ginter hit a grounder to the first baseman who then threw it to the catcher, Victor Martinez, who came to play in Boston in 2009, to get the runner out at home. Martinez threw it back to the first basemen in time to get that runner out and end the inning. It was really something to see.

From there, it was slow going. In the bottom of the second, Cleveland managed a single and drew walks to load the bases with one out. A sacrifice fly drove in one run.

The score and pitchers stayed the same with a walk and strike out scattered here and there, but no hits until the seventh inning. Cleveland manufactured another run in the seventh. We both decided to root for Oakland so we hadn't given up hope, but it was getting late and the A's had only been able to get two hits so far in the game.

In the bottom of the inning there was a two-run homer to double the lead for the Indians. Okay, four runs is not impossible. We were still hoping. Bob Wickman came in for Cleveland. Eric knew of him and said that in his time Wickman was a formidable closer. He was actually the closer who saved the game back in 2002 at my very first game at Fenway when the Indians beat the Red Sox. My hope was diminishing. But then Wickman gave up a double and walked two to load the bases with just one out. One big swing could tie this up! Apparently the manager thought so too, because he pulled Wickman and brought in David Riske.

Riske had successfully pitched an inning against the Angels the last time we were in Cleveland, so we were nervous that it would be a shutout. Nick Swisher was up to bat. He got a hit to drive in a run. Bases were still loaded, the score 4–1 Indians, but there were two outs. Charles Thomas came in to pinch-run for Swisher, so the A's weren't ready to give up yet. But at nearly 11 PM, all hope was lost with a ground ball to second to end the game.

The Indians had broken their losing streak in front of not even 20,000 against the Oakland A's. We were both now convinced that Eric was a good luck charm for the Indians, as he had never seen them lose, ever, at any game he attended. Baseball is a game of superstitions, after all.

We headed west for about an hour before we found a place to stay in Sandusky. We wanted to get a good night's rest, this being just the first night of a five-day trip.

Saturday morning we had breakfast at the hotel and headed out for our six-hour drive to Milwaukee. We knew traffic would be bad near Chicago so we expected it would take longer then the mapping program suggested. We did stop and enjoy some time outside en route. With that and the traffic, we arrived at the game almost too late to see it start.

The stadium itself was very nice, obviously fairly new, maybe a year or two old at the time. To our surprise it had a retractable roof, the first one I had seen. The weather forecast was questionable, but the day had turned out to be nice, a little cool but no rain. They kept the roof closed anyway.

We made our way to our seats from the parking lot, which was difficult because Eric had a sudden migraine, which made it nearly impossible for him to see. He said his migraines usually lasted anywhere from several hours to several days. I was concerned and went to first aid to see if I could at least get him a couple of aspirin. We were both surprised and grateful that his headache subsided swiftly.

We had pretty good seats even though they were in the middle of a row. It was a sellout crowd of well over 37,800 fans. Ben Sheets was pitching for the Brewers and Wandy Rodriguez was pitching for the Astros. I went into the game not knowing who I was going to be rooting for and of course was initially distracted by Eric not feeling well. Ironically, that would be the only time I would see either of the pitchers pitch.

Houston got off to a good start and manufactured four runs. It seemed like it would be another disappointing day if I were thinking of rooting for the Brewers. In the bottom of the inning the Brewers got one run back. At that point I decided to go to first aid for the aspirin for Eric and missed the next couple of innings, not getting back to my seat until the top of the fourth. Eric said I really hadn't missed much, because neither team got a hit.

In the bottom of the fourth the Brewers were at it again. They cut the lead in half, which provided more hope if one were rooting for the Brewers, which I found myself doing without really making the decision to do so. The Brewers gained more ground on a pair of doubles to make it a one-run game, adding some more hope for me!

The hope didn't last long. Despite a couple more pitching changes, the Astros scored five more runs. So much for that one-run lead; it was suddenly a six-run lead.

Junior Spivey hit a solo home run in the bottom of the inning to lessen the gap by one and help keep some hope alive. One of the cool things about seeing a home run hit by a Brewer was seeing Bernie the mascot slide down the slide in the outfield, another one of those unique things I enjoy at the different ballparks. I was told it was brought over from the previous stadium.

In the bottom of the eighth the Brewers managed to get a couple of solo home runs. Wahoo! A couple of more slides down for Bernie made the score Astros 9, Brewers 6. Still down by three, but that inning really lifted my spirits.

A perfect top of the ninth got the Brewers right back up to bat while the bats were hot! Unfortunately the game was wrapped up in short order by Brad Lidge. I asked Eric if Lidge was one of the Killer B's, and Eric said he was that night. The final was score Houston 9, Milwaukee 6.

It was a good game even though the Brewers weren't able to turn it around. It had only taken about two and three-quarter hours for the game. Even though Eric was feeling better we just headed back to the hotel to get some rest as the next morning was going to be an early one.

Chicago was only a two-hour drive away but it was an early 1:20 PM game at Wrigley so we wanted to get there with plenty of time to visit with Eric's friend and his wife before we all headed to the game, so we got up fairly early. We grabbed breakfast at the hotel and went out to load up the car.

When we got outside we saw a beautiful rainbow. As we stood there admiring it, we began to see a second rainbow just below it. I had never seen a double rainbow and it was quite a sight. It was comforting, a great way to start off the day.

Traffic was light, much to our delight, and we arrived early. We found out that Eric's friend's wife was out of town so he had invited the neighbor to go with us in her stead, which was fine with us.

Eric's friend drove to the game which was a relief to Eric. We had covered a lot of miles in the past two days. Eric and I had walked around Wrigley on our visit to his friend's back in 2003 but it was my first time to actually see a game there. I really liked how you could see into the field from the street and how so many of the buildings in the area have bleacher seats on their roofs that are filled for most every game. To top it off, the Cubs were playing the Rockies, whom I hadn't seen yet.

These tickets had been the hardest to get off all the games I had seen. I signed online at 10 AM Friday morning and didn't get tickets until 2:00 AM

Saturday morning. At that point I couldn't even get four seats together. I got two seats, one behind the other, in two different sets of rows. At least we were all in the same section. There had been other times we had tried to get tickets to Cubs games to no avail, so I was pleased to have gotten these. Eric's friend had gone to many games and usually had better seats than we were able to get, but I think he was still glad to get to go with us.

We parked the car and walked to Wrigley. I admit I was pretty giddy by then. We went inside, got some refreshments, and found our seats. We all sat together until the stands began to fill up with a sellout crowd of 40,000. Soon the game was underway.

The Cubs were on a two-game winning streak and I was rooting for them. I was confident that I was finally going to see the team I wanted to win to actually win for the first time on this road trip. The view of the skyline from our seats was amazing. I was on top of the world.

The Rockies managed a two-run homer to take an early lead. Was I in for another disappointment? Eric was sitting next to me in an obstructed view seat. No one ever came to sit there. The no-show afforded us a chance to sit next to each other. Eric was more worn out than he wanted to admit, and promptly fell asleep. I teased him relentlessly, saying he should be thankful the pole was in front of him so none of the players could see him sleeping!

In the bottom of the second inning the Cubs got one run back. In the top of the third a Rockies solo homer took the run right back away from the Cubs. Darn it!

In the bottom of that inning, the tables turned. The Cubs came up with two runs to tie the game. The tie score let me take a minute to breathe. In the top of the fifth inning, Colorado was at it again with a home run to regain the lead. Darn it! In the bottom of the fifth a two-run homer jumped the Cubs ahead for the first time that day. The place went wild and woke Eric up from his nap. He was embarrassed, to say the least.

In the top of the sixth inning, the Rockies scored two more runs to take back the lead. Oh my! In the bottom of the sixth, the Cubs broke the game open, scoring five runs, three of which were from a home run. Todd Walker gave another one a ride in the seventh to make the score Cubs 11, Rockies 6. At that point our driver wanted to beat the traffic so we left. I was so happy to finally have the team I was rooting for win. We listened to the rest of the game on the radio. I wanted to make sure that was the final score. It was.

We went back to the house and some other friends came over. We had Chicago-style pizza and talked into the wee hours of the morning. We got a good night's sleep. We were happy to be able to sleep in some the next morning. We said our grateful goodbyes then headed across town to the early afternoon game on the South side.

This was our second time to "the Cell," as U.S. Cellular was affectionately called around Chicagoland. The first time we were late and sat next to some rude people who were not at all interested in the game. We were certainly hoping for a better experience. We were seeing the Angels play the White Sox, a potentially exciting game.

It was a sunny, cool day, perfect for a ball game. We were seeing our fourth in four days. How crazy was that? And we weren't done yet!

Mark Buehrle was the starting pitcher for the White Sox and Jarrod Washburn was the starting pitcher for the Angels. This was the first time I had seen either of these pitchers in person, but Eric seemed to think it was a good matchup. If the first inning was an indicator he was right as both pitchers only faced three batters.

In the top of the second inning we noticed a cool thing. Bengie Molina and Jose Molina, two of three Molina brothers who are big-league catchers, were in the lineup at catcher and at DH respectively. This was the first time we had seen brothers playing on the same team in the same game. In that inning, the Angels managed to get two on, but couldn't score.

Washburn started off the bottom of the inning with a walk, which came back to bite him when the White Sox brought the runner around to score. He continued to struggle, giving up two more walks, one of which was to Frank Thomas to load the bases. Thomas was playing for the first time in a year due to an injury. I was pleased to hear the crowd go crazy when he came up to bat. Their cheering was akin to what I had experienced at my very first game in Boston, when Manny Ramirez returned from a long absence due to injury. Eric and I had seen Thomas hit a home run in 2003 against Texas. I had realized then that he was truly one of the greats. I certainly couldn't blame Washburn for not wanting to give Frank Thomas anything to hit. But a subsequent long double brought home two more White Sox runs.

In the top of the fourth, the Angels retaliated with a leadoff home run for their first score. I found myself rooting for the Angels for no particular reason. Washburn posted a pair of easy innings. The Angels were not going quietly. In the top of the sixth they gave Buehrle more trouble and generated another run. Each team only got a single in the next two half-innings.

The score remained the same until the top of the ninth. Buehrle was still pitching for Chicago and had gotten one out, but had also put two men on. At that point the managed decided that Buehrle had had enough and made a pitching change.

The next batter grounded into a fielder's choice, which I asked Eric to explain. We had seen this sort of play a few times already, and I wanted to be sure I understood it. The runner, who should have been out, ended up on base because of a throwing error by second baseman Iguchi. Oh my, things were getting interesting. A single scored another run and the bases were still loaded. Then the White Sox walked in the go-ahead run. I could hardly believe my eyes! I thought the Angels might actually win the game!

Chicago brought in another relief pitcher. The new guy was able to get the final out of the inning. Okay, three more outs and the Angels would steal a win. They were up by one, so the White Sox had to score in the bottom of the ninth. The Angels brought in Scot Shields to pitch, and made a few defensive substitutions. Willie Harris pinch-hit for Juan Uribe. He drew a walk. Uh oh. Joe Crede drew a walk. Oh *no*. Podsednik hit a sacrifice fly to advance the runners. Not looking good! Carl Everett hit for Iguchi and ended up striking out. Okay, two outs … can we just end this thing already? Next up was Timo Perez. He had played a few years for the Mets, so I found it hard to root against him. I just covered my eyes and peeked out between my fingers. The little guy hit a single to drive in the two runs needed to win the game. I could hardly believe it. I didn't feel too badly because it was a good game and neither team was my favorite. But it was the third time that trip the team I was rooting for lost. The home crowd of more than 38,000 was a fair sight more excited than I was.

It was only about 6:00 PM; things were going according to schedule. We would drive toward our next destination until we got tired and then find a place to get some rest. It was still daylight when we drove past Miller Park. I tried to get a couple of pictures but they didn't turn out very well. The wrong side of the highway in a moving car isn't much of a vantage for quality photos, it turns out.

We drove on until about midnight, and then found a place to stay. We had made more progress than we had expected, so we would have a good deal of time to do some sightseeing in Minnesota on Tuesday.

Eric had wanted to take me to the Mall of the Americas. He had been there a few years earlier on a business trip and was quite impressed. We mostly window-shopped, but there was one store that we actually went into. The shop had something to do with the radio show *A Prairie Home Companion*, a program that we both listened to. There were so many neat things in there. That was enough shopping for one day, so we walked around the mall's amusement park for a while before heading toward the Metrodome to see some sights around there.

The Mississippi River runs through Minneapolis. We actually climbed down the banks to put our hands in the river. This was rather exciting because we had plans to see the river again in late June on our trip to Missouri to see both baseball teams in that state. The "mighty Miss" was really something. The game wasn't until 7:10 PM that night, so we went to find something to eat. We found a really cool place very close to the dome. I am a Minnesota Vikings fan, so the restaurant's collection of Vikings gear was a cool bonus for me. I took some great pictures.

Afterward we walked all the way around the dome, which was very big. I was curious about the whole structure because I had never been inside a dome before. As soon as the gates opened, we went in so that we could wander around inside. You have to enter through a revolving door, because air pressure is part of what holds the dome up. The seating capacity was only about 46,564, but it seemed so big compared to Veterans Stadium, the only other multi-purpose stadiums I had visited at that point. Our seats were way up in the top tier, but almost directly behind home plate. The cheap seats were a result of five games in five days—we had to keep costs down where we could.

One of the neatest things we saw in Minnesota was a huge sign hanging high in the stands that read "Take me outside to the ball game," in support of building a new outdoor stadium for the Twins. The new park came to fruition in 2010. On our visit to the Metrodome, the Twins were playing the Indians, so we were both fairly sure who was going to win, especially with Eric in the house. But we were hoping for a good game, despite Eric's uncanny ability to cause the Indians to win. The inside of the dome was interesting, but I wondered if the white ceiling made it difficult for outfielders to see fly balls. The whole interior was fairly plain, with just a few championship flags and banners scattered around.

I was in for a real treat: C. C. Sabathia was going to be pitching for the Indians. Carlos Silva was pitching for the Twins. The closer it got to game time, the more apparent it was that it was going to be a really small crowd. Only about 16,000 people turned out that night. The paltry crowd made me really sad.

The first inning only saw a single from each side. The second inning was not so easy for Silva. It started with a double, followed by a couple of singles, one by Victor Martinez (a future Red Sox). Martinez's hit brought home the first run.

The Indians scoring first was no surprise with Eric, their good luck charm, in attendance. The Twins managed some damage of their own in the bottom of the second, plating two runs for a lead. They held the advantage until the top of the fourth when an Indians solo home run tied it up.

Sabathia was giving up singles here and there, but that was about it. The game remained tied until the top of the sixth. Silva was still on the mound. Martinez hit a very long home run with one out and one on to claim a two-run lead. The game seemed to be going really fast. I wasn't sure if it was because we were so high up that our judgment was skewed. Maybe it really was going fast.

Sabathia gave up one more run in the seventh. Only down by one, the Twins had a chance to break the curse against anyone playing the Indians whenever Eric was around. The relief pitchers did their jobs and only gave up one more hit in the bottom of the ninth.

But a Twins comeback wasn't to be. The final score was Indians 4, Twins 3, accomplished in a mere two and a half hours. It was a good game even if the Twins didn't win. I decided I would have to remember to take into account the Eric factor next time I planned to see the Indians play.

Leaving the dome felt like being pushed out the revolving door by the air pressure. It was a really weird feeling. I wanted to go back to the place we had lunch to get more pictures before we left. We even parked on the street heading in the direction we wanted to be going after the game. That move paid off, although the traffic wasn't very bad in the end. Maybe it was the small crowd, or maybe it was the detour we took to get more pictures, but either way we were pleased.

We decided to try to get beyond Chicago before stopping for the night, in order to miss the morning traffic. But that was a good six hours away from where we were at 10 PM. Eric started out driving. I am a light sleeper, so I tried to just rest. Eric did very well and we cleared Chicago around 4:00 AM. We stopped for a little break and decided it was silly to try to get a place to rest at that hour. So we just keep going, trading off driving. I took over and was only able to drive for a couple hours before I was too tired to continue. I had drifted onto the rumble stripe once and it really scared me. I pulled into a rest stop and was going to try to get a little shuteye, but Eric woke up feeling rested enough to drive. I think at that point I was so tired I was able to get some real sleep. We made it home safely around 6:00 PM Wednesday evening, having switched back and forth driving a couple more times. It sure felt good to sleep in a familiar bed that night. I couldn't help but lay there smiling before I went to sleep. We had done it—five games in five days in five different stadiums in four states! Wow!

GIANT GAME

Just three days later we were to head to New York to see the Giants play the Mets, a day trip for a day game. As it turned out, Eric was unavailable so I decided to attempt it myself. I felt disappointed for him that he would yet again miss the Giants. It was never fun to lose my traveling partner just before a trip.

It was a beautiful day, and there was no place better to be than a ball game. The drive down went well and I arrived early enough to avoid the heaviest traffic. I had a neat surprise that day that made me glad I'd made the trip. One of the pitchers, Pedro Martinez, who played for the Red Sox for ten years before joining the Mets, was getting an award at that game which was neat enough. But to make it even better, the president of the Dominican Republic (Martinez's native country) was there to throw the ceremonial first pitch. It was wonderful to be there and be a part of all that with 37,000 other fans on a warm June day.

I had seen Tom Glavine lose a start the first time I was at Shea Stadium. Noah Lowry pitched well for the Giants in August 2004 against the Phillies so I wasn't feeling really confident. But any team can win against any other team on any day. Time would tell.

In the top of the first Glavine gave up two hits, which made me nervous. But no runs crossed for the Giants. In the bottom of the inning, the second batter, Mike Cameron, who came to play for Boston in 2010, hit a long home run. Wahoo—the apple popped up in centerfield! I love to see that apple.

There was a woman with her young son sitting next to me, and the little boy was also excited to see the apple pop up.

Both teams threatened in following innings, but no more runs scored until the top of the fourth when Moises Alou jacked a leadoff homer to tie the game. I really like Alou but that was not a good thing against the Mets. Fortunately, that was the only run Glavine gave up.

In the bottom of the fifth, with Lowry still pitching for the Giants, Jose Reyes hit a deep double. Good things happen when Reyes gets on base, I told myself. Cameron walked, Carlos Beltran hit a sacrifice to advance the runners, and Mike Piazza hit a single to bring home two runs! Another single by Cliff Floyd advanced Piazza to third. Then David Wright scored Piazza with a single, and the Giants decided that was enough for Lowry. In came Al Levine.

The Mets immediately tried a double steal—both Cliff Floyd and David Wright advanced! What a beautiful thing to see! Chris Woodward struck out, and then Kaz Matsui was intentionally walked to load the bases for Tom Glavine who grounded out for the final out of the inning. Oh but what an inning it was, giving the Mets a three-run lead.

In the bottom of the seventh, Jim Brower came in to pitch for San Francisco and only gave up one hit. Glavine pitched part of the eighth and managed the first two outs on a double play. At that point Mets manager Willie Randolph thought it prudent to bring in Roberto Hernandez, who only allowed one hit and got us out of the inning.

In the bottom of the eighth the Mets got another run, making it Mets 5, Giants 1. Aaron Heilman closed the game out for the Mets. It was Tom Glavine's 266th win, tying him with Eppa Rixey at thirty-fifth on the all-time wins list. That wouldn't be the last milestone I would be present to see Tom Glavine achieve.

The drive home is always better coming off a win, but the traffic getting out of town was the pits. It required patience and some aggressiveness. Once I got across the George Washington Bridge, traffic lightened up and I was home in about three hours.

A couple of weeks later Eric wanted to make up for his absence, so we ordered tickets to see the San Diego Padres against the Washington Nationals at RFK Stadium for a Saturday in August. We also exchanged the Yankees tickets from the previous season (when Tampa Bay couldn't get there for the doubleheader) for tickets to upcoming games. We were able to get four tickets, two for a game against the Rangers for Eric and I, and another set for Eric and a friend of his that he wanted to take to a game. Pleased with our exchange, we grabbed some lunch and headed to Coney Island for the rest of the day.

I had never been to Coney Island, so it was a nice treat for me. We rode some rides, sat on the beach, played in the ocean, and snacked on some boardwalk food before heading back home. It was a good day. We spent time at the beach and got free tickets to two games. What else could we have wanted?

TIME TO TAKE FLIGHT

My next game wasn't until July 2 in St. Louis. I was growing weary of Eric not being able to make the games we had planned, so for this trip I made other arrangements. We hadn't really made specific arrangements, and I had bought the tickets, so I didn't really feel bad about excluding him, as he had bailed on me a few times already.

I had a cousin who lives near Kansas City, Missouri. I talked to his mother, my great-aunt, eighty-three years young at the time, to see if she would like to go with me. She was a baseball fan and I really wanted to see Busch Stadium before the Cards moved into the new park (with the same name) being built right next door. We talked to Dougie (her son, my cousin) and plans were made.

We were going to fly out and stay with Dougie. Then we would drive the four hours to St. Louis for the game, stay overnight there, and come back the next day in time for the game in Kansas City that night. We would be at Dougie's for the Fourth of July, and then I would fly back home on the following day. Eric was disappointed, but it worked out for the best in the long run.

Dougie bought his mother's airline tickets on Southwest Airlines, so we had to drive three hours to Albany to get the flight, which had a stopover in Chicago. We got to the airport and grabbed some lunch before the flight. We were both excited to be underway. Dougie met us at the airport in Kansas City, and we stopped for a bite to eat on the way back to his place.

It was so good to see him. He and his twin brother are only eighteen days older than I am, and we were all fairly close growing up.

On our first day there Dougie took us on a tour of Kansas City. The fountains were so beautiful. I was majorly impressed. We went to a casino on the Missouri River and I made my way down to the water to stick my hand in, just like I dipped into the Mississippi River in Minnesota.

We also went to the Negro League Baseball Hall of Fame. They had just that week put Satchel Paige's uniform on display. It was such a neat place, but they wouldn't let us take our cameras in because of the damage the flash can do. It was a truly wonderful experience even without pictures.

Dougie had made reservations at Harrah's for us the night of the game in St. Louis. There was a train that ran from the hotel to right outside the ballpark. He and his girlfriend drove the four hours to St. Louis with us. They were going to stay and have dinner there while Auntie (as I call Dougie's mother) and I went to the game.

We drove over in the morning and did some sightseeing around the Gateway Arch. There was a festival going on nearby, which resulted in a long line, too long to go up in the arch and still make it to the game in time. We walked down to the Mississippi River, and I stuck my hand in it again. I had just done that when Eric called to see how things were going. It was nice to hear from him.

We went to the hotel and got ready for the game. That was Auntie's first Major League baseball game in person. I was hoping it would be a good one. Dougie and Penny walked with us to the train platform, and we were on our way. It was an interesting ride on the train, followed by an easy walk to the park.

Our seats were on the second level. It was a nice stadium; I really didn't understand why they felt they needed a new one. Busch Stadium was forty years old, which is getting up there for a ballpark. The Rockies were in town, and I really wasn't sure who I was going to root for. I just wanted to see a good game and hoped Auntie had a good time. I went to get us some dinner and then we settled in to watch the game. It looked like a pretty big crowd was turning out. I found out later in the game that there were almost 48,000 people there.

Jason Marquis was pitching for St. Louis and Jamey Wright was twirling for Colorado. This proved to be a good matchup because by the top of the sixth inning, there was still no score and there had only been six hits, three for each team. It was a nice warm night to be at a ball game. Auntie and I cooled off with some Dippin' Dots as we watched the scoreless game.

With two outs in the top of the sixth, the Rockies manufactured two runs. In the top of the seventh, a homer by J. D. Closser added to the Rockies' lead. The Cardinals might get shut out at home in front of a huge crowd. It wasn't until the bottom of the seventh the Cardinals got their only run of the game.

We thought it prudent to leave early to beat the huge crowd. So we made our way out of the park in the top of the ninth, heading across the street to the train platform. I am so glad we got a head start, because it was just an absolute zoo. Three trains passed before we were able to get on. People were pushing and shoving so much that it took me a little while to muster the courage to push and shove back enough to get Auntie and I on the train together. I told her to take my arm and not let go no matter how hard people pushed, and we finally made it on. We were packed in so tight that we couldn't even turn around for several stops. I was trying to hold on to the ceiling with my fingertips to avoid bumping into fellow passengers as the train swayed.

After a few more stops we were able to find a seat and relax for the rest of the ride back to the hotel. We went back to our room, and I fell fast asleep, as I hadn't yet adjusted to the Central Time Zone.

The next morning we went to the breakfast buffet at Harrah's. It was the biggest buffet I had ever seen. There was row after row of every kind of food you could imagine, as well as stations where you could have things prepared just the way you wanted them. It was difficult to decide what I actually wanted to eat. There was no way you could even take a taste of a third of what was there and not explode.

We headed back toward Dougie's by mid-morning. I was pleased that he let me help with the driving on that leg of the trip. It was a four-hour drive but pretty much a straight shot on the highway. We stopped at one rest stop. The restrooms there had fully automated sinks and everything. Auntie and I had been in the restroom at the same time as another lady, who couldn't get a faucet to come on. I joked and said maybe telepathy was required to make it work. We tried the one on the other side, which worked. The silly thing squirts soap followed by water, so one doesn't have to touch anything. A grand idea! We had a good laugh about it.

We made it back to Dougie's in time to relax a little bit before heading to the next game in Kansas City, the Royals against the Angels. Dougie joined us for that game. Kauffman Stadium was a really short drive from their house. The others went in while I took a walk around the park. It wasn't much to see from the outside, but on the inside it was beautiful. The fountains were very nice. The scoreboard was a bit outdated. It was built in 1973.

Our seats were directly behind home plate but in an upper deck. I walked around inside a little bit before heading to our seats. The weather looked a little suspect, and we kept an eye on it all night. I kept waiting for the crowd to arrive, but it never did. There weren't even 15,000 people there. The place looked so empty. I felt sad that such a beautiful stadium was so empty.

Jarrod Washburn was pitching again for the Angels; I had just seen him that previous May against the White Sox. I wasn't sure who I would be rooting for. Perhaps because my cousin was rooting for the Royals, I could root for them as well.

In the top of the second inning the Angels went ahead by one. In the top of the fourth the Angles scored two more runs for a 3–0 lead. The weather was looking even more threatening. We made the decision to get out of there before we got wet. It started to rain before we got to the car. It was raining very hard on all of the short drive back to Dougie's. There was lightning and hail as well. We were really glad to have bagged it when we did. We listened to the game on the radio on the way back. The Angels scored two more runs before the umpires called the game after the fifth inning.

The next morning, the front page of the paper carried a half-page picture of one of the pitchers, standing on the mound, rain coming down hard and lightning striking in the background. I was even happier that we left when I saw that.

We enjoyed a Fourth of July cookout and fireworks the next day at Dougie's. Our visit was over and we headed to the airport the next morning. We said our goodbyes to Dougie and Penny as they accompanied us to the security checkpoint.

Next thing I knew the guards had pulled Auntie aside and were patting her down. The attendants then asked me to step aside and start going through my purse. I had a very small screwdriver for glasses in there. They decided it could be used as a weapon and confiscated it. On the other side of a glass partition, Dougie was watching, fuming at what the guards were doing to his mother. But Auntie was fine. A nice security guard explained that they do random searches every so many people, and she just happened to be the one. The guards were sensitive to her and even offered to let her step behind a screen to be patted down. She chose not to and took it all in stride. She tells that story and laughs about it all the time. All in all it was a great trip. Spending time with Auntie, Dougie, and Penny and seeing two baseball games in two new stadiums was great. I had to admit I wished Eric could have been there to share the experience. I know he would have loved it. But it wasn't to be.

On our flight back, stopping over again in Chicago, we flew right over U.S. Cellular Field. I was able to get a bird's-eye picture of the stadium for my collection.

DODGERS IN NEW YORK

Back in March we had gotten ticket to another game at Shea, Mets against Dodgers on July 23. Just a couple of Saturdays later, Eric and I were off again. It was a mid-afternoon start, so we took our time heading out in the morning. The drive down was normal except when we got closer to the city, traffic seemed to be busier than usual. I hoped they weren't all going to the game.

I would get to see Pedro Martinez pitch for the Mets for the first time. It was an exciting thing for me to see a player that I had gotten to know with the Red Sox take the hill for my favorite team, the Mets. Martinez wasn't off to the best start in New York. I was used to seeing him dominate, but that year and the years that followed it seemed to take him at least an inning to find his stuff. This first inning was an example of that. He gave up three hits and walked one, which led to three runs for the Dodgers. A three-run top of the first was so disappointing to see. We reminded ourselves that Martinez would be himself later in the game.

In the bottom of the first, the Mets got one run back. Jose Reyes singled, and then stole second base and advanced to third on a throwing error by catcher Jason Phillips, a former Met. A single brought Reyes in. Things happen when Reyes gets on base! It was hard for me to see Phillips make the error. He played for the Mets and I felt a fondness for him. Even though he was playing against the Mets, I couldn't feel happy when he didn't do well. That attachment continued to be difficult for me. I get really attached to players on the teams I follow. When they leave by choice or are traded, it's a hard adjustment for me to make, as it is for many fans I am sure.

Martinez came back in the second inning with a one-two-three inning. Unfortunately, so did the Dodgers' starter. In the bottom of the third, Reyes got a single. He really was a spark plug for the team. Reyes scored again! The Dodgers led 3–2 after three innings. There was still plenty of time.

In the fourth inning, Jason Phillips hit an RBI single to make it 4–2. I didn't like the score, but was okay with seeing Jason Phillips do well. Eric told me I can't have it both ways. But it really was a hard concept for me. I don't have a switch to turn off my affinity for a player once he wears a different uniform.

After two quick innings for both sides, Martinez gave up a home run in the sixth before sitting down the next three batters. In the bottom of the sixth, David Wright started things off with a double. Doug Mientkiewicz sacrificed to advance Wright. Ramon Castro grounded out but Wright scored on the play.

The Mets being down two runs going into the seventh made me nervous. Martinez came back out to the mound. I flashed back to 2003, when Grady Little left Martinez in too long in a crucial playoff game. Eric just made a face and told me to cross my fingers. Martinez managed to get through the eighth inning fairly easily, much to our delight and relief.

In the bottom of the inning, up came a pinch hitter in Martinez's spot, confirming he was done. The sub drew a walk. Jose Reyes then hit a triple to tie the game. I was holding my breath. Los Angeles brought in Wilson Alvarez to pitch. I felt like the Mets had the Dodgers on the run, but didn't want to say anything to jinx it. Carlos Beltran hit a single to score Reyes, giving the Mets the lead for the first time in the game.

Next in to pitch for the Dodgers was Duaner Sanchez, who came to play for the Mets in 2008. Beltran stole second and Cliff Floyd was intentionally walked. But Wright hit into a rare double play to end the inning. Drat! But it was still a one-run Mets lead with two innings to play.

Roberto Hernandez took the mound for the Mets. We had seen him pitch one easy inning for Philadelphia the prior year, so I felt pretty good. He made quick work of the eighth.

In the bottom of the eighth, Mientkiewicz doubled, and Ramon Castro sacrificed him to third. Miguel Cairo drew a walk and proceeded to steal second. Jose Offerman pinch hit for Hernandez and grounded into a fielder's choice to erase Mientkiewicz at home, but Cairo advanced to third. My heart was pounding! Reyes hit a single. Cairo scored an insurance run, and Offerman made it to third. The crowd went wild! Reyes stole second.

Braden Looper came on to close the game for the Mets, which made Eric extremely nervous. Looper struck out the first two batters, and the third grounded out, which was a great relief to Eric. That was a great end to the game. 43,000-plus joined us as we made our way out of Shea on a warm Saturday afternoon.

We got to the car thinking we would get out of the city to find a place to eat dinner. Feeling good about the Mets win, Eric suggested that we do something in the city. I had never done much in the city. He took me to Chinatown for dinner. It was neat, except I was sick to my stomach before we got back on the road. I made a beeline for a garbage can and made it in time, but unfortunately the trash can had messy sides. I had to clean off my shoes before getting back in the car. Eric found all of this hysterical. My Chinatown misadventure turned out to be another one of those stories he loved to tell to anyone who would listen.

A week later, my company took a group outing to a Binghamton Mets game. It turned out we were in for special treat. Steve Trachsel of the Mets was rehabbing with Binghamton that night. That was the only time I got to see him pitch. He wasn't 100 percent, but did pretty well. A co-worker's daughter was an intern for the B-Mets at the time, and she made sure that some of the kids in our group were selected to participate in some of the on-field events. She also made sure I was selected as the female fan of the game. She presented me with a rose as my special status was announced over the loudspeaker. I was shocked when I heard my name. The moment made the night even more special.

BASEBALL BACK IN OUR NATION'S CAPITAL

Less than a week later Eric and were to catch our next game in Washington DC. We decided to take extra days off to hit the beach. We headed out on Thursday and drove to Delaware to spend some time on the sand. After checking in at the hotel, we headed straight for the ocean. We started out at Rehoboth Beach. It was extremely crowded. We found a place on the board walk to get some lunch. We walked along the beach and decided to try someplace less crowded. We drove south and found a less packed stretch of sand. The water was so shallow that practically had to lie down in it to get completely wet. We decided to give up on the idea of the beach for that day.

We went back to the hotel and decided to try the restaurant next door for dinner. They were about to close but offered to serve us anyway. We didn't know where else there was to eat, so we went ahead and sat down. The meal was good, although we were intent on eating fairly quickly so as to not detain them any longer than necessary.

The next day we planned to visit Cape Henlopen, where we had camped in 2003. We took hot dogs to grill for lunch and scallops to cook for dinner. We were able to cook the hot dogs in the parking lot for lunch, but when we wanted to cook the scallops we were asked to put the grill out and leave. Neither of us noticed the sign saying that grilling wasn't allowed in the parking lot. Oops!

We had a great day sitting on the beach and playing in the water. We had come to like the area, and the beach was very nice. They kept it clean and the bath houses were also well maintained.

Later that night, after we got back to the hotel, I wasn't feeling very well. I took a shower to get all the sand off me and then lay down. Eric was very sweet. He went to get us something to eat and pick up something to ease my headache and calm my stomach. I was afraid I wouldn't be well enough for our trip to DC, so I just stayed put the rest of the night. Thankfully, I was fine by morning. We headed to DC after breakfast.

We found a place to park that had no meter or posted time limit. We figured we'd be able to stay parked there all day. We set off on foot to find a bite to eat and use the restrooms. We walked all the way from RFK Stadium to downtown to the Capitol without finding either one. That meant we had to trek back to the ballpark in the same condition we started out in. We made it back and relaxed under a tree outside the stadium until the gates opened. What a relief that was, let me tell you!

It was a warmish day in the mid-eighties, but partly cloudy, about perfect in my book. From the outside, the stadium was okay, definitely on the older side. If I remember correctly, RFK was built in the 1960s as a multi-purpose stadium.

This was another game where I didn't have any vested interest in either team winning. I determined that I'd root for the Nationals, formerly the Expos, if for no other reason than to see them do well in their new location under their new name. San Diego was in the race for the National League West and the Nationals were in the lower half of the standing for the NL East. So my choice was probably influenced by my thing for underdogs. A pretty big crowd came out, just over 38,000.

Our seats were in the second section from the top, right behind home plate—our preferred spot. We had a good view of the whole place and all the action on the field. The game started off slow, with only a couple of hits and no runs for the first two and a half innings. In the bottom of the third, Washington showed some spark and scored the first run.

The Padres got the run right back with the help of a player who would become a familiar face playing second base the following year in Boston, Mark Loretta. He hit a sacrifice fly with two on to tie the game. Washington battled back in the bottom of the inning with a solo home run for the go-ahead run. In the top of the sixth, San Diego tied it up again.

That score held until the top of the seventh when a pair of doubles scored what turned out to be the winning run for the Padres. With only three more hits, the final score was San Diego 3, Washington 2.

Some of the players I saw that day would become familiar to me in coming years. Xavier Nady played part of 2006 with the Mets, and Ryan Church was a Met in 2008 and part of 2009. There were also some old favorites like Dave Roberts, one of the heroes from the 2004 Red Sox, and Damian Jackson, who played with Boston in 2003. I was pleased with how I was getting to know the players and remember where they had played. It always helps when they've played for my beloved Mets or Red Sox.

We made our way back to the car, just a block away from the stadium after all that time, free of parking tickets. We drove as far as we could and found a place to sleep. The hotel was probably one of the worst ones I had ever stayed in, but it was a short stay. We survived and made it home the next day at a reasonable time.

BACK TO NEW YORK AND ADD ONE MORE

The following Friday night we had tickets for the Rangers-Yankees game at Yankee Stadium. We left work early and headed to the city. It was a down-and-back trip. Veteran Al Leiter was pitching for the Yankees, and Chris Young was pitching for the Rangers. The stadium was packed with almost 55,000 fans. Our seats were way out in right field, one deck from the top of the stadium. It was a warm night, and we were happy to be higher up where there was some air movement.

Of course I was rooting for Texas to win, not because I was fond of them but because they were playing the Yankees. Texas led off the first inning with a single but couldn't do anything with it. The Yankees did no better in their half of the inning. In fact Young struck out three of their top hitters: Derek Jeter, Robinson Cano, and Alex Rodriguez all went down on strikes.

In the second, the Rangers took advantage of two Yankee errors to score three runs. Way to go, Texas! The Yankees came right back with their first run. In the third inning a home run by Alfonso Soriano made the score Rangers 4, Yankees 1. The Yankees scored another run in the bottom of the third inning. It would have been two runs but Hideki Matsui was thrown out at home plate for the second out. Even though Matsui was out, Eric looked at me askance, because I had once said that I liked Matsui. Some things I would never live down.

Another single scored another run. Darn it! If that wasn't bad enough, Bernie Williams promptly hit a home run to take the lead. I looked at Eric in disbelief. He just shook his head and muttered "Damn Yankees."

The Rangers tied the game in the fourth inning, giving us some hope. But in the home half of the inning, Jeter hit a home run to put the Yankees back in front. Bad words! Despite three more hits by Texas and only one by New York, there were no more runs scored. That Jeter homer, unfortunately, was the ball game, which took a long three and a half hours.

Because we had been through city traffic a few times now, Eric was ready to try a better way to leave the city. Instead of heading back toward the bridge like everyone else, we went away from the bridge and through Harlem to beat traffic to the bridge. It worked great! I think that Friday was the fastest we had ever gotten out of a baseball game in New York City.

It was over a month before our next adventure. In that time we decided that it might be nice to tack on another game and extend our season. We had gotten tickets in May to see the Red Sox in Baltimore on September 24. Because the weather was still looking nice, we decided to try to sneak in one more beach day in, and hit a Monday night Mets–Phillies game in Philly, as the division was running tight. We put in for the time off and ordered the tickets.

We headed out Saturday morning and made our way to the Baltimore harbor to do some sightseeing and get lunch before the game. We walked around for a while and found a neat place overlooking the water for lunch. We chatted with some of the other patrons and had an enjoyable afternoon until it was time to make it to Camden Yards.

After we parked, we passed several street vendors and came across a shirt that Eric just had to have. It said "Baltimore: A drinking town with a baseball problem." He thought it was funny, so he bought it.

Our seats were way out in left field but we didn't care. We were seeing the Red Sox who were very much in the division race. It was a full house of well over 48,000 people. There was so much red in the stands that it was practically a home game for the Sox.

As the crowd filled out, a group of people from the same workplace arrived to occupy the two rows in front of us. One gentleman in particular stood out, as he was rather loud and covered in Yankee gear. Before the game started, the Yankees-Jays game ended with Toronto winning. The place went crazy with cheers. The man in the row in front of us, whom I will call Yankee Bill, became very agitated. Eric and I chuckled to ourselves.

The announcers made reference a number of times to how much red there was in the stands and throughout the game referred to Camden Yards as Fenway South. With the Yankee loss, the Red Sox would be tied for first in the AL East with only seven games left, provided they won the game against Baltimore. Boston had a four-game series against Toronto and a three-game series against the Yankees remaining. The Yankees had a three-game series against Baltimore before facing the Red Sox for the final showdown. It doesn't get any closer than that.

Matt Clement was the starting pitcher for Boston and Erik Bedard was the starting pitcher for Baltimore. This was the first and only time I would see Matt Clement pitch. We were impressed with the number of Red Sox fans in the stands, but when the "Star Spangled Banner" was sung there was still the drawn-out "O" from the fans, an Orioles tradition.

In the first inning, the Red Sox loaded the bases in front of Manny Ramirez. Wahoo! Yankee Bill was stewing in his seat. Ramirez hit a sacrifice fly to score the first run. A wild pitch scored another run. Two runs in the first inning—a nice start!

There wasn't another hit by either team until the fifth inning. Of course, Yankee Bill had something to say about many of the plays in the meantime, or I should say, the same thing to say. At the end of each inning he would stand and proclaim "Yankees Rule," much to the annoyance of most of the people around him.

In the bottom of the seventh, Craig Hansen came into pitch for Boston. One of Eric's favorite players, John Olerud, came in to play first. Unfortunately, Melvin Mora hit a home run with one on to tie the game, which prompted more pitching changes. By this time people were being verbally abusive and throwing things at Yankee Bill. Not me, of course, although I was tempted.

The Red Sox brought in closer Jonathan Papelbon in for the eighth inning. He gave up a single to the first batter. The Orioles brought in a pinch runner hoping to get something started. I was holding my breath. The next batter bunted unsuccessfully for the first out. Okay, I took a little breath. Papelbon struck out the next batter and my man Jason Varitek threw out the pinch runner trying to steal second. Inning Over!

B. J. Ryan came in to pitch for Baltimore. Uh oh! A couple of singles followed by a walk loaded the bases with Red Sox. Okay boys, make it count! Yankee Bill was very upset by this point. A single scored two runs! Up by two—now we just need to hold on.

In the bottom of the ninth, Mike Timlin came in for Boston. We had seen Timlin many times before. As comfortable as we were with him, I was still nervous. Alex Cora also came in to play second. That was the first time I had seen Cora play for Boston, but we had seen him play for Cleveland earlier that year. He also would come to play for the Mets in 2009 and 2010. Timlin walked the first batter. Nothing good can come from walking the leadoff guy! Eric agreed. A pop-up out and a groundout followed, but the walked batter made it to second. Again I was holding my breath. One swing could tie this thing up. Just one more out, Timlin! Next batter hit a double, knocking in a run. I looked at Eric with fear in my eyes. A pinch runner came in, hoping the next batter could follow suit. By that time the fans around us were taking some of their frustration out on the somewhat deserving Yankee Bill. His comments turned uglier as the game went on. Timlin came through and got a fly ball for a dramatic end to a just-under-four-hour game. The Red Sox won and tied the Yankees atop the division. We were very excited and wanted to savor the moment. We left and made our way to the hotel in preparation for our beach day on Sunday.

We went to the beach the next day. We brought a little propane grill and a radio. We stopped to get some clams and set everything up before taking a dip in the water. The ocean was cool but still a lot of fun. We were able to get the game on the radio, making for a perfect afternoon. We heard the Red Sox beat the Orioles again that Sunday. At one point we saw the Fuji blimp fly overhead. What could be better than cooking clams on the beach while listening to the Red Sox win a game on the radio and playing in the ocean in September?

We drove back to the beach on Monday, even though it wasn't as nice, just to take one more walk around before we headed to Philadelphia. On the drive to the game, we decided we should find a hotel for after the game and drive back on Tuesday fresh, rather than drive all the way home after the game, especially with rain in the forecast perhaps causing rain delays. That was what we did. We ended stopping at the same place we had stayed at before, the one that double-charged us. The hotel was under a different name and ownership.

We went to get something to eat and found the same diner we had eaten at the last time. We relaxed for a while and then headed to the game. Finding free parking about a block away from the exit to the highway, going in the direction we wanted to head, was a big plus. We always travel with our rain suits, and this was one time we were exceedingly glad we had them. It was drizzling off and on, and on the cool side. We carried the rain suits into the stadium, as we weren't sure if our seats were under a roof or not. As the fans filtered in it was apparent it was going to be a smallish crowd. The attendance ended up being just under 29,000, which was a little more than half full for Citizens Bank Park.

Brett Myers was pitching for Philadelphia and Jae Seo was pitching for New York, a matchup that figured to favor the Phillies. Myers started the game well, allowing just one hit in the first. Seo, on the other hand, gave up a home run to Jimmy Rollins, the first batter he faced, extending Rollins's impressive thirty-one-game hitting streak. We looked at each other and decided it was going to be a long night. A couple of hits and a walk netted another Phillies run. Ugh! We were down by two at the end of the first inning.

In the second inning, rookie Mike Jacobs, who was playing in Binghamton just a month earlier, slammed a home run with one out to cut the lead in half. I was so happy, and felt a bit of pride for the young lad. That score was short-lived, as the Phillies came right back.

The rain was getting harder, so we decided to put the rain suits on. This was the first time I had worn my rain suit, and the pants were way too long. I had to cuff them about four inches and hold the pants up when I walked, because they were too big around the waist. But I was very glad to have a fashion problem instead of getting soaked or having to watch the game on TV from the concourse.

The next couple of innings went quickly. Neither team got another hit until the top of the fifth inning, and that runner was promptly picked off. In the bottom of the fifth inning the Phillies capitalized on a walk to score another run—not what we were hoping for. The Phillies were up 4–1 and the rain was coming down. At one point the sky opened up and they covered the field for over an hour. We went to the concourse to get a snack and drink and wait out the rain delay. We talked about leaving, but because we already had a hotel and it was the last game we were going to see that year, we decided to stay.

In the top of the seventh inning, the Mets came alive. David Wright drew a walk with one out. Mike Piazza advanced Wright to third on a single, and Jacobs drove him in on a fielder's choice. The darn Phillies came right back with a home run by Pat Burrell, how frustrating! In the top of the eighth, the Mets got it going again. Down 5–2, they started the inning with a double. Jose Reyes drew a walk. A long double scored a run and put Reyes on third. I was getting excited, because things happened when Reyes was on base. The next play looked like something from a Three Stooges movie. Carlos Beltran hit the ball toward second base, which was retrieved by Chase Utley. But Utley overthrew first base, so Beltran was safe at first, Reyes scored, and Cairo advanced to third and then scored because of a second throwing error by Utley. Now it was Phillies 5, Mets 5 with no outs. Aaron Fultz came in to face Cliff Floyd, who hit a hard single to advance Beltran to third. Wright made the first out. Piazza was hit by a pitch and was replaced on the base paths. Jacobs hit another sacrifice to drive in the go-ahead run. What a night for Mr. Mike Jacobs—three at-bats and three RBIs, one of which was a solo home run! 6–5 was the final score. The Mets came back to beat the Phillies! We were so glad we stayed to see it. Plus the Phillies announced that night that we could send our tickets in and exchange them for a game before mid-May of next year. We couldn't have been happier as we headed back to the hotel.

The Mets didn't make the playoffs, and the Red Sox took the AL Wildcard playoff spot, even though they'd tied the Yankees (the Yankees had won the season series, which was the first tiebreaker). The Sox went out in the first round, courtesy of the White Sox. As some consolation, the White Sox did go all the way that year.

All in all, it had been a pretty good baseball year. I had accomplished part of my mission by seeing all the teams in major league baseball. It was exciting to be able to say that. I had also seen half the major league stadiums so I was on my way to meeting the second part of my goal! On December 10, my birthday, we bought tickets for a game at Fenway in April of the following year. What an excellent way to start my birthday celebration! I knew my quest would continue.

NIXED IN 2006

Eric and I started off 2006 at a football game at the Meadowlands between the Jets and the Bills. During our drive down and back, we talked about what baseball games we were planning to catch the following season. We would have to travel farther to see the rest of the stadiums, so that meant we might have to see fewer games overall. Florida became our next target. We even talked about possibly taking a couple of days to go to the Bahamas, as we would be so close. I began to do the research and plan things out.

But Eric disappeared on me early in 2006, so I had to make the plans for myself. I had two tickets to the game at Fenway in April, and was planning to send the rain-game ticket into the Phillies to get tickets to a game that spring, so I had a start on the season. I requested tickets to a Saturday game in Philly when the Giants were in town, in case Eric might be around to come with me.

As the year went on, it became clear that Eric was out of the picture. I went ahead and made plans to get to Atlanta, Florida, and perhaps Texas on my own. My sister and I talked about going to Toronto to see the Red Sox play late in the season. We bought inexpensive tickets for a game in Toronto in February. The trip was still tentative, but we didn't want to risk not being able to get tickets later in the year. The Georgia trip was also of interest to my sister, as we have an aunt and uncle that live about four hours outside of Atlanta. We decided to plan our trip so we could spend some time with them in addition to seeing a game. My uncle went to college in Boston, so when he heard I was planning on getting tickets to see the Red Sox play in Atlanta, he was really interested in going to the game with me, as was his son. Plans were taking shape. My sister wasn't a big baseball fan (yet) so she made plans to spend the time with my aunt doing other things. By the end of March, I had made plans to go to Florida to see the Red Sox at Tampa and the Dodgers at the Marlins. I left Texas up in the air for a while, to see how things went traveling alone before filling my calendar with solo jaunts.

Late in March I had lunch with Eric's mother. She indicated that he wasn't interested in going with me to Boston, so I gave her the cost of his ticket to return to him. I had hoped things would go differently, but that was reality. I had to deal with it.

I decided to take a couple of extra days off work for my Boston trip so I could visit an old high school friend who lives in Bristol, Vermont. On Saturday I would drive to Boston for the game and head home afterward. I didn't ask my old friend to go with me to the game, as he wasn't a baseball fan. He had already taken Friday night off for my visit and I didn't want to impose on him.

When the time came, I headed north to Bristol. It saddened me to be going without Eric, but there was nothing I could do about that. My friend and I had a nice time. We had lunch with one of his friends from work whom I had been looking forward to meeting. We went to one of his favorite places in Bristol for dinner that night.

The next night we drove over the mountain to a very unique place for dinner. I saw my very first moose, which was standing right next to the road as we drove by. On Friday we went shopping in a nearby small town that had some unique little shops. Eric's mom called me while we were there, and was surprised to find out that I was out of town and still planning to go to the game. Perhaps Eric had changed his mind. But it was too late for that.

My friend and I had lunch at a great place overlooking a small lake. That night we just relaxed and caught up while cooking dinner. He did most of the cooking, and it was a very good meal. I had a long day planned for Saturday, and he had to work Saturday night, so it was good that we kept the evening low-key.

On Saturday morning I headed for Boston via Vermont and New Hampshire. It was about a three-hour drive. I had brought an audio book to keep me company. I was convincing myself that Eric was the one missing out, even though I was missing him especially going to Boston. The drive went well and I got into town easily. I began looking for a place to park along Commonwealth Avenue but wasn't having any luck. So I turned onto a side street, where I happened across a garage offering parking for $10, which was very reasonable in my experience. The garage was just one block from the onramp to the interstate that was my route home. I began my walk toward Fenway.

The excitement started to kick in, as it always does, when Fenway came into view. The first game of the year really gets my blood pumping. I stopped in one of the Red Sox shops to look around but decided not to buy anything, as my ticket was for standing room and I would have to hold whatever I bought for the entire game. I went inside and got something to eat. There weren't many people there yet, so I sat in a seat to eat my lunch and relax for as long as I could before I had to stand up for the entire game.

There was a nice surprise during pregame that day. It was mascot day, and that was when I became familiar with Lefty and Righty. If you don't know about them, they are red socks, one with the toe part facing right and the other facing left. So incredibly cute! I took a bunch of pictures and was really enjoying myself. Then the people whose seat I was borrowing arrived, and I had to move. I was standing in the standing room area at the top of the steps when a woman who was sitting two rows down walked by and said she had a ticket that would be going unused. Hmm, did I want to sit in a seat for three hours, or stand? What a tough decision. Of course I took the seat.

It was a warm and sunny day for April, and I was very excited to be officially starting my baseball travels for the season. It was only my second time seeing Seattle so I wasn't overly familiar with the players other than Ichiro Suzuki. Tim Wakefield, whom I had seen pitch two other times, was pitching for Boston. This time was he was not pitching to his usual catcher Doug Mirabelli, but to Josh Bard. Time would tell if that would be a problem. Joel Pineiro was pitching again for Seattle.

The first inning went quickly. Wakefield faced only three batters. Pineiro faced five batters, giving up two hits but no runs. Wakefield had more trouble in the second, as he gave up two singles and a stolen base. But no runs scored. In the bottom of the second, the offense got started with a walk, a ground-rule double, and another walk to load the bases. But the Red Sox still couldn't score! I didn't know what to think.

In the third inning it became clear that letting Doug Mirabelli go had been a mistake. There is a talent to catching a knuckleballer. As good as Josh Bard and Jason Varitek are, catching Wakefield was difficult for them. The first batter hit a double. Ichiro Suzuki struck out swinging but took first on a passed ball. The runner also advanced to third. Suzuki stole second. Stealing bases is easier against a knuckleballer as well. The runner scored and Suzuki took third on yet another passed ball. I couldn't believe what I was seeing. I had felt catching Wakefield was going to be a problem after the team let Mirabelli go, but I didn't expect it to be that bad. The next batter lined out for the first out of the inning, which gave me some hope. This was short lived, as the next batter hit a ground-rule double to score Suzuki. Not good! Another single followed to score the third Mariner run of the inning, two of which were due to difficulty catching the knuckleball. Why oh why did they trade Mirabelli?

The damage was done. Despite a few more hits by each team, 3–0 was the final score. Tim Wakefield pitched the whole game to take his second loss in three games. Seattle brought in two relievers, J. J. Putz with one out in the seventh and Eddie Guardado in the ninth. Boston brought in Varitek to pinch-hit for Bard in the ninth, hoping to change their luck. It didn't work. The Red Sox were shut out at home in front of more than 36,000 fans in just under two and a half hours. It was not the result I was hoping for, but it was still nice to be in Boston for a game on such a beautiful spring day.

I made my way back to the car. It took twenty minutes to get around the block and get on the interstate. On the five-hour-plus drive home I stayed focused on the positive aspects of the trip, like my visit with my friend in Bristol, the nice lady that let me sit in her spare seat, and the beautiful weather, instead of letting myself get upset at Eric for not being there. I knew I would be going through the same thing again in just a couple of weeks in Philadelphia.

There was no contact with Eric in the weeks leading up to the Philadelphia game. I caved the morning of the game and called to see if he was interested in going with me. After all, he had paid for the original ticket and was entitled to one of the tickets. I called but he wasn't home, so I headed out by myself again, determined to make the best of it. It was a night game, which meant I would have to find a place to stay or drive all the way back home after the game. I was going to play it by ear. I left early in the afternoon to get there in time to take a walk around.

I got to the park and took my walk before going in to find my seat. There are so many neat things around Citizens Bank Park, like street signs for "Phillies Drive," and the Phillies bar lights in the windows of a nearby tavern.

My seat was in the top deck, just like last September, right behind home plate about three rows back from the thick glass that fronted the deck. The excitement of the day was that Barry Bonds was chasing Babe Ruth's home run record. He had only hit four home runs so far that year, the last one just four days prior to that game, leaving him just two home runs shy of tying Babe. Maybe, just maybe, he would do it that day.

It was a comfortable night, although it felt like it could rain. The rain stayed away, even though I did bring my rain suit into the game. Ryan Madson was pitching for Philadelphia, and Jamey Wright was pitching for San Francisco. I had seen both pitchers the previous year.

Madson faced six men in the first, giving up two singles and walking two (including Bonds), but somehow managed to get out of the inning without allowing a run. Wright did a little bit worse, giving up a one-out home run to Chase Utley before getting out of the first. I did like seeing and hearing the home run bell ring, especially at night. Both hurlers settled in until the third inning, when Madson had to face Bonds again. The batter in front of Bonds hit a single, so the Phillies pitched to Bonds. He hit into a double play! Darn it. I was really hoping to see some history, or at least see him get one more home run closer to making history. In the bottom of the inning, Wright took more damage. A couple of singles and a hit batsman loaded the bases. I could hardly believe my eyes when Wright walked Utley to score another run. Pat Burrell hit into a double play, but Jimmy Rollins scored before a groundout ended the inning. I was sort of rooting for Philadelphia but also was rooting for Bonds to get a home run. It was a mixed-up game for me.

There was only one more hit for each team in the next few innings. Bonds flied out in the fifth. Both teams scored a run in the seventh. The final score was Philadelphia 4, San Francisco 1. It was clear early on who was going to win, but I wanted to stay and see if Bonds was going to hit again. He came up in the top of the eighth and hit a single. I did get to see Tom "Flash" Gordon close out the top of the ninth for the Phillies, posting a perfect one-two-three inning. All this came in front of over 44,000 fans in under three hours.

As luck would have it, Bonds hit his 713th home run the very next day in Philadelphia. Two weeks later he hit 714 to tie Babe Ruth. I was only sort of close to being present for history. I made my way back to the car and felt awake enough to start home, as it was not even 10 PM yet. I drove all the way home, stopping only once to take a break and get some more caffeine. I was tired by the time I got home at 1:30 AM, but I felt good that I was continuing on with my quest, even if I was traveling alone. I really wanted to achieve my goal..

SOUTHERN BOUND

My next trip was a month and a half away. Having my sister go with me added another dimension to my traveling, as she was usually the one who took care of things on the home front when I hit the road. I asked a good friend of mine from work to fill in, and she was happy to do it. I reciprocated the favor in August when my co-worker went on vacation.

My sister and I were really excited to see my aunt and uncle. We hadn't seen them in several years. They had been in a serious accident in their tractor trailer the year before, so we wanted to see firsthand how they were really doing, and help out however we could. I was concerned about how my uncle was going to handle sitting for long stretches of time, owing to the damage to his back from the accident. He assured me he would be fine.

His son, my cousin, was going too. It was going to be a great time. The game was scheduled for a day game but was moved to the Sunday night game of the week. With the daytime temperatures over one hundred degrees the week before, that was out to be a good thing.

My sister and I mapped out our route. We planned to drive as far as we could, find a place to stay, and get to our aunt and uncle's place at a reasonable time the next day. We headed out on Friday about 6:00 AM. We stopped just before dark at an Econolodge to spend the night.

We got an early start the next morning and made it to our aunt and uncle's by midday Saturday. We had a nice time catching up, although it was difficult hearing about the suffering they had gone through in the accident and its aftermath. I just wanted to hug them and make it all better. If only it were that easy!

It was a four-hour drive to Atlanta from their place and they wanted to take me to the Varsity Club for dinner before the game, so we headed out early. The Varsity Club was a very neat place, although it seemed everyone else had the same idea because the restaurant was unbelievably packed. We sent my uncle in to get us seats and my cousin and I stood in line to order. The food was good and beyond that, it was great to experience a new place in the company of family. Times like these are wonderful additions to my baseball adventures.

We parked in a nearby lot and took a shuttle to the park. I was concerned about the impact all of this would have on my uncle's comfort. But he was such a trooper. I was so honored that he did all of that with me, especially on Father's Day.

We were in for a major treat. The starters for the game were Curt Schilling for Boston against John Smoltz for Atlanta. Talk about a pitching matchup! I had never seen a faceoff of that caliber before, for sure. I had seen Schilling the year before in Boston and Smoltz two years prior when the Braves were in Philadelphia. I knew it was going to be a good game!

I sent my uncle and cousin to the seats, and took a little walk around to get some pictures. It was a "cool" eighty-three degrees in a stadium packed with almost 49,000 other fans, making us especially grateful that it was a night game.

Turner Field was a neat place, not overdone, definitely a ballpark. There were unique touches along with references to team history all around. Our seats were in the second section up from the field, just past third base. I thought they were good seats, even though I tend to prefer the first base side.

Most of my all-time favorite players were Red Sox at one time. The game in Atlanta re-introduced me to a future favorite, Mike Lowell. I had seen Lowell play for Florida two years earlier against the Mets. Back then he had had a couple of hits and an RBI, knocking in the run that beat the Mets. I wasn't sure what to think of Lowell when he was killing my Mets, but seeing him play well for Boston won me over.

The games started with two quick outs from Smoltz until the third man up, Big Papi, gave the ball a ride out of the park via center field. We were overjoyed! High fives came from everywhere. I love it when the team I am rooting for jumps out to an early lead, even if it is only one run.

Schilling gave up a single to the first batter, but then settled in nicely, setting down the next three in order. Smoltz started off the second with walk and a single before getting out of the inning. Schilling allowed the same exact events in the bottom of the inning, a single and a walk but no runs. What a matchup it was!

In the top of the third, Smoltz gave up a one-out single but then induced a double play to end the inning. Schilling had a rougher time of it in the bottom of the inning. A single started things off, followed by two groundouts that put the runner in scoring position. A single scored the tying run. There were two outs and one on. A double and another single scored two more runs. Uh oh: Braves 3, Red Sox 1 after three innings. In the top of the fourth, Manny Ramirez sent one sailing for Boston's second solo home of the game, closing in on the Braves. The place went crazy! More high fives! The energy in the park was amazing.

Over the next couple of innings, things settled down a bit, with each team getting just one hit and no runs. The top of the sixth started off with Smoltz issuing three walks. It was time for the Red Sox to take full advantage. Jason Varitek grounded into a double play but brought Ortiz home to tie the game. Phew! The place was going crazy again. I was so pleased to see lots of Red Sox fans there. The young man sitting next to me was from Boston but attending college near Atlanta. He had gotten tickets to all three games of the series. Seeing a whole series was something I had never done. Hmm, I might add that to my to-do list.

In the top of the seventh, Smoltz handled the Red Sox dandily. Manny Delcarmen relieved Schilling in the bottom of the frame, getting the first two batters out and then giving up a single. Javier Lopez came in to relieve Delcarmen and proceeded to walk the next batter. Ugh! Rudy Seanez came in with two outs and two men on. He immediately gave up a three-run home run to Jeff Francoeur, who came to play for the Mets in 2009. Oh no! The score was Braves 6, Red Sox 3.

Macay McBride relieved Smoltz in the top of the eighth inning. He struck out our big guns, Ortiz and Ramirez! I couldn't believe what I was seeing. But then McBride walked the next two. Maybe we would make something happen. Coco Crisp hit a long single to bring one home and move a runner to third. That brought Chad Paronto to the mound for the Braves. Mike Lowell pinch-hit. That at-bat was what made him stand out in my mind. He drove a double to right field, scoring two runs and tying the game. Lowell was a double-hitting machine! What a play! Another of my favorites, Alex Cora, pinch-hit, knocking a single to score Lowell with the go-ahead run. Sox take the lead again! Cora advanced to second on a throwing error. Kevin Youkilis, another one of my favorite players, came to bat and hit a home run to bring in two more runs! I was so excited that I was jumping up and down. Mike Remlinger came in for Paronto. Just leave him in! We really liked Paronto, as Sox fans. Mark Loretta hit a single to left to welcome Remlinger. David Ortiz, batting for the second time that inning, was hit by a pitch, putting two men on for Manny Ramirez. The excitement dwindled just a bit as Ramirez popped out. But still, eleven men to the plate and six runs isn't a bad inning!

Mike Timlin took the mound for Boston in the bottom of the eighth. Lowell took over third, Cora took over shortstop, and Youkilis moved over to first. At the time I barely understood the moves, but came to be so impressed with the versatility of this Boston team, especially Youkilis.

Ryan Langerhans got a hold of a pitch for a deep double, followed by a single by Marcus Giles to drive in a run for Atlanta. Renteria jabbed a single to advance Giles to second. Here we go again! Chipper Jones pinch-hit for Remlinger, reaching on a fielder's choice and advancing Giles to third. Uh oh! Andruw Jones hit a single, and Giles scored. The big gun came in for Boston—Jonathan Papelbon got the last out of the inning! Phew!

In the top of the ninth, Kenny Ray took the mound for the Braves. Nixon singled. Varitek grounded out, moving Nixon to second. Crisp singled and Nixon scored. Insurance runs are always good! Papelbon gave up a two-out double before sealing the deal. The Red Sox won 10–7. What a wonderful and exciting game! I was so happy to have shared it with such dear family members.

We left the park and were able to get right on a shuttle back to the car. I was pleased about our luck, as Uncle Steve was likely feeling the effects of sitting for a long time. We headed in the direction of home and found a place to grab a bite, as all the excitement had made us hungry. Being truck drivers, my relatives knew the best places to eat, any time of day or night. We had a good meal and finished the trek home. We arrived in the wee hours of the morning having wound down during the four-hour drive. I was ready for some serious shuteye.

The next day we relived parts of the game. I felt that we really had shared something special. The following day it was time for Cindy and I to head north, so we said our tearful goodbyes. The drive went smoothly, and we kept plugging along. We stopped once at a diner for a meal, but then just ate snacks the rest of the way home, stopping every couple of hours only to stretch our legs and use facilities. Cindy kept me going with trivia questions, everything from state capitals to Harry Potter. We ran into some construction which delayed us about three hours, but all in all it was a good trip home. We arrived at home in the early hours of the following morning, exhausted but happy.

The end of July meant it was time for a family reunion. Another one of my cousins was also a huge Mets fan. She was married to a huge Yankee fan, which resulted in lots of friendly teasing. We talked about going to a game at Shea Stadium. I told her that after I got back from my Florida trip we would talk. I was excited at the possibility of another trip to Shea.

FARTHER SOUTH

The next trip was in early August. I was bound for Florida to see both Dolphin Stadium and Tropicana Field. I decided to stay in St. Petersburg to see the Devil Rays (before they dropped the "Devil") on Saturday night, and then drive over to see the Marlins' Sunday afternoon game and back. Perhaps I would get to the beach on Monday before I flew back on Tuesday.

Eric's mother had been in touch, and told me that her daughter, Eric's sister, was taking the family to the Bahamas in August for her birthday. Well, if that wasn't a kick in the teeth! Eric would get to go to the Bahamas after all. Funny how that worked out. They were leaving around the same time as I was. I didn't know where they were flying out. I just hoped I didn't run into them at the airport. I didn't.

The flight down went fine; everything was going according to plan. When I got to the motel, I wanted to get a real meal. I knew that later I would just have a snack (part of my ritual at each new park is trying a hot dog). I asked at the front desk if there was something a bit better than fast food to eat nearby. They pointed me to a restaurant a few buildings over. I walked up to the restaurant, which didn't appear to be open. I turned to leave, but a man came out and asked if he could help me. I said I was just looking to get some lunch. He said they would make something.

They were still setting up the tables, so I sat at the bar. I was already wearing my baseball fan outfit. The TV was on and the bartender asked if I wanted the remote. I changed the channel to a baseball game. The owner, the man who had let me in, started talking to me about baseball. He had grown up in the northeast and was a Boston fan as a young man. Then he moved to the Houston area and became a Mets fan. We had two teams in common. The whole staff was so nice. One of the waitresses said that the bartender must have liked me because he never gave up the remote for anyone. The food was very good, just what I was looking for. It was nice to have someone to talk to.

I headed to the game in plenty of time to take my usual walk around and get pictures. I was excited to see the Red Sox play again. Tropicana Field was an interesting place. On the outside it was somewhat generic, but had some neat features. I particularly liked the entrance, a huge rotunda with a beautiful painting all the way around it. It was very neat. There was a petting tank for real devil rays in the outfield concourse, which was very cool.

I made my way to my seat, which was in the lowest section in left field a bit past third base. It was a great seat. While watching the guys warming up on the field, I noticed David Ortiz, Manny Ramirez, and Wily Mo Pena talking. A few minutes later David and Manny were jogging back from a sprint. Wily Mo passed them going the other direction and then turned around, snuck up behind Manny, and tickled his neck. Manny just about jumped out of his skin. All three of them started laughing. What a neat experience it was seeing them have fun with each other.

I was fortunate enough to be sitting next to a family of Red Sox fans. It was fun to have someone nearby to celebrate the good plays with. They were from Boston but had relocated to Ocala, Florida, which, according to them, has a large population of New York transplants who also happened to be Yankees fans. When they had their driveway redone, they put a ten-foot Red Sox logo in the center of it. That was such a cool thing! I can relate to being deep in enemy territory, coming from upstate New York where Yankees fans were everywhere.

This game was only the second time I had seen Tampa Bay play, so I really wasn't familiar with many of their players. Casey Fossum was pitching for Tampa Bay and David Wells was pitching for Boston, neither of whom had I seen before. The place was jam-packed. There was a different feel to seeing a game in a dome, something I'd first experienced in Minneapolis.

The game started off with a bang. Coco Crisp hit a ground ball to third base and should have been out at first, but due to a throwing error by B. J. Upton, Crisp was safe. Crisp then stole second. Mark Loretta hit a single and Crisp took third. We all got really excited because Big Papi was up next. With Crisp on third and Loretta on first we were sure the Sox were going to take an early three-run lead. Ortiz struck out to a collective sigh from what seemed like half of the crowd of over 30,000. There was still hope as Manny Ramirez came to the plate. Manny hit a sacrifice fly to allow Crisp to score, giving the Red Sox a one-run lead.

David Wells started three hitless innings, and Fossum also did well after the first. In the bottom of the fourth, things started to fall apart for Wells. The first batter hit a single, and the second batter made it safely to first on a throwing error by Ortiz, who was playing first base because Ramirez was at designated hitter that game. I had seen Ortiz play first base in Philadelphia in September 2003, before I knew that he usually didn't play in the field. His error set things up nicely for a single to score a run and tie the game. Okay, not good, game tied, two on and no outs yet. Javy Lopez, who was catching for Boston that game, caught a foul ball for the first out. Here we go, I told myself. But a walk loaded the bases. Not a good situation, especially for the struggling Wells. Three more singles drove in three more runs, giving Tampa the lead, 4–1.

Fossum had found his stride and pitched well for the next two innings. Wells settled back in by the fifth inning. In the sixth, however, he gave up two hits, one of which was a home run that extended the Tampa lead by one. The family beside me had never seen the Red Sox play other than at Fenway, and this was their kid's first game, so they were really hoping for a win.

In the top of the seventh, Shawn Camp came in for the Devil Rays. Wily Mo Pena hit a single and then went to second on another throwing error by Upton. We assured ourselves it was going to get things going. Boston would surely take advantage of the error. Kapler struck out but Pena took third on a wild pitch. Good! We were on a roll now. Alex Gonzalez struck out, keeping us on the edge of our seats. But then Crisp hit a double to bring home the second run for Boston and keep the inning going. The Boston fans were definitely making their presence known. Loretta grounded out to end the inning and silence the Boston fans. The Tampa fans were making some noise by then as well.

Julian Tavarez came in to relieve Wells. I rather like David Wells, and except for the trouble in the third inning, I thought he had pitched well. Tavarez made us sweat by giving up two singles, one erased by a very nice double play, before getting the final out of the inning.

In the top of the eighth Ortiz hit a single. Good, good. Ramirez followed that up with a long home run to the deepest part of the park! The place erupted with cheers of hope. Tampa's third pitcher of the night, Jon Switzer, got two outs and then walked two before Tampa's manager replaced him with Brian Meadows. All of this gave me a feeling that Boston had them on the run, and they knew it. Meadows got the final out of the inning, but we were only down by one.

Craig Hansen came in for the bottom of the eighth for Boston. First out was no problem, but the second batter hit a single and stole second. The steal proved irrelevant because Hansen then walked Upton. Josh Paul slammed a double to bring in two runs, extending the lead to three again. He ended up on third on the throw to home, and all of this came with only one out. We were stunned. The icing on the cake was a sacrifice to bring home one more run. This was not good! I had seen the Red Sox score six runs in one inning before, so I knew a comeback was possible, especially because we had the top of the order coming up. Coco Crisp led off with a ground ball, first out. Ugh! Loretta lifted our spirits with a long double. The whole place was on its feet with the best two hitters in the league coming up next, Ortiz and Ramirez. Papi smacked a long single and Loretta scored! Way to go guys—keep it going! Manny did just that with another nice single! Kevin Youkilis drew a walk to load the bases! Let it be another great comeback win, I prayed. It was not to be, as Lopez grounded into a double play to end the inning and the game. We all looked at each other, speechless. We finally regained our composure, admitted it was a good game nonetheless, and said our goodbyes (with hugs) before making our way out of the stadium. My new friends had never seen Boston lose, so I felt bad for them, but no team can win every game.

I drove back to the hotel to find the desk clerk at the door as I pulled in. He came up to me with such a concerned look on his face. I was afraid that somehow he had bad news for me. It turned out he was just worried about me. He knew I had left several hours ago and was traveling alone; he had thought I had gotten lost or worse. His worry was sweet but something I definitely didn't expect. I assured him that I would let him know when I left the next day, explaining my plans to drive to Miami and back.

The next morning, I drove over to the east coast of Florida. The drive was interesting. I have driven in Boston and in New York, but I have to say, Alligator Alley was crazy. Cars were passing on both shoulders, no matter how fast traffic was going. I kept my composure but was forced to drive a little bit faster than I might have otherwise.

I made it to the game early, as was my custom. I had time to walk around the stadium and take it all in. The Marlins weren't drawing much of a crowd, so they offered free parking as an enticement. I am not sure that it was working. The parking lot was very empty, though I was early.

Dolphin Stadium was obviously an older multi-purpose stadium. It was fairly plain on the outside, and had more of a football stadium feel to it, not counting the Billy Marlin blow-up mascot at the entrance.

After my walk around and picture taking, I went into the park to get some lunch before the game. I had remembered to put on sunscreen. I wasn't sure if my seat was under a roof or not. I was glad I was cautious, because my seat wasn't too far up from the field and definitely in the sun. I had just sat down to eat my lunch when there was a cloud burst and people made a mad dash for cover. I had a soda and hot dog on a tray, so I was hurrying to put my cup in the holder and get myself up when a young man who was running by stopped to ask if he could help me. I thought that was a very nice thing to do. I thanked him and said I was all set. I did get a bit wet and there were two more similar cloud bursts before the game started. It was ninety degrees and partly cloudy the rest of the day. The rain had washed off my sunscreen, and I did get a burn on both of my legs. This made for an uncomfortable and very long four-hour drive back to the motel.

This was only the second time I had seen either the Marlins or the Dodgers, so I wasn't very familiar with the players. I had thought I would be rooting for the Dodgers, for no particular reason.   Scott Olsen was pitching for Florida and Mark Hendrickson was pitching for Los Angeles. That was the first and only time I saw either of them pitch. The crowd of a little over 14,000 looked extra small in the large stadium.

The Dodgers started things with a run, helped out by a Marlins throwing error and a wild pitch. Hendrickson pitched a quick one-two-three inning. Olsen had more trouble in the second and loaded the bases before striking out the next three batters. Hmm. That was something, seeing him work out of that kind of trouble.

Hendrickson ran into trouble in the bottom of the second inning and allowed two runs for the Marlins to take the lead. There was a family a couple of rows in front of me that were having a loud discussion and playing musical seats, which was fairly distracting. I decided to get out of the sun briefly and get another drink.

The score held until the bottom of the fifth. Hendrickson started it off by walking a batter, which inevitably came back to bite him when the walked runner scored, making the score Marlins 3, Dodgers 1. The game was not going the way I had wanted, but I wasn't that invested. I was still distracted by the family in front of me. That score held until the top of the seventh inning.

That's when things really started to happen for the Dodgers. Los Angeles played some pretty good small ball, taking advantage of a passed ball and a couple of walks. Even with a couple of pitching changes, the Dodgers brought home six runs to turn the game around. This was the second time I saw two players who would come to play for Boston the following year, J. D. Drew and Julio Lugo.

I was starting to get uncomfortable in the sun, so I decided to watch the rest of the game from the top of the stairs. As it turned out, I should have done that earlier, as my legs were painfully burned. There were only a couple more hits and a few more pitching changes the rest of the way. The final score was Dodgers 7, Marlins 3. I made my way out of the stadium and to the car. It was one of the easiest escapes from a stadium I ever had, and I attributed it to the small crowd. I endured the four hours in the car and looked forward to getting some ice on my legs.

When I got back to the hotel, the desk clerk was glad to see me get back safe. It was kind of nice to think someone was thinking of me. I had taken an extra day off to perhaps get to the beach while in Florida. Unfortunately, the weather on my free day was expected to be full of thunderstorms. I had also had a bad night due to the sunburn. So I decided rather than getting caught at the beach in a storm, I would settle for the swimming pool and a good book.

I decided I had to get something for my legs, so I walked over to a nearby drug store to get some lotion. It was only a couple of blocks away, so I headed out on foot. When I got back to the hotel, I headed back to my room. In the elevator there were two young men, and one had a Boston hat. I asked him if they were in town for the game. They weren't. They had just gotten into town for a last break before heading back to college for the fall semester and didn't even know the Red Sox were in town. They had missed out. They were a bit bummed but they had some cool stuff planned for the week anyway. They were staying on the same floor as I was. We all got off the elevator, and I told them to enjoy their stay.

I waited for the storm to pass, got changed, and went down to the pool. I went for a swim and then sat outside in the shade reading my book. Two of the young lads from the elevator came out to have a cigarette. They noticed me at the pool. After a brief conversation, they went up to get their friends and came down to go swimming. We all chatted and swam for a while before the rain came through again. It was fun, and I was glad to have company for a little while.

I split the rest of the day between the pool and my room, depending on the weather. I turned in early and headed back to the airport for an easy flight home the next morning.

MORE SHEA

After I got back, I contacted my cousin Jen to see if she still wanted to go to a Mets game. It was going to be just us two women, as her husband Lane—a Yankee fan—had no interest in seeing the Mets. We compared schedules and settled on a game. I set about getting the tickets. We had decided on a Saturday game against the Dodgers. That week my sister and I decided we could definitely go to Toronto, so we firmed up those plans too. I was excited to be going to two more games that season.

The day came for the Shea trip. Lane dropped Jen off and we headed to Flushing. It was looking to be a nice day, and we were both excited to be going to a game. We chatted about how we had become fans, which only made us more anxious to get there. The drive went fine, even with heavier traffic due to the US Open tennis event. We parked and headed for a brief walk around so Jen could get some pictures. It was a warm, sunny day, but then again we were at a baseball game, so the perfect weather only added to the experience.

We went to our seats, stopping on our way up the ramp so Jen could take in the sights as well as have a look at the US Open going on across the highway. We made it to our seats in the upper deck and took in the view of the field. It was exciting for me to share her first experience at Shea.

I had to take the usual pictures from my seat, and then we went to the team shop for Jen to find a t-shirt she liked. We got back to our seats just in time for the first pitch.

It was another good matchup, with Orlando Hernandez pitching for the Mets and Greg Maddux pitching for the Dodgers. The first batter Hernandez faced hit a deep double. Uh oh, we both said. But that was the only hit he gave up until the sixth inning. The game was moving fairly fast. Over the first five innings, Maddux only gave up one run, which came on a home run by Carlos Delgado in the second inning.

Jen was enjoying taking pictures of the players and seeing them on the big screen along with some of their stats. I didn't want her to miss a minute, so when it came time to get something to eat, I went and got food.

In the sixth inning Hernandez had some trouble. The inning started off with a single followed by a rare throwing error by Jose Reyes, landing a second runner on base. A sacrifice followed by a single brought home the first Dodgers run and tied the game. Nomar Garciaparra kept things going with an infield hit toward third base, which was gathered up in time to get Maddux out at home. J. D. Drew drove in the go-ahead run with another single. Jen and I were nervous that the whole thing might fall apart, but we kept telling each other we could get that run right back.

In the bottom of the next inning, the second batter up, Jose Valentin, another player I became very fond of, hit a double. Carlos Beltran was intentionally walked, and the Dodgers brought in a relief pitcher. That pitching change made me feel a little bit better. Delgado flied out, and the runners advance to second and third. We were getting excited! The situation prompted another Dodgers pitching change. We could feel the energy in the air! David Wright hit a single, and both Valentin and Beltran scored to take back the lead! The final score was Mets 3, Dodgers 2 in an exciting game of just about two and a half hours, played in front of a crowd of just over 47,000. I was pleased to have seen Billy Wagner in a Mets uniform for the first time, and also to see Lastings Milledge in a major-league uniform after seeing him play in Binghamton the year before.

We made it back to the car and waited for our turn to get out of the parking lot. The drive home was uneventful, except for the exit we took to take a break and get a bite to eat. It was one of those exits where you have to drive several miles to get to the restaurant they have a sign for at the exit, which always annoys me. We made it home. Lane came to pick up Jen. We visited a while, talking about maybe all going to a Mets-Yankees game the following year. I was very interested in that. We said our goodbyes, and I got some rest after a long day away from home.

O CANADA

The next game was in Toronto with my sister. I was doubly excited because Rogers Centre was another stadium I had not seen before, and this was Cindy's first major-league game. It had been fun to share Jen's first major-league experience a couple of weeks before, and I hoped it would be the same for Cindy's.

We left early Saturday morning for Toronto. We mapped out our route and allowed extra time, not knowing what we would run into at the border. I had gotten my passport, knowing I would be making the trip at some point. But Cindy only had her birth certificate and driver's license, so we wanted to have extra time in case we were detained at the border for whatever reason. At every stop on our way we saw people in Red Sox gear, which only made us more excited. I had my Red Sox t-shirt on. Cindy didn't have any Red Sox fan clothing yet, but she wore as much red as possible.

We got to the border and were welcomed to Canada swiftly. We stopped to exchange some money and made our way to the hotel. We had driven by the stadium on our way in to scope out parking. We were disappointed at the prospects, even at that time of the day. When we got to the hotel we found out the bus route and proceeded to the stadium via public transportation. A nice lady on the bus was very helpful, explaining which transfers we needed to make. The bus took us to the subway, and that took us directly to Union Station, right next to Rogers Centre. We took a walk around the outside and took some pictures of the CNC Tower next to the stadium. We toyed with the idea of going up in the tower, but there was too much of a wait. We didn't want to miss any of the game.

After taking sufficient pictures of the very neat fountains outside and the beautiful stonework on the outside of Rogers Centre, we went in, grabbed a snack, and found our seats. They were way up in the top section, only a few rows from the edge, which made Cindy very nervous. As a matter of fact, she didn't leave her seat once until the game was over because it bothered her to stand up way up there.

Cindy enjoyed watching the Blue Jays mascot as I took some more pictures. The stadium was an amazing place. The roof was open, because it was a nice, almost clear night, temperature in the mid-seventies. Cindy wasn't really a baseball fan yet, so I wasn't really sure how watching the game with her was going to go. Boston and Toronto were vying for second place in the AL East, and both pretty much out of the wild card race, so the game wasn't of great significance.

We did get to see Devern Hansack pitch in his major-league debut for the Red Sox and A. J. Burnett pitch for the Blue Jays. Burnett made me a little nervous because I knew he was very good. My concerns were soon set to rest, at least temporarily. The first Red Sox batter to face him, rookie Dustin Pedroia, hit a home run! Burnett struck out Kevin Youkilis and David Ortiz before Mike Lowell hit a single, which only served to remind me how good a pitcher Burnett was. Lowell was hitting behind Ortiz because Manny Ramirez was not in the lineup that night. Cindy really liked Big Papi. I cheered really loudly for Trot Nixon when he came to the plate.

A woman a couple rows in front of me had a t-shirt on with Nixon's number on it. She turned and said, "Hey, he was my guy!"

I laughed and told her she had made an excellent choice.

Hansack did well until the fourth inning, only giving up a couple of singles to that point. Then in the fourth he gave up back-to-back home runs to Lyle Overbay and Troy Glaus, giving the Blue Jays the lead. Oh Boy! I really wanted Cindy to see her Red Sox win.

In the top of the sixth inning, the Red Sox got a little something going. Lowell, who had moved up on my favorite players list, made it to first on an error by Overbay, followed by a double by Trot Nixon that moved Lowell over to third. We were getting excited. Cindy was enjoying the game, which made me happy. She was asking questions, just like I did when I was learning the game. I was thrilled to be able answer them, feeling grateful that Eric was so patient with me over the years. Next up was Jason Varitek, the captain of the Red Sox, one of my favorite players of all time. Unfortunately, he hit into a double play, but Lowell scored the tying run before Nixon was thrown out at third. Yeah! I was cheering as loudly as I could.

Hansack didn't have any better luck in the bottom of the sixth inning. After he gave up a double and a single, Terry Francona brought in Javier Lopez to face Overbay. Overbay hit a grounder to second, erasing one runner. But the go-ahead run scored. Ugh! Bryan Corey came in to relieve Lopez and faced Troy Glaus. Glaus hit a grounder to third and Overbay was called safe at second. An error was charged to Lowell, which brought Terry Francona out to argue the call. That was the first time I had seen Francona ejected from a game. From our seats you could see Francona vibrating just before the umpire gave the universal gesture for "you're outta here." It looked so funny from where we were sitting. Finally, a double play ended that dreadful inning.

Burnett had a little trouble in the top of the seventh. He gave up a single to Eric Hinske, who was booed by the crowd, having played in Toronto before going to Boston. Then, to my surprise, they announced Manny Ramirez was pinch-hitting. The whole place went nuts! I explained to Cindy about Manny, and she was happy to get to see him as well. I was really happy she got to see him too. Gabe Kapler came in to run for Hinske. With Manny up to bat anything could happen! Manny drew a walk and they brought Alex Cora into run for Manny, who was nursing a knee injury. None of that netted the Red Sox anything, but it was exciting to see anyhow.

In the bottom of the eighth, Mike Burns came in to pitch for Boston. A single followed by a triple scored another run. An intentional walk and a sacrifice scored one more, leaving the Red Sox down by three heading to the ninth. I kept reminding myself that anything could happen, but wasn't feeling very confident.

Toronto brought in B. J. Ryan to close the game. I was downright fearful, having seen him the last three years in Baltimore and having seen how good he was. Kapler started the inning off with a single. Mark Loretta pinch-hit for Alex Cora and hit a single. Okay, two on with Pedroia up. He lined out, as did Youkilis, dashing some of the hope we had built up. David Ortiz was up next. Could he? We hoped so! He hit a single to drive home Kapler and move Loretta to second. But the comeback wasn't to be, as Lowell struck out for the final out of the game. Final score Toronto 5, Red Sox 3 in just about three hours, in front of over 42,000 fans, more than half of which I swear were Red Sox rooters.

Cindy and I made our way out of Rogers Centre and around the block to the subway station. We stopped in a sports shop so Cindy could look for a gift she had wanted to pick up. She found something, and we continued toward the station. As we rounded a corner, we encountered a man playing guitar in a suit and well-shined shoes, with a paper bag over his head. His guitar case was open, collecting bills and coins from passers-by. It made me smile and think of Eric. Often in our travels Eric, a musician himself, dropped a bill or two into the case of a street musician.

We got on the subway and headed back to the hotel. We had to wait a while for the bus to pick us up at the station after getting off the subway, which wore on us. It had already been a very long day. We finally got back and were about ready for bed, but I had to check the TV for highlights of the day's games before I could turn the lights out.

The next day we made our way out of town to visit Casa Loma. Casa Loma is a famous Toronto castle with over 90 rooms, secret passages, towers, beautiful gardens and stables at the end of a very long tunnel. We wanted to do some other sightseeing while in Toronto and we both thought it looked really interesting. We had a good time wandering around the grounds and inside the castle, taking pictures of everything. We had a sandwich at the snack shop in the basement and decided it was time to head home. We exchanged our money back to American currency and got in line to cross the border, which took much longer than it had the prior day. Finally, after a couple of hours, we made it into New York.

On the way home we stopped for dinner at a truck stop. We figured it would have a variety of decent food and that the meal would get us the rest of the way home. We were pleased to see a salad bar and both ordered that. As we were talking over our meal we both noticed something on Cindy's plate was moving! The fruit salad had bugs in it! We called the waitress over and she removed the fruit salad from the bar immediately. Neither of us could eat anything else, so we just paid the bill and left. We did stop for a snack later on, but it took a while to get over that meal experience.

The playoffs that year were disappointing. The Red Sox didn't make it into the playoffs. The Mets did, but they were knocked out by the Cardinals in the NLCS. I watched the World Series anyway. I missed Eric as another baseball season came to an end. All I could do was move forward and make some plans for the following year. It was going to be a big baseball year!

ELEVEN IN 2007

As soon as the tentative schedules came out, I started to make plans for my trip to the West Coast. I had lots of decisions to make, and the logistics took a long time to work out. I had to map the distance between parks, and finding dates where most of the western teams were at home that would allow me time to travel between parks kept me up many a night running different scenarios. It was a wonderful distraction for the void that is the off-season.

By March 25, I had a firm plan: flights scheduled, game tickets ordered, and hotels booked. Early June 2007 was the date for my trip to California and Arizona to see six games in eleven days. I was excited but also nervous about taking such a long trip by myself. It had always been my hope that Eric would be traveling with me on this trip, because he had never been to the West Coast either. It would have been extra special to experience it together. I had sent him an e-mail before I finalized things asking if he would consider it, but he said no. It wasn't long after that I found out the reason why he wasn't interested. He was moving to Illinois.

Once he moved, he did get in touch with me. We were going to make an effort to rebuild our friendship. It would take some effort on both our parts but we had been through so much together. The distance would make it even harder, but where there is a will there is a way.

I get many e-mails about opportunities to enter drawings for chances to win or purchase highly sought-after tickets. One such chance came in

March 2007, when I had a chance for tickets to Yankees against Mets at Shea in May. I forwarded it to my cousin Jen, remembering what we had talked about the year before. Well, she was selected and she and Lane asked me to go with them. Even though Lane is a big Yankees fan, he and I get along very well on every other subject except baseball. We both take baseball very seriously even though we are fans of opposing teams. Jen likes the Yankees just fine as long as they aren't playing her Mets. It promised to be an interesting day. How could I say no?

We made our plans and anxiously awaited the day of the game. We decided to make it a real baseball experience and tailgate, as it was a late afternoon game on a Saturday afternoon. We figured out who would bring what for the cookout as the weekend got closer.

By April, Eric and I were talking regularly. Early that year he had gotten two tickets to Toronto to see the Red Sox play the Jays. Having moved away and started a new job, he didn't think he would be able to get time off. So he sent me the tickets. They were really good seats, so I talked my sister into going back to Toronto with me. It was a Monday night game which meant we both had to take a couple of days off work, but it was early enough that scheduling the vacation time wouldn't be hard. We started looking into other places we could see and planned to go up on Sunday to do some sightseeing. That time we were going to see the Ontario Science Center as well.

In May Eric and I decided we should get tickets to see two games in one day. Because he lived near Chicago and the Chicago teams were close to each other, that became our target. There was only one time they were both home on the same day and not playing at the same time, in late August. I booked a flight and ordered tickets to the games on August 20. The Cubs were playing the Cardinals at 1:00 PM, and the White Sox were playing the Royals at 7:00 PM. It would work out perfectly, or so we thought.

Meanwhile the New York game with Jen and Lane was approaching. We were going to leave mid-morning but had decided it would be best to talk that morning to see what the latest forecast was. There was a chance of rain that day, but we decided we would go ahead with our plans to tailgate. Things started out badly. My little portable gas grill was missing a regulator, so I had to run to the store to see if I could get one. No luck. I had to get a whole new grill if I wanted to follow our plan. I bought it and made it back home before they arrived at the appointed time. We were all set to go. As we were loading the trunk, Lane noticed the Red Sox pillows and Red Sox throw that I keep in the trunk. He joked that he couldn't ride in such a car! There was bantering back and forth about the fan of the losing team riding in the trunk on the ride home. Eric called twice that day, once while we were driving down and the second time during the game, which was nice. It was sort of like having him along at the game.

The next snag was the directions. I brought the wrong directions! We had to find our way from the atlas. We found our way to a parking lot under the highway that required us to take a little shuttle to the ballpark. We found a parking spot where we could have our cookout, albeit a little rushed. Lane was an excellent cook and was great about getting everything going while Jen and I found a port-a-potty. We ate and then got ourselves ready for the game. Thus far it wasn't the best start to a game, but we were there and making the best of it.

It was also the first time since 2003 that I hadn't started the season at a game in Boston. With the big trip planned for June, I couldn't spend too much more on baseball.

We took the shuttle to the park and found our seats in time for the first pitch. We had hoped to see some batting practice but at least we were there in time for the game. It promised to be an interesting one.

It was cool and still drizzling, so we were grateful that our seats were under an overhang. I think we were three rows from the top of the stadium. The only problem with seats like that is that you can't see where fly balls go. As Eric always said, if the seats are on the inside of the stadium, then they are good seats. But some are just a little bit better than others.

Shea was packed with over 56,000 fans. We had gotten an extra ticket, which I planned to use as a peace offering to Eric before I knew he was moving. I couldn't find anyone else available to go, so we had an extra seat to put our stuff in. The spare spot came in handy with such a huge crowd.

It was going to be an exciting game. Tom Glavine was bidding to record his 295th career victory. Of course Jen and I were rooting for that, but not Lane. The starting pitcher for the Yankees was Darrell Rasner.

Glavine started off walking the first batter, which is never a good thing. A one-out single and another walk loaded the bases. Lane was enjoying the game already, but Jen and I were sitting there in disbelief. We knew it would be a very long day if that continued. A grounder scored the first run, but resulted in the second out as well. A fly ball ended the inning, much to our relief.

In the bottom of the inning Jose Reyes hit a single and then stole second. Endy Chavez hit a single and advanced Reyes to third. Now, I know I have said it before, but things happen when Jose Reyes gets on base. That time was no different! Jen and I were cheering as loudly as we could in hopes of drowning out Lane's jeers. The Yankees didn't give Rasner much of a chance to get work himself out of trouble and promptly brought in Mike Myers to pitch with two on and no outs. Carlos Beltran hit a sacrifice, Reyes scored! Tie game! Carlos Delgado struck out for the second out. David Wright hit a two-run homer! The Mets took the lead. Knowing full well that the score would change again and probably soon, Jen and I celebrated while we could. It looked like the Mets weren't done when Shawn Green made it safely to first on a Robinson Cano throwing error and then stole second, but Paul Lo Duca flied out to end the inning. All of that in just the first inning!

The top of the second started off with a home run by Robinson Cano. I had come to call him Uh Oh Cano, because he is always a threat! It looked like the Yankees were going to inflect more damage with a few singles, but groundouts did them in before a run could score. Phew, the Mets still had the lead!

The bottom of the second inning was another good one for the Mets. Speedy runners and a Yankee throwing error added another run to the lead. Lane was not happy but Jen and I certainly were.

In the top of the third inning Glavine faced three batters, giving up a single but then getting out of the inning on a double play. The bottom of the inning was more fruitful for the Mets. It kicked off with a single followed by *another* two-run home run by David Wright! Mets were up by four! But you can never count the Yankees out, ever! Jen and I still celebrated, but a little less, because we knew that if this turned around Lane would make us eat our words. Myers walked the next batter and that was it for him. The Yankees brought in Luis Vizcaino, who got them out of the inning with relative ease. I was getting to see a lot of Yankee pitchers that I had never seen before.

The fourth inning was as easy as the third for Glavine. The bottom of the fourth was similar to the third for the Mets. A couple of singles were followed by a double, and another run scored. Wright was getting some respect and was intentionally walked. A groundout brought in another Mets run, putting them up 8–2. Jen and I were starting to feel bad for Lane, so we kept our cheering to an absolute minimum. The top of the fifth was a one-two-three inning for Glavine. If the Mets held the lead, he would get his 295th win.

In the bottom of the fifth, Ron Villone came in to pitch for the Yankees and had himself a one-two-three inning. Glavine came out for the sixth, allowed two hits, but got out of the inning without any runs scoring. Villone got out of the sixth inning without allowing a run after intentionally walking Wright for the second time in the game.

Glavine was back out there for the seventh. The first batter hit a single. Doug Mientkiewicz pinch-hit for Villone, prompting the Mets to bring in Scott Schoeneweis to replace Glavine, who received a curtain call. This was first time I had seen that happen in person. Tom Glavine was happy to oblige. A couple of groundouts landed the runner on third! Not good, guys! A single scored a run for the Yankees. Now it was Mets 8, Yankees 3, and Lane was getting excited. I started to worry!

Brian Bruney came in to pitch for the Yankees. He issued a walk but didn't allow a run. Schoeneweis didn't do as well in the top of eighth. He was greeted with back-to-back home runs! How rude, don't you think? Okay, not really. He walked the next batter, so that was it for him. Pedro Feliciano came in to get one out, but then a double scored another run and brought the Yankees to within two. Lane was having a much better time by then! Jen and I were still happy the Mets were ahead, but we weren't going to rain on Lane's parade. Jason Giambi pinch hit for Bruney and advanced the runner to third. Ugh! Next, a walk! Would this inning ever end? Aaron Heilman came in to face Jeter, who grounded out to end the pain for the Mets.

Kyle Farnsworth took the mound in the eighth for the Yankees. Now I was happy to I got to see him, as I would consider him a great player. But I can't say I wasn't worried with him on the mound. Jen and I took deep breaths and watched quietly. He started out with a groundout and then a walk to Beltran. Another groundout advanced the runner to second. Wright was intentionally walked by the third Yankee pitcher!

Then a wonderful, exciting thing happened. Julio Franco came in to pinch-hit for Heilman! I had seen Franco play for Atlanta in 2004, and I was so happy when he came to play for the Mets. I considered him to be one of the most interesting players to play the game. He was approaching his forty-ninth birthday that August. I was so excited about taking pictures that I almost missed the double steal by Beltran and Wright! I was on the edge of my seat. Franco hit a single, allowing both Beltran and Wright to score, and then advanced to second himself as they tried to throw out Wright at home. I don't think I have ever screamed so loud. It was such a beautiful inning! The Mets widening their lead to four making it 10–6! My heart was pounding, but the game wasn't over yet! Lane was again slumping in his seat and cursing the Mets.

Billy Wagner came in to pitch the top of the ninth. Wagner, the Mets closer, and one of the best in the game, came in even though it wasn't a close situation. They definitely wanted to get Glavine that win. Wagner gave up a one-out single to Alex Rodriguez, then another deep single to Posada, advancing him to third. I didn't check but I don't think Jen was breathing either! Abreu hit an infield grounder to Wagner, Rodriguez scored, and Posada was safe at third because of a throwing error by Wagner! Fortunately, Wagner struck out the next two to end the game. Although not an official save, Wagner did preserve the win for Glavine, his 295th career win. We were there to see it!

Out of respect for Lane, Jen and I only celebrated by sneaking high fives behind his back and out of his sight while we made our way to a few shops and then back to the car. We stopped at one shop near the offices. I could hardly believe it when I saw Omar Minaya walk by with a big smile on his face. Jen and Lane were in the shop, but I was waiting outside because it was crowded and I wasn't looking to buy anything. I was a bit stunned. I looked to see if I could get Jen's attention but couldn't, so I looked back, smiled, and nodded in his direction. He nodded back and kept on walking. A happy day for all!

I was anxious to get back to the car because it wasn't in a regular parking lot. I was nervous after seeing signs that said they would tow people an hour after the game ended. Jen found what she was looking for in the shop, and thankfully the car was still there when we got back to the lot.

The ride back home was fairly uneventful. No one had to ride in the trunk despite prior threats. Lane was able to get some rest on the way back as Jen and I chatted. The route home was familiar to me by now, and it really wasn't a bad drive. But it's always nicer to have someone along to keep you company.

CALIFORNIA, HERE I COME

Two weeks later, I headed to California for the adventure I had long saved and planned for. My sister took me to the airport on Saturday morning. She took pictures and had some breakfast with me after I checked my luggage.

My flight left on time, headed to Philadelphia on the first leg of the trip. As we were making our descent into Philadelphia, we flew over Citizens Bank Park. I couldn't get my camera out fast enough, so I missed the opportunity to get the picture. I saw a plane coming toward us at a 45-degree angle, and then all of a sudden we pulled up hard and the engines revved. We had to abort our landing attempt. The pilot came on the intercom and explained that one of the planes had to be called off, and it was us. So we circled around again and guess what, I was able to get the picture of the stadium after all! I was happy about that, but even happier that we weren't involved in a midair collision!

My flight out of Philadelphia left on time and I was on my way to California. I sat by the window. The gentleman next to me and I began to chat. He had moved to Los Angeles a couple of years ago and had started a Web site company. He said it took him a while to get used to the traffic on the freeways, which made me think about how a country girl like myself was going to do. It was a long flight. With the time change, I decided it was best to try to get a little shuteye before landing.

After the plane landed, my fellow traveler was kind enough to show me where the baggage claim was and where to catch the shuttle to the car rental place. He even gave me his card in case I ran into trouble while I was in town. I told him I wouldn't be in Los Angeles long, but that I would be back in town on the last day of my trip. I wished him luck with his business and thanked him for all his help. I expect to see him on the cover of a business magazine some day.

I picked up my rental car and headed to the hotel. I called home to let them know I made it safely to the hotel, and then called Eric to let him know as well. I sang him a little song I had made up just for the occasion. It made him laugh, probably at my singing, as much as the actual song.

The hotel was fairly close to Disney World. There were plenty of places nearby to get a snack. I walked around the block and found a neat place to get a sandwich. The place didn't have anywhere to sit, so I took my food back to my room. I spent some time outside, enjoying my first night in California before allowing myself to get to bed. I was spending only one night in Los Angeles, seeing Angels Stadium the next day and heading south to San Diego right after the game. I had a hard time getting to sleep because I was so excited that I was actually there on the West Coast, ready to see some baseball games in stadiums I had only seen on TV! I was starting a wonderful adventure that would include six games in two different states, over 1,000 miles by car, some time on the beach, and lots more.

The next morning I packed up and headed to Angel Stadium. It was a 12:35 PM game against the Orioles. I decided to get something to eat before going into the park. The top of the big "A" in the Angels Stadium parking lot could be seen from blocks away. I knew I was getting close. I had started out in shorts for the day, but once I got to the park I decided it was too cool for shorts and changed into pants. The weather was in the low seventies and overcast.

I walked around the stadium taking pictures. The main entrance of the park was really something to see. I had seen it on TV, but it was way better in person. It has concrete baseballs lining the sidewalk and two huge Angels baseball caps on either side of the entrance. The roof to the entrance was held up with two sets of three huge bats. It was so cool!

Neither team was one of my favorites, but I thought I would root for the home team, mostly because the Orioles are in the same division as the Red Sox. A couple of the players I had gotten to know when they played for the

Red Sox were playing that day. Kevin Millar was playing for the Orioles and Shea Hillenbrand was playing for the Angels. It was nice to see them.

I was reminded of all the different names the Angels have had. They started out as the California Angels, then they were the Anaheim Angels, and then they became the Los Angeles Angels of Anaheim. The reason for the new, long name was stressing their status as the American League representative in the Los Angeles area. Personally, I thought the Anaheim Angels had the best ring to it, but they don't consult me on such matters.

My seat was in the second section up from the field, just past first base in the fifth row a few seats from the aisle. The section was in front of the Panda Express restaurant, the scent of which was tempting me to choose Chinese food instead of my traditional hot dog. I had to force myself to resist. This was one of the biggest temptations to break with my tradition of having a hot dog at every new stadium.

One of my favorite things about the inside of Angels Stadium was the waterfall in center field. There was a picnic area beyond the waterfall which also looked really cool. This was my first West Coast stadium, and so far I was impressed. As they were getting ready to bring the players out, they played the song "Calling All Angels" by Train. They also showed pictures of past players on the screen in center field, which was very moving. It brought tears to my eyes. I really liked that song before, but it had even more meaning for me after that. I thought it was a great way to start the game.

Another thing stuck out for me: during the performance of the "Star Spangled Banner," the Orioles fans in the crowd made sure to draw out the "O" just like they do at Camden Yards! I had never seen the O's play outside Baltimore, so I didn't know they did that. It was just one of those cool and unique things that a team's fans do, like when the fans sing "Sweet Caroline" in the middle of the eighth inning at Fenway.

The pitchers were Ervin Santana for the Angels and Jeremy Guthrie for the Orioles. It was the first and only time I saw either of them. It was a good matchup. There was only one hit until the top of the third inning. This was a good thing, because the group around me was playing musical seats. I am not sure where they were supposed to sit, but they kept trying different seats until the people who actually had those tickets made them move. Finally, the usher escorted them out of the section, presumably to their real seats. It was really distracting for all of us who were in our correct seats. There was a father with three young kids sitting next to me who was also frustrated with all of it. We chatted about different stadiums. He said one of the best he had been to was Fenway. His youngest was maybe two or three years old. The little guy would high five me on the arm whenever the crowd cheered. It was cute. They didn't stay until the end of the game, as the kids got restless, but I enjoyed them while they were there.

With two out in the top of the third, the Orioles manufactured the first run of the game. In the bottom of the inning, the Angels tied the game with the help of a throwing error. In the top of the fourth, the Orioles went ahead on a solo home run. Okay then. In the top of the sixth, the Orioles were at it again, plating another run. Perhaps the game wouldn't turn out like I had hoped. Neither of the players that I knew from their time in Boston had gotten a hit, so there wasn't a great deal to cheer about. In the top of the eighth inning, Hillenbrand hit a single to start things off and came around to score. Okay, just a one-run lead for Baltimore.

A new pitcher for the Angels posted a quick one-two-three inning to get the Angels right back up to bat. A leadoff single followed by a walk-off home run by Vladimir Guerrero! The Angles won! It was good to see the home team win in front of a fairly full stadium (41,000-plus) in just over two hours. This would be within two minutes of the shortest full game I ever attended. I called Eric to fill him in on what I had just seen. He was a Guerrero fan and thus was happy too.

I made my way out of the park and back to my rental car. I reviewed the directions before I left the parking lot. I was amazed at how easy it was to get out of the lot and onto the highway, which was really nice, as I had a few hours' drive to San Diego.

I scheduled a free day in San Diego so I could do some sightseeing and maybe even go horseback riding on the beach, always a dream of mine. The drive was pretty straightforward so I took the opportunity to put on my Bluetooth and call my uncle in Georgia. He and my aunt were truck drivers after all, so he wanted to know specifically where I was. He amazed me by describing in great detail exactly what I was seeing at each exit. He told me in about five miles I would see something special on the right. He was on the phone with me when I got my first sight of the Pacific Ocean! It was such a beautiful sight to this East Coaster! It brought tears of joy to my eyes, and I was especially touched that I got to share that moment with my uncle, even over the phone. The water seemed so much bluer than the Atlantic! I was so looking forward to getting to actually touch it the next day. He gave me some additional information on good places to eat along the way before we said our goodbyes. I was very happy!

I got to the hotel easily and had dinner at a Denny's, breaking my rule to stay away from chain restaurants. It was right next to the hotel, and I really didn't want to drive any farther that day. I got a really good laugh when my waiter's name was Jose Reyes! I asked him if that was his real name and if he was a baseball fan. He said he was aware of the Mets player but not really a big fan. I thanked him for his good service and told him he did the name proud.

While I was sightseeing I had passed the Coronado Bay Bridge. I am not a big fan of driving over bridges but it looked so neat on the other side I mustered all the courage I had and headed over the bridge. It was really high, but the view was beautiful. I made it across and drove around the manmade island until I came to the beach. I found a place to park and walked down toward the water.

There were benches on the beach so I sat and just listened to the water. It was still fairly early in the day and still hazy. I could have listened to the water for hours. I was dressed in jeans and sneakers. I had to take my socks and shoes off and roll up my pants to wade in the water. The water was cool but still wonderful. I really wanted to play in the waves, but I didn't want to go all the way back to the hotel for my suit, so I settled for walking along the beach for a while. I took a picture of the ocean on my phone to send to Eric, knowing he was at work. At least he could enjoy it with me in some small way.

I noticed something breaching the surface of the water. It was black. The more I watched the more I was convinced it was a pair of dolphins. I was wrong; it was a family of dolphins! The big one jumped, and then the baby jumped! It was such a special sight. I tried to get a picture of the baby but was not successful. It will live in my memory forever, though. At that point I called Eric. Of course, faking disbelief, he teased me about always thinking I was seeing dolphins. Others were starting to walk the beach from the resort or the neighborhood nearby, and they stopped to watch the family of dolphins also.

After sitting at the beach for a while longer, I decided that I would head back to the hotel and either get proper clothing to be at the beach or find something else to do. As I was heading back across the bridge, I noticed what looked like a tour boat for the bay. I decided to see if I could find a place to take that. It was turning out to be a beautiful day to be on the water. I found the launch site and bought a ticket for a tour. I had time to eat some lunch before the next tour left.

The director had served in the navy and was very knowledgeable. The first half of the tour was around the navy shipyard. I took a lot of pictures to share with my cousin Norman. He had been an airman in the navy. I got to see the USS *Midway*, which had become a museum, and spotted the USS *Ronald Regan* being built. Petco Park was also visible from the bay, so I got some good pictures of the park as well.

The other leg of the tour took us about as far west as you can go in the bay, Point Loma if I remember correctly. We got to see some sea lions and their babies. It was a very nice and informative tour. As always, I enjoyed being on the water.

I went back to the hotel and walked over to Denny's again to have some dinner. Jose Reyes the waiter was there, but he didn't wait on me that time. Afterward I sat down to watch some baseball and plan out the next day. It was a night game on Tuesday, so I was going to spend the day at a beach somewhere. The clerk recommended a beach not too far up the coast at Mission Bay. There was a little boardwalk there with shops and things to do, so that was to be my destination for the next day.

I found I had adjusted fairly well to the time change and woke up at a more reasonable time in the morning. That was good, because it was going to be a late night with going to the game. I headed out mid-morning and made my way to Mission Beach. It was a really nice place. There were some shops, restaurants, and games going on. I wandered around to see what was available before I chose a place to have brunch.

The place I picked had a balcony overlooking the ocean, so I took my time and enjoyed the entire experience. Afterward, I found a spot on the beach and relaxed until the haze completely lifted. I had brought a book to read (*Big Papi* by David Ortiz). As the haze lifted, I decided that I really needed a hat. I went into one of the shops to get one. I found a really cool t-shirt that I had to have also. It was a tie-dyed one that said San Diego, perfect for commemorating my time there. The only hat I could find that fit was very pink with a big brim. I bought it, already thinking of ways I could tone it down when I got home.

By then the haze was completely gone and it was a beautiful, warm, and sunny day. I made my way to the water and played in the waves like a kid. The water was refreshing. I returned to my spot on the beach to read a little more before heading back to the hotel to prepare for the game. On my way back to the hotel, I had an idea of what to do with my hat. I was going to scan all the tickets from the trip and then make a collage and print it onto an iron-on transfer. Then I could plaster them all over the hat! That would make it less pink it, and much more unique!

I was going to take public transportation to the game, so I had to factor in the travel time. I had booked a hotel very near a trolley station which offered free parking. I was fortunate not to have to make a transfer to get to the stadium. I wanted to get to the park with enough time to walk around.

When I got to the station, I met a nice older couple who were also going to the game. They didn't live too far from there but preferred taking the trolley to driving downtown. We sat together and visited on the trolley. They walked to the stadium with me, and then I took my leave to walk around the outside of the park to take some pictures. The stadium was sort of jammed in the center of town and didn't offer too much from the outside, although the marquee at the entrance had some flair, similar to the one at Citizens Bank Park in Philadelphia.

When I got inside the park, I wandered around a little bit and found one of the most touching things I had seen at a ballpark: a tribute to ball players who served in the military. I took a picture of it for my cousin, and zoomed in on his hero Ted Williams. I couldn't help but stand there in silence in gratitude for what all servicemen and servicewomen have done for this country.

I made my way to my seat. Who was sitting in the next section, only a couple rows back, but the couple from the trolley! We chatted again, and they said they usually leave after the eighth inning, if I wanted to go back with them. I told them I would wait to see because I didn't usually like to leave until the end of the game. My seat was in the second section up under cover but not so far back that you couldn't see where fly balls were going, on the end of a three-seat row. A really good scenario, if you ask me.

One of the unique features of this park was the building in left field, Western Metal Supply Co. There are seats on each level outside the building and bleacher seats on the top. I took some pictures from my seat and then headed back up to get my usual hot dog before settling in for the game.

Just before the game started, the older couple who had seats next to me came in. We chatted a moment, and then the game started. Nomar Garciaparra was playing for the Dodgers. Because he was one of the players I came to know when he played for the Red Sox, I was leaning toward rooting for the Dodgers.

The first inning started with a walk and a stolen base but no score. Hmm. Not the start I was hoping for. The next couple of innings went quickly and no runs scored. The first hit of the game came in the bottom of the second off the bat of Geoff Blum, who, at the time, was one of only two active players to have multi-home run games while playing second base, short stop, and third base. The other, I was pleased to hear, was Jose Valentin. Blum thankfully only hit a single, and no runs scored that inning. All of this was giving me and the couple next to me a chance to chat. They were season-ticket holders so they knew I wasn't a regular. They asked where I was from. As it turned out, he was also from upstate New York but had married a woman from California and she wouldn't move back east. They had just celebrated their fiftieth wedding anniversary. I thought it was a sweet story and thanked him for sharing it with me.

The next hit came in the top of the fourth, but still no runs for either team. Each side only had one hit so far in the game. There had been plenty of base runners, with each side walking their fair share. In the top of the seventh inning, I thought the Dodgers were ready to make their move when they got a couple of hits and a walk, but nothing was doing. It was one of the longest innings of the game.

In the top of the eighth, Garciaparra got a hit, which was exciting for me, as I do love to see his at-bats, especially when they are fruitful. But the

Dodgers couldn't do anything with it. In the bottom of the eighth a pinch-hitter was hit by a pitch, giving the Padres a runner. He stole second base and then scored on a single. The place went nuts as San Diego plated the first run of the game.

I looked back to see if the couple from the trolley were still there, and they were. She yelled down to me that they would wait and go back with me, which I was pleased about not only because I enjoyed their company but because I felt better with them knowing where to go. All of a sudden the whole place went dark. Then a real gong and "Hells Bells" started to play. This was typical when closer Trevor Hoffman came in, but even seeing it on TV didn't prepare me for the live experience.

As the lights came back on, two young guys ran onto the field. They managed to elude the security staff for a couple of minutes before being tackled and led off in handcuffs. I am not sure what possesses people to do such things. That was the first time I had seen that happen. Hoffman closed out the game with little trouble. Even though it wasn't the outcome I thought I had wanted, it was an interesting game for the 31,703 fans present.

I made my way up the aisle to the couple who were waiting for me, and we walked together back to the trolley station. I was glad they were with me, as it was a fairly dark walk. We caught the second trolley, and it wasn't many stops later that we were able to sit down and chat. She asked where I was from, and I told them of my travels and my goal of seeing all the stadiums. She told me that her husband had Alzheimer's, which meant she had to learn to drive and many other things. They had enjoyed going to games for many years and would continue to go as long as they could. I let them know how much meeting them had meant to me and asked if it would be okay to include them in the book I was writing. They were pleased and said that would be fine. They took my name to make sure they could look for it when it came out.

We arrived back at the station where we were parked, wished each other luck, and hugged as we said our goodbyes. They watched until I got to my car and unlocked the door, and then we waved goodbye again and headed our separate ways.

On the short drive back to the hotel, I prayed for them, and I have thought of them often, hoping that they are still doing well. They are two of the many people who have touched my life in a very positive way during my baseball adventures.

The next morning I was heading north to catch games in Oakland and San Francisco. I got up early enough to get beyond Los Angeles before rush hour, or so I thought. I was wrong. I had thought about taking Route 1, which follows the coast, thinking I would make the most of the drive and my time in California. But when I got to the exit leading to Route 1, traffic was backed up for miles. I was already too far committed to try to sneak over the two lanes to that exit and squeeze in without causing even more trouble by blocking another lane.

Traffic was bumper-to-bumper on a six-lanes-each-way highway, moving less than twenty miles per hour. All I could do was settle in and ride it out. It took me a while to clear Los Angeles, but once I did, things opened up nicely. I was able to see the Hollywood sign from a couple of spots but wasn't able to get a picture. I wish I had, but at the time I thought it best to just drive and not try to take pictures while on the freeway.

There were many beautiful sights on that drive. I passed through some mountains. At the point at which I decided to check in at work, I lost signal on my cell, which made me laugh. It was the only time the whole trip I didn't have a signal, and it happened while I was talking to my boss!

San Luis Reservoir State Recreation Area was amazing. I was able to get some pictures of the reservoir. It was such a beautiful sight. Shortly before I got off the exit to head toward the reservoir, while I was still on Route 5, I saw traffic slow down. I didn't think I was close enough to a major city to be running into traffic again, so I couldn't imagine what was wrong. We were being stuffed over into the two rightmost lanes and the other side's traffic had all but stopped. As I moved closer, I could see a tractor trailer sideways on the opposite side of the highway blocking all but the outside lane. As I got even closer I saw what had happened. The tractor trailer had somehow pushed a car through the concrete barrier which was what was blocking the four lanes on our side. There was an ambulance there, and an injured person on a gurney. I didn't think it was a fatality, as the victim was moving, but you wouldn't know it from the sight of the damaged car. I passed slowly enough for me to get a fairly good look. I said some prayers for all involved and was happy to be moving beyond the area.

All in all, the drive went well and I arrived at the hotel at a reasonable hour. I checked in and had a wonderful chat with the desk clerk. I had asked him about the BART system and explained my plans to take it to the games the next two days. He was a baseball fan, but even more of an Oakland Raiders fan. At the time, both the Raiders and the Athletics played at the same place, McAfee Coliseum. He told me the A's were planning to build a new stadium just down the road in Fremont for the 2011 season. I thought that was rather neat. I made sure to note the location of the hotel so that when it came time to see the new home of the Athletics I would be prepared.

He recommended a place to get some dinner and was very helpful with directions to the BART station. He directed me to a mall, and I treated myself to Hawaiian BBQ for dinner, which I enjoyed very much. I headed back to my room to unpack and settle in for the next couple of days. The only driving I planned to do was to and from the BART station until I headed back to Los Angeles on Friday.

Getting to the BART station was fairly easy, and finding a parking spot was even easier. I had left plenty of time in case I ran into trouble but all went better than planned. I arrived at the Coliseum in plenty of time to walk around and take lots of pictures. It was fairly plain from the outside. What else you would expect a multi-purpose stadium to look like?

I came back around and got in line to go into the park. The couple in front of me and I started talking because they were Red Sox fans also. They had just flown up from Los Angeles to see the game. They were big fans and tried to see the Red Sox as often as they could. She even had a Red Sox tattoo on the back of her calf. She let me take a picture of it!

My seat was in the second section up from the field, almost even with third base. When I got to my seat, I realized that I had forgotten my hat and was going to be facing the sun all afternoon. It was a warm, sunny day without a cloud in the sky. It was a forty-five-minute BART ride back to the hotel. I knew I would never make it there and back in time. So I went to the MLB shop to see if I could buy an inexpensive hat that I would wear. I didn't find anything. I decided I would have my hot dog and think on it. I had a Pepsi with my hot dog ... in a paper cup. Hmm, I drank the Pepsi down and went to the rest room, where washed and dried the cup out, ripped it down the seam, and tucked it under my headband. Voilà, instant hat. Eric would have gotten a kick out of it.

A couple of guys that had seats right behind me were definitely Red Sox fans. I gave them a thumbs-up and we began to talk. We talked about the players, their record so far that year, and of course the wonderful World Series win just three years prior. The two men had gone to college together in Boston and had vowed to get to all the ballparks, but life had taken them in different directions. They were content to get together a few times a year to see a game. I told them about my quest, and they wished me luck.

A group of people who apparently worked together filled the seats in front of me. They chatted about work throughout most of the game. At one point a woman in the front row who was on her cell phone was the topic of the conversation after she stood up for several plays, blocking the view for many of us. At that point, one of the guys found it necessary to comment that women should just stay home. I wanted to tell him not to judge all women by her example, but I kept my mouth shut.

I was so excited to be seeing the Red Sox on the West Coast! Curt Schilling was pitching for Boston. I had just learned that he was one of only two major league players who were born in Alaska. I just thought that was an interesting fact. Joe Blanton was pitching for the A's. I had seen Schilling pitch each of the previous years, but this was the first time I was going to see Blanton. I knew it was going to be a good game.

To make it more special, Lars Ulrich, the drummer and a founding member of the musical group Metallica, threw out the ceremonial first pitch. I was so excited to be there on that beautiful day, seeing the Red Sox play for the first time that season, I was wiggling in my seat.

In the first inning Blanton got the first two batters, Julio Lugo and Kevin Youkilis, to ground out. Lugo was tied for second in the AL with 17 stolen bases so we definitely needed to get him on base. Youkilis was a hitting machine and at that time tied with Ichiro Suzuki for the AL lead with twenty-six multi-hit games. There was lots of hope yet. Next up was David Ortiz. On the first pitch he hit a home run! The Red Sox scored first with Papi's 204th career home run, fifth all-time among designated hitters. That was followed by a single by Manny Ramirez. According to the stat on the scoreboard it was Ramirez's 1,875 major league career game and that single his 2,129 career hit. He was second to Lou Gehrig in career grand slams with twenty at the time. Wow! J. D. Drew lined out to end the inning. Curt Shilling had a perfect first inning.

In the second inning Blanton only faced three batters, even though there was an error when Jason Kendall dropped a foul ball hit by Mike Lowell. At that time Lowell had the best all-time career fielding percentage as a third baseman (.975). He was also the top run producer that year for Boston, and the only Red Sox third baseman to post consecutive 20-home-run seasons. He had already become one of my favorite players, but when he stayed in Boston because "it was a matter of heart not my bank account," it touched me deeply. To me, that was what it was all about. And to think, he came up with the Yankees in 1998! I'm so glad he came to Boston, so very glad! Lowell grounded out, Jason Varitek flied out, and Alex Cora grounded out to send Boston down scoreless in the second.

Schilling faced three in the bottom of the inning, allowing no hits and striking out two. In the top of the third, Blanton walked Youkilis with two out before Papi grounded out for another Red Sox inning without a run. In the bottom of the third inning, Schilling faced the minimum again. It dawned on me that he hadn't given up a hit, but I didn't want to focus on that, as it was only the third inning. The top of the fourth was another one-two-three inning for Blanton. In his half, Schilling struck out one more, again with no hits. The fifth inning was another three-batter inning. Blanton's first strikeout of the game came with Coco Crisp at the plate.

In the bottom of the inning, Schilling faced four. He struck out one and a man reached first on an error on Lugo, but no hits were allowed. He still hadn't given up a hit! In the sixth, Blanton stuck out Lugo, got Youkilis to ground out, and walked Ortiz before Ramirez flied out to end the inning.

Schilling had another no-hit inning. The Red Sox were up 1–0 and the A's weren't hitting so the game was flying by. The guys behind me were talking about different players that were on the 2004 champs and where they were now. They asked me if I knew where Trot Nixon was, and I told them he was playing with Cleveland. The guy in front of me who had complained about the women standing down in front turned around with a stunned look on his face. He began chatting with me, saying he was impressed. I explained my mission and the number of games I had seen each year, including the game the next day in San Francisco. He said he was going to that game also.

In the top of the seventh, Blanton gave up hits to Drew and Varitek but they didn't score. In the bottom of the seventh, Schilling had yet another no-hit inning. In the eighth inning, Blanton was still on the mound. He walked Youkilis with one out. That was enough for a pitching change for Oakland. That pitcher faced only Ortiz, who grounded into a fielder's choice, erasing Youkilis. Another pitcher came in to face Manny Ramirez. He grounded out to end the inning. The bottom of the eighth inning was the same as all the others. No one dared say the words in fear of jinxing it: Schilling was working on a no-hitter, and I was there!

Colby Lewis pitched a no-hit ninth for Oakland. I don't think anyone was breathing in the stands when Schilling came out for the bottom of the inning. The first two batters grounded out! Every eye was on Schilling. He shook off Varitek. Wait, did we really see that? Yes, he shook him off! The batter was Shannon Stewart. He hit a single to ruin Schilling's no-hitter, just one out away from completion! The whole crowd of over 31,000 exhaled loudly. The next batter fouled out to end the game. The Red Sox won 1–0. Schilling had the third one-hitter of his career. What if he had just listened to Varitek? We will never know for sure, although Schilling said in an interview afterward that he wouldn't shake Varitek off ever again. Attaboy Schilling! Jason Varitek knows his stuff. After all, he is the only catcher in the history of the game to call *four* no-hitters! So very impressive, Mr. Varitek, so very impressive!

The guy in front of me shook my hand on the way out, saying that he was glad he met me and perhaps he would run into me the next night. I felt a little proud to have scored one for women everywhere. That was the shortest full game I have ever attended, at two hours and ten minutes. With only five hits in the game, it was bound to be quick.

I made my way to the BART and enjoyed my ride back. I was so excited that I could hardly sit still. I had some difficulty finding my way back to the hotel but finally got there. The helpful desk clerk was still there, and I was happy to fill him in on the game. He seemed happy to hear about my experience even though his team didn't win. Perhaps he was just being polite. Either way I enjoyed chatting with him.

I walked over to the nearby strip mall and had Mexican food for dinner after Eric called and I filled him in on the game. I knew I would need to get myself settled down and try to get a good night's sleep, because the next day was going to be a long one. I was going to go over to San Francisco early to do some sightseeing before the night game between the A's and the Giants.

The next morning I couldn't contain myself with the excitement I was feeling about getting to AT&T Park. It always looked so beautiful on TV so it had to be even better in person. I headed out late in the morning, thinking I would get lunch somewhere in San Francisco when I got there.

I had one transfer and then it was a straight shot to the stop near the park. I got to chatting with a German student on the train who was backpacking around California and Mexico. I wasn't paying attention and missed my stop. The student was getting off at the next stop, and assured me he could get me where I needed to go. I knew I had plenty of time, so I was fine with it. The detour would just give me more opportunity to sightsee.

We got off at the next stop, Powell Street. I laughed as Powell was my maiden name. There was a street map on the corner, so we walked toward that. I realized I was only a few blocks away from the stadium, so I decided to walk it even though he tried to discourage me. We said our goodbyes and wished each other luck.

As I was at the map plotting my course, another gentleman walked over to do the same thing. We were heading in the same direction so we decided to walk together. His name was Jeff and we chatted as we walked. I was happy for the company, as at a couple of intersections there were groups of young people hanging around.

Jeff and I made it to the stadium and we took a walk around it, seeing the bay and coming back around front. We both were thinking of lunch by then. But he wanted to head farther to the pier for chowder, and I wanted to take a closer look at the stadium and get pictures before I ate. So we parted company, wishing each other luck. These were two more nice people who shared my path just when I needed them.

I strolled around the park again, taking tons of pictures and admiring the bay. I love being by the water, so standing with a baseball stadium on one side and a bay on the other was heaven for me. I enjoyed the rivers in Pittsburgh and in Cincinnati, but somehow the bay was different.

There were plaques in the sidewalk celebrating milestones such as championship runs and Barry Bonds's batting accomplishments. It took me a while to get the pictures I wanted of those. The whole place had a wonderful baseball feel to it. I was looking forward to getting inside.

My hunger got the best of me, so I searched for a reasonable place to eat. One place had the menu on the door and listed a salad for $14, so I kept on looking. I came upon a pub. They had a decent menu and good prices, so I went in and took a seat at the bar, not wanting to take up a table at lunch time for just one person.

I ordered and looked at some of the pictures I had taken on my digital camera. The waitress noticed and began asking me questions. I enjoyed sharing my story with her and she stopped by with more questions in between customers.

A businesswoman came in and sat near me at the bar to have her lunch. She noticed the camera and we began to chat. Turns out she was a baseball fan and had tickets to the game that night too. She had just relocated to San Francisco after a divorce and was taking her son to the game. She was a very nice woman. She finished her lunch, gave me her card, and told me to look her up if I was ever out there again or if I decided to move out there and needed a job. We wished each other luck and she left.

At the end of the bar was a man in a Mets t-shirt. I asked him what he was doing there. It turned out he was from Flushing! It wasn't clear what brought him to the area, but he was doing a bar crawl. He was waiting for his friends, so we chatted a bit about our beloved Mets.

I finished my lunch and did some additional sightseeing. When I got inside I took a stroll around and then made my way to my seat. I wanted to make sure I knew where to catch the Muni when the game was over. I talked to one of the ushers and she recommended that I go back out and get my Muni ticket now, so I wouldn't have to fight the crowd later on. I knew leaving the stadium and returning was prohibited at most parks, so I checked with the women at the gate. She said it would be fine and stamped my hand so I could get back in. It turned out it was a good thing that I got my Muni ticket then.

After such an exciting day, I decided to get something to eat and settle into my seat to watch batting practice.

My seat was just a little right of home plate, in the second section from the field, in the middle of a row. That isn't my favorite spot but it would certainly do. The park was even more beautiful than I imagined on the inside. I was taken back by the images of cars on the outfield wall. There was a huge bottle of Coke and giant baseball glove beyond the outfield area that was especially neat when lit up at night. The all-star game was going to be there the following month, so there was signage about that every where. What an amazing place it was!

It was another beautiful day. I was just so excited to be there, even though neither team was one of my favorites. It was an interleague game and there was a rivalry similar to the Mets and Yankees, hence the beyond-sellout crowd of over 42,400 fans.

At first I didn't mind being in the middle of the row. As the game went on, however, between the man to my right (I will call him "Hands" because he couldn't seem to utter a word without using both of his hands, and he talked most of the game, which meant he elbowed me constantly) and the man in front of me (who I will call "Yo-Yo Bobblehead" because he jumped up at about every play), being packed in was not my favorite thing.

I had not seen either starting pitcher before, but had heard of Tim Lincecum who was pitching for the Giants. Chad Gaudin was pitching for the A's. Each pitcher only faced three batters in each of the first two innings. Not a bad start. In the third inning Lincecum had some trouble and Oakland scored two runs. Gaudin had some trouble of his own in his half of the third inning. He loaded the bases but was able to limit the damage to one run. He loaded the bases a second time before Barry Bonds made an out to end the inning.

Lincecum gave up another run in the fifth, making the score Oakland 3, San Francisco 1. The interesting part of the inning was when the run scored, because Nick Swisher plowed over Bengie Molina at the plate. Another walk was enough for a pitching change, and for Eliezer Alfonzo to replace the shaken-up Molina. As you can imagine, all of this was keeping Hands talking up a storm and Yo-Yo Bobblehead springing up to comment on every play. It was frustrating, but the game was interesting.

In the bottom of the sixth I really thought the Giants were going to make their comeback when they managed to load the bases, but they couldn't get anyone home. Just before the seventh inning stretch, I called Eric. He had asked me to call so he could sing "Take Me Out to the Ball Game" with me. It was nice to have him there with me like that.

In the bottom of the seventh, here come the Giants. They brought in two runs to tie the game! Barry Bonds drove in the second run on a single, and then stole second base! Oh, what an inning! In the top of the ninth, score still tied, the A's didn't score. Okay, time for the home team to strike. A triple and a couple of walks loaded the bases. Was Oakland *trying* to lose this game? In came a reliever, who quickly got out of the inning.

We were headed to extra innings in what was already a long game. I was watching the clock, knowing that I needed to be on the train by 11:45 PM. If I missed the last train, I would be so out of luck. I vowed to watch one more inning or another half hour, whichever came first. At that point, I was especially glad I had gone out to get the Muni ticket. That would make things go a lot faster when I did leave.

I am so glad I stayed, because the game got even more interesting in the top of the tenth inning. A double started the inning, which brought in a pinch runner. A groundout advanced the runner to third, and a fielder's choice led to the runner being thrown out at home. The play featured great block of home plate by the backup catcher, but unfortunately he was hurt in the process. Now what? Molina had already been taken out back in the fifth. I had never seen this happen before. What they did was bring third baseman Pedro Feliz in to catch, move Daniel Ortmeier from right field to center field, moved Randy Winn from center field to third base, and put Noah Lowry, a pitcher, in right field. They were out of position players! That was really something to see, but worrisome at the same time. The game resumed. A couple of singles scored two runs—Oakland had the lead. A foul out ended that scary inning.

It seemed like no one dared leave the park. We all had to see how it was going to turn out. I kept a close eye on the time. In the bottom of the tenth, Travis Buck moved to right field, Swisher moved to first base for Johnson who was pinch run for in the top of the inning, and Shannon Stewart played left field. Alan Embree came in to pitch. I had come to like Embree when he pitched in Boston in 2002 through 2005, so I felt confident that the game would end in that inning. But I couldn't bring myself to leave. I was correct:

he faced three batters and it was over. I was relieved that I could start my trek back to the hotel, after an almost three-and-three-quarter-hour game. I was still reeling from all the player switches.

I was able to get on the second Muni and make it onto the first BART train that came. Making my connection was going to be close, but barring any delays I would just make it. I got there with a whole two minutes to spare! I felt like I could finally relax on the last leg of the trip before getting to my car.

That wasn't entirely true, thought. Coming out of the station parking lot, I proceeded to get lost. It took me a while and a lot of prayer, but I finally came upon a street name that I recognized and was able to find my way back to the hotel. When I got there, the desk clerk was outside smoking a cigarette. He was pacing. When he saw me get out of my car, he came right over to me and asked how it went. I told him about the game and just making the train, but left out the part about the wrong turn. I jokingly asked if he was waiting for me. He nervously said he was on a break. There was another clerk at the desk for the late shift, so maybe he really was waiting for me. I was grateful either way. I needed to get some rest. The next day I had to drive back to Los Angeles to catch my flight to Phoenix for the next leg of the adventure. But what a day it had been!

QUICK TRIP TO ARIZONA

The next morning I made the six-hour drive to LAX to catch my flight to Phoenix, where I would see the Red Sox play the Diamondbacks. I left myself plenty of time, even though it was a Saturday. I didn't know what the traffic would be like on the freeway. I made really good time until about ten miles from the exit I needed. I hit eight lanes of traffic moving somewhere between five and ten miles an hour. I was really glad I left early. I made it with time to spare and had a very relaxing flight to Phoenix.

I loved the way the plane took off over the water before turning and heading east. It was a short flight. The view was beautiful, plus we flew over Chase Field. I wasn't quick enough to get a picture from the plane.

I called for a shuttle to the motel, which wasn't too far from the airport. That was part of the reason for choosing that particular mote, which also had a restaurant right next door. I was planning to take the bus to the game.

When I was checking in, the desk clerk confirmed that I was going to be checking out Monday morning. He said that was good, because the place had been sold and was closing on Wednesday. I was shocked. The Methodist Church had bought the place and was turning it and the hotel next door into a homeless shelter. The restaurant that was next door was closed and being renovated to be a soup kitchen. I had dinner out of the vending machines that night. They offered to have the shuttle take me to a local eatery, but it was late. After what they had just told me, I didn't think I wanted to go anywhere and eat alone anyway.

The next morning I inquired about the bus schedule while enjoying the breakfast buffet offered in the lobby. There were two bus stops nearby. I choose one and picked a time to leave, a time I felt would leave me enough time to wander around the park and take pictures before I returned to my room to prepare. I like to minimize the amount of things I carry with me, only bringing absolute necessities, pretty much only what I can stuff in my camera case.

I made my way to the bus stop early, waving to the desk clerk as I went by. It was a beautiful sunny day, over a hundred degrees. It was true that the dry heat was much easier to take. I opted to leave my hat at the motel, because it was advertised that the roof would be closed. Thankfully, this time it was the right decision. I didn't have to fashion any more hats out of paper cups.

Chase Field was another stadium I was really looking forward to seeing, not only because it was fairly new (the park opened in 1998), but because it had a retractable roof. So far I had seen the retractable roofs at Rogers Centre in Toronto and Miller Park in Milwaukee.

It was a short bus ride to the ballpark, and I arrived early enough that the bus wasn't packed. I had a two-block walk when I got off the bus. That last approach to the park is, in my experience, part of the thrill, knowing you are getting close and seeing even part of the stadium in the distance. My excitement grew as I started seeing Diamondbacks flags on the light poles. The outside was fairly plain, aside from the colorful tile pictures of baseball players. I took a walk as far around the outside as of the building as I could before heading into the park.

Inside, Chase Field had an interesting feel about it. Chase had fewer windows than Miller Park, but it was still very neat. I got something to eat and found my seat. It was again in the second section from the field, on the aisle (which was I was happy about after the crowd at the previous game). I ate, watched batting practice, and took some pictures. The usher was very informative about the retractable roof and the structure. Despite the temperature outside, it was a very comfortable seventy-five degrees inside.

One thing that stuck out was the snake that slithered along the scoreboard every so often. I am not a fan of snakes, so it was good that the graphics weren't realistic.

Before the game I saw J.D. Drew come out onto the field and shake hands with a diamondback player that was walking towards him. I realized it was his brother Stephen. That was such a neat thing to see.

As the lineups came up on the screens, I had a wonderful surprise. Daisuke Matsuzaka was going to start for the Red Sox! It was his first year with the team, and the first time I would get to see him pitch! It was my understanding that he was a pitching phenomenon at an early age, so I was really looking forward to seeing him pitch in person. I was getting to see so many of my favorite players: Jason Varitek, Mike Lowell, David Ortiz, Dustin Pedroia, Kevin Youkilis, Manny Ramirez, and well ... you get the picture.

Oh, and pitching for the Diamondbacks was none other than Randy Johnson, who I hadn't seen since my third major league game in 2002. The Big Unit against Dice-K, what a matchup! Of course I was rooting the Red Sox, but I knew the Sox weren't in for an easy time that day. The game was scoreless with only a couple of hits until the fourth inning. I was thinking it might end up being a really quick game at that rate, even though it seemed Dice-K took a lot of time between pitches.

In the top of the fourth inning, the Red Sox scored the game's first run when Manny Ramirez drew a walk and Mike Lowell's double drove him in. In that inning, the Big Unit intentionally walked Dustin Pedroia. What a sign of respect that was!

Dice-K started off the bottom of the inning with a walk to Orlando Hudson. That has been the biggest frustration with Dice-K: he walks a lot of batters. Then he walked *another* batter. Uh oh! Two on with one out! Stephen Drew, the brother of Boston's right fielder J. D. Drew, hit a long single. A run scored to tie the game.

The game stayed tied until the bottom of the sixth. Dice-K started his half of the inning off with another walk! Grrrr! A one-out double scored the go-ahead run. Tony Clark pinch-hit for Johnson, so his day was done with Arizona ahead by one. He had walked three and struck out nine. Not too bad for a forty-three-year-old pitcher! Clark struck out, making nine strikeouts for Dice-K as well.

The Diamondbacks broke the game open in the eighth against Mike Timlin. I was concerned about Timlin, because he had been on the disabled list. This was his first game back. What a way to come back: down one with two on and no outs. Still, I tried to have confidence in the experienced veteran. I was disappointed when another three runs scored. The final score was Arizona 5, Red Sox 1. So much for what I thought was going to be a quick game! It ended up taking almost three and three quarter hours, and was played in front of a crowd of 46,600.

I checked the bus schedule and realized I had just missed a bus. It would be a while before the next one, so I took my time getting to the stop two blocks away. I took some additional pictures and walked around a little bit more.

FINAL GAME IN LOS ANGELES

My flight Monday was on time. I was looking forward to the next and final game of the trip. It was a quick, smooth flight and the view was just beautiful. I made my way to the car rental shuttle and picked up the car I reserved. The drive to the hotel that time was only about a half-hour but the routes were confusing. There were US-101, CA-110, I-110, and I-101 all intersecting and going in every direction. Only by the grace of God did I find my way.

I found the hotel and went to check in. I knew it was not the greatest neighborhood because the clerk was behind thick glass. I asked him what the best way to get to Dodger Stadium was. He rudely said "You have a car. Drive it."

I was taken aback, but then a nice younger gentleman came out and asked what I needed. I told him I had checked out the bus route and I understood that it was only a couple of miles to the stadium. He asked if I was going alone. When I said yes, he indicated driving would be the safest way to go. I thanked him, took my room key, and went to the room.

After I settled in, I took a little stroll to see if there was a place close by to get a little something to eat. My only choice was a mini-mart-type place. I grabbed a salad and a drink to take back to the room.

I ate and took a little nap to be fresh for the game. Before I left I reviewed the directions and headed out. The parking attendants at the stadium wouldn't let the cars line up before the lots opened so I had to drive

162

around for about ten minutes to kill some time. By the time I got back, cars were starting to line up and I was happy to be one of them.

Dodger Stadium has to be about the most unique setting for a ballpark that I had seen. I loved the "Think Blue" sign on the side of the hill, similar to the Hollywood sign. I took some pictures from outside but was very anxious to get inside. There were big posters everywhere depicting the players, two of whom I was very familiar with because they played for the Red Sox—Derek Lowe and Nomar Garciaparra. Unfortunately, neither were playing that day.

I made my way to my seat, took in the view, and then went to get something to eat. Once again my seat was close to Panda Express, and the smell was tempting. Of course, I stuck to tradition and had a Dodger Dog. I thought the Dodger Dog was the second-best stadium hot dog, behind only the Monster Dog at Fenway.

My seat was twenty-two rows up but directly behind home plate in this forty-five-year-old gem of a ballpark. It was a nice evening and I was glad I wore pants instead of shorts, as it was a cool sixty-six degrees. There were breaks in the rows so it made it easier to move around during the game. The stadium was only about three quarters full so that helped as well.

Randy Wolf was pitching for the Dodgers, and Orlando Hernandez was pitching for the Mets. I had seen both pitchers pitch before, so I knew it was a good matchup. Before the game they were showing shots of people in the crowd on the screen and they came upon famous comedian Jerry Seinfeld. He was enjoying a hot dog but was nice enough to wave, even though his mouth was full.

In the top of the first inning, Reyes hit a single then advanced to second on a passed ball. Things happen when Reyes gets on base, I reminded myself. He was the first player in club history to have consecutive seasons with sixty-plus steals. I think he really helps spark the team. A single by Green, and Reyes scored! That's not to diminish Green: he was one of only five players to have hit forty or more home runs in a season in both leagues. Beltran, who at the time was just one RBI shy of 800 for his career, flied out. Green stole second and then took third on a throwing error with David Wright coming to the plate. I was so excited! Wright singled, getting a hit for the thirteenth straight game. One more hit would be his five hundredth!

Green scored! David Wright was the fourth Met to have consecutive 100-RBI seasons. The others were Gary Carter, Darryl Strawberry, and Mike Piazza.

The Mets were up by two with only one out and a man on first. I was thinking it was going to be a good game. Carlos Delgado fouled out, but Wright stole second for the thirteenth successful attempt out of thirteen overall. Paul Lo Duca, who had his one thousandth career hit less than two weeks prior and had the best average in the National League at the time at .389, lined out to end the inning, but it was a good start.

Hernandez had a one-two-three first. As Wolf made his way back to the mound, they showed some of the crowd on the screen again. Lo and behold, Hilary Swank was in the crowd as well, and wearing a Mets hat! She smiled and waved.

Jose Valentin started off the inning with a bunt single. I really liked him. He was one of four shortstops to have four straight seasons with at least twenty-five home runs. He was in the company of Cal Ripken, Alex Rodriguez, and Miguel Tejada. Next up to bat was Carlos Gomez. He had been signed by the Mets organization at sixteen years old, and I had seen him play for the B-Mets in 2006, where he was MVP that year. Unfortunately, he flied out. Hernandez hit a sacrifice bunt to advance Valentin, who then took third on a wild pitch. Here we go again! Sadly, Reyes grounded out to end the inning. Oh well, can't expect every inning to be big.

In the bottom of the second, Hernandez walked the first batter and then retired the next three, two on strikeouts. Wolf settled down and had a quick one-two-three third himself. Hernandez followed suit in the bottom of the inning in that game, which was his 201st appearance of his career. He even struck out Wolf.

Delgado started the fourth with a double. Lo Duca flied out and Valentin grounded out, but Delgado advanced to third on a throwing error. Here we go again. Gomez singled and Delgado scored before Hernandez struck out to end the inning. Mets up 3–0!

That all changed in the bottom of the fourth, when the first batter walked, stole second, and scored on a single. Uh oh! The next batter flied out, giving me a little hope that the rally would lose steam. But Luis Gonzalez doubled, which tied him with Eddie Murray for career doubles. A runner scored for the second run. Andre Ether then hit a single, and Gonzalez scored to tie the game with still just one out! The damage was done. Ugh!

In the top of the fifth, Reyes fouled out. Green hit a single, and Beltran followed suit with a single that bounced off Wolf's ankle. That looked like it really hurt. Here we go. Not to be, as Wright flied out and Delgado struck out. Hernandez got through the bottom of the inning unscathed, even after giving up a single to Wolf and a walk.

They again were scanning the crowd between innings and showed basketball legend Kareem Abdul-Jabbar. I was certainly in good company that night.

In the top of the sixth, even though Lo Duca singled and advanced on a Gomez sacrifice bunt, we couldn't add to the score. The Dodgers had better luck. Hernandez gave up a double to Gonzalez, putting him one career double ahead of Eddie Murray. James Loney hit a triple, and Gonzalez scored the go-ahead run! Oh no! Only one out! Tony Abreu bunted a pitch-out attempt, and Loney was tagged out at home on the play. But in trying to double up Abreu, Lo Duca made a throwing error that allowed Abreu to make it to third. Ugh! At least there were two out. Wilson Betemit pinch-hit for Wolf and drove Abreu home on a single, giving the Dodgers a two-run lead. A few more pitching changes and no more hits the rest of the way, and the Dodgers won the game, 5–3. That trip wasn't so good for the teams I wanted to see win, but at least I had seen one of my favorite teams in three of the six games. The Red Sox had managed to win one for me.

One of the unusual things about Dodger Stadium is that everyone has to go *up* to get out of the stadium. That was a strange feeling. I was looking for another escalator, and an usher told me to go out through the offices, which was a fairly quick way out. On the way to the parking lot, I could smell a funky smell—let's just say it wasn't tobacco. The lady next to me in the crowd said she hadn't smelled pot in a long time. The gentlemen nearby who was the source of the smell offered us a drag, but I declined.

It wasn't too bad getting out of the parking lot and back to the hotel. I was happy when I got back to the room and ready to get some sleep, as it had been a long day. The following day I was heading for home. I had mixed feelings. I was sad that the trip was over but also sort of pumped that I had actually done it!

The next morning I got up and turned on the TV to see some news while I dressed. They mentioned on the traffic report that there was an accident at an exit slowing traffic. I wasn't sure whether it would affect my getting to the airport, so I decided to head out early. Either the accident was cleared up by the time I got there or it hadn't been near my route to the airport. Regardless, I preferred getting to the airport early and killing time there to having to rush or miss my flight. It was a good thing I got there when I did, because they had changed my flight to an earlier one. I didn't bring my computer or have any way to check my e-mail. If I hadn't heard about the accident and headed out early, I would have likely missed my scheduled flight home.

As one could predict, we left the gate only to sit on the tarmac for two and a half hours because there was a ground hold in Philadelphia due to stormy weather. We finally took off, and it was so cool. We took off heading out over the ocean again. That was just the neatest feeling!

When I got to Philadelphia, we had to wait on a flight crew to get in from Pittsburgh. I didn't get into Binghamton until after 2:00 AM. My sister had left my car at the airport once I knew there was going to be a delay. There was no sense in her sitting there waiting for me all that time. It sure was good to crawl into my own bed that night, but I am sure I could have slept anywhere after that travel day.

I couldn't feel too sorry for myself, because I had met a couple on their way home from Alaska who had been in airports for thirty-six hours already and wouldn't be on a plane toward home until the next afternoon! That was in addition to another layover before getting there. The hotels were full, and there were no rental cars to be had. Those poor people had it much worse than I did.

MORE WEST COAST

The other trip I had planned for that year was a jaunt to Seattle. I had been discussing it with Eric and he said he would like to join me. Of course, that meant getting a couple of days off of work. He checked it out and they were willing to give him the time off. He had worked a fair amount of overtime, so he felt he could afford do it. We made plans for a quick trip to Seattle to see the Red Sox play there. It would be another stadium for me, and Eric and I would get to see some of the West Coast together for the first time.

I was flying to Chicago on August 2. From there we would fly out to Seattle the next day with a layover in Arizona. I got the game tickets, booked the flights, made the hotel reservations, and reserved a car. We were all set. We hadn't seen each other in over a year and a half, so the coming reunion was exciting.

I had enough reward points for a free flight, so I was flying a different airline to Chicago. That was the only time my luggage was lost. I was bringing a birthday gift for Eric's housemate that Eric has asked me to pick up for him. Go figure. Eric met me at the airport. When we went to get the bag I had checked (with the gift in it), it wasn't there. I had my clothes in a carry-on; at least that was okay. We went to the airline baggage claim desk, and the clerk there was not a great deal of help. I tolerated the attitude for a while, but eventually told him firmly to stop blaming me and get started finding my bag. He finally did. My bag hadn't left the airport back home when I did, so it wouldn't arrive in Chicago until the next day. We were heading out the next day from the same airport, so the clerk suggested I just pick it up then. I told him I was not interested in toting another bag along on the next leg of my trip, so they would have to get it to Eric's house for me. They agreed and we were on our way.

We were on our way to get something to eat when a friend of Eric's housemate called his cell phone. He handed it to me to answer because he was driving. She wanted us to come back to the house so she could meet me. So we aborted our dining plans and headed there. We had something to eat and chatted with them for a while. After that I think Eric and I talked until the wee hours of the morning. It was really great to see him again.

The next morning, we headed back to the airport to start our trip to the West Coast. The flight was fine and I think both of us were able to sleep for part of the trip. When we got to the car rental desk, they told us for just a couple of dollars more we could upgrade to a convertible. Well, I usually don't go for things like that, but we knew we were going to try to make it to the beach while there, which meant we'd be making at least one long drive. So we said sure. We had a red Mustang convertible to drive around Seattle!

We had made dinner reservations at the Space Needle, so we checked in, got cleaned up, and off we went. We could see the Needle, but do you think we could find it? Nope. We eventually did, no thanks to me, and had a very nice dinner with a breathtaking view.

The next day was the game. We had tickets to a night game, so we allowed ourselves to sleep in and get acclimated to the time change. We wandered around a bit then headed toward the stadium. From the outside, Safeco wasn't as stunning as I would have thought. Of course it has railroad tracks along one entire side. But when we got inside, it was really neat.

As we looked around from our seats, which were only two rows from the very top of the stadium but behind home plate, we noticed a group sitting in the stands in right field all wearing the same color shirt. Later on in the game, we found out this was a group of students from Japan to see Japanese stars Daisuke Matsuzaka and Ichiro Suzuki. Jarrod Washburn was pitching again for the Mariners. I had seen Dice-K pitch in Arizona in June, but it was the first time Eric was getting to see him.

In the first inning, Washburn only gave up one hit, a single to Kevin Youkilis, and struck out both David Ortiz and Manny Ramirez. Eric and I exchanged a concerned look. Matsuzaka also had a one-two-three first and struck out two. Washburn faced only three in the second. Matsuzaka struck out one but then gave up a home run in his half of the inning. Now Eric and I were expressing our concern verbally. Washburn dashed a momentary hope in the next inning.

In the bottom of the third, Dice-K caused us even more stress. He hit the first batter, who then took second on a single. Ichiro Suzuki advanced the runners on a fielder's choice. Boy, the fans really like Suzuki. The place got noisy when he came to the plate. Another single loaded the bases with only one out. I still have a hard time watching Matsuzaka because of the number of base runners he allows. He got out of the inning without allowing a run. Phew!

In the top of the fourth, Big Papi got it started with a single and took second on an error. Manny drew a walk. Okay, here we go! Mike Lowell popped out but Jason Varitek hit a deep double to score both Ortiz and Ramirez. My man Tek to the rescue! Red Sox took the lead.

Dice-K gave up two more hits in the next two innings, and Washburn continued to handle the batters until the sixth inning. Youkilis started that inning off with a double. Ortiz hit a single to score Youk and ended up on third himself after with some heads-up base running after a throwing error. Manny topped the inning off with a double to score Ortiz. Red Sox were ahead 4–1!

Matsuzaka had another stressful inning, starting the sixth off by hitting the first batter and walking the next before getting the next three batters out. In the top of the seventh, after walking Pedroia, Washburn came out of the game. The next pitcher struck out Youkilis and Ortiz. In the bottom of the inning, Yuniesky Betancourt hit a home run, the second one Dice-K had given up in the game. He handled the next three batters to limit the damage.

In the bottom of the eighth, Eric Gagne came on to pitch for Boston, which caused Eric much stress as he had no faith in Gagne. The former star closer didn't do well and allowed a Mariners run to score, cutting the lead to one! Jonathon Papelbon came on to close out the game for the Red

Sox. He struck out Suzuki and Jose Vidro and then walked Jose Guillen. Adam Jones came in to pinch-run for Guillen. I had faith in Papelbon, but I was a little nervous. Jones stole second! Papelbon walked Raul Ibanez before Adrian Beltre fouled out to end the game. Red Sox won but wow, what a close game.

We hung back a little while, letting some of the 46,000-plus fans in the stands clear out so we could enjoy the stadium a little longer. As we were leaving, a panhandler approached us handing out a pamphlet about something. Eric is very soft-hearted and usually stops to listen when that kind of thing happens. He took the flyer and gave the guy a couple of bucks. The guy thanked Eric and then shook his finger in my direction saying if I didn't marry that man, pointing back at Eric, he would put a curse on me. We both had a good laugh about it as we continued toward the car.

The next morning we took off for the beach. It was almost a three-hour drive to Ocean Shores, so we wanted to get a fairly early start. Most of the way we had to keep the top up, as it was sprinkling. It was still overcast when we got there, so we found a place to get some lunch. It was always my job to pick the place we ate, so I chose a little diner. It was good and over lunch we talked about our options to get to the ocean. We found one place to park where we could hike to the ocean, so we did that. We both stuck our feet in the water, for me just a toe, as it was extremely cold. It was still a hazy day but we were determined to enjoy the Pacific Ocean, as neither of us knew when or if we would see it again.

We made our way farther south to a better beach area that had horseback riding! If I had known, I would have come more prepared to go for a ride. But we had our beach attire on, so horseback riding was out of the question. Farther down the beach was an old station wagon with wooden side panels that caught our attention. Apparently a wedding was taking place. We joked that our invitations much have gotten lost.

We enjoyed sitting on the beach for a while and got our feet wet again before we headed back to the hotel. The whole way back we had the top down, as the rain had stopped and the sun had come out. I enjoyed driving the convertible very much. At one point I threw my hands in the air and shouted a big "Wahoo!"

The next morning we made our way to the airport. We turned the keys in to the beautiful red Mustang that had added so much to the trip. At the gate there was a slight delay. The flight being overbooked, the airline staff were asking for volunteers to take a later flight. Eric had to work the next morning so we decided he had better not take advantage of the free flight offer to get bumped.

I returned to the airport the next morning to make my way home. It was a good to see Eric again. Knowing I would be back in Chicago a couple of weeks to see two games in one day made saying goodbye a little bit easier.

TWO BY TWO

On Friday, August 17, I was back at the airport to fly to Chicago. We didn't really have any plans other than the games on Monday, so we decided to do some sightseeing in Chicago on Saturday. We spent the day at Navy Pier, and it just so happened that they had an air show that day, which made it extra special. We enjoyed the Ferris wheel and the sights it offered, including Wrigley Field, which is visible from the top of the wheel. After wandering around the pier and watching the air show, we decided to take a stroll downtown and ended up at the Hancock Building. We went up to the observation deck. It was a drizzly day, so the view was limited but still neat. On the way back to Navy Pier, where the car was parked, it really began to rain, so we decided to stop and buy an umbrella, which turned out to be a very expensive umbrella. We got back to Navy Pier and had a bite to eat at Bubba Gump's. Eric bought us Bubba Gump glasses to commemorate the occasion.

Sunday was a day to relax and firm up plans for Monday. It was the first time either of us had been to two games in one day, except that Mets doubleheader, which wasn't the same thing. The Cubs game was at 1:20 PM and the White Sox game was at 7:11 PM, so there would be time to get across town even in the event of traffic. We had a route planned even if we needed to take the train. We were pretty sure we had thought of everything.

We went out for breakfast on Monday at a small diner near Eric's before we got ready to head into the city. We decided to drive so we would have a little bit more control over our day. Off we went to Wrigley, almost giddy at the day ahead. Eric's neighbor, Kelly, admitted he was a bit envious. We would have loved to have him join us.

We made it to Wrigley and headed inside to our seats, which were twenty rows up in the second section from the field, way out in left field but on the aisle. The St. Louis Cardinals were playing the Cubs, and the Royals were playing the White Sox in the later game. The Cubs had Ted Lilly starting and the Cardinals had Joel Pineiro on the hill, so it promised to be a good game. I was excited because the last time I was at Wrigley, we had left early because our friends wanted to beat traffic and I hadn't gotten to see the full game.

We were rooting for the Cubs. The Cardinals putting two on base with no outs was not the start we were hoping for. A crowd of a little over 40,000 were there for the game. We regained some hope when Albert Pujols popped out and Juan Encarnacion fouled out, but hope was quickly dashed when Scott Rolen hit a deep double to score two. Hmmph.

Lilly settled in after walking Yadier Molina and got out of the inning easily. I was pleased to see Yadier Molina play, because that meant I had seen all three Molina brothers play. Pineiro gave up back-to-back home runs to tie the game! Okay, we are back in it! The tie didn't last long, as the Cardinals got those two runs back in the top of the third inning.

It started sprinkling. We looked at each other. *What if there was a rain delay?* Neither one of us wanted to acknowledge that possibility. The Cubs came back in the bottom of the inning to get one of the runs back. The rain came down a little bit harder, but the next inning went quickly. We were hopeful that the game would get done in time for us to head across town to see the next game. Pujols started the top of the fifth inning off with a homer to extend the lead back to two. They next two half-innings were quick ones, with neither team getting a hit. But it was still raining, and the rain was coming down harder. We finally had to accept the possibility that there could be a delay.

In the bottom of the sixth, Troy Percival took the mound for St. Louis. The first Cub batter, Derrek Lee, hit a home run to bring them back within one. We were excited, as we wanted the Cubs to win. We were mindful of the time and worsening weather. The next pitcher for Chicago gave the run right back with a home run. That brought in Kerry Wood to pitch, and he got the next three batters out. The rain was coming down really hard, and the grounds crew came out to cover the infield.

We had to discuss our options. We decided to wait out the rain delay and hope it wouldn't be long. We could still beat the traffic to get to the next game on time. We decided that 4:45 PM would be our deadline to make it to the south side in time to get settled for the next game.

Unfortunately, the rain continued and we had to bail, regrettably. I had yet to see a full game at Wrigley Field. There was an almost two-hour rain delay before the game resumed, so we wouldn't have made the second game if we had stayed. The Cardinals ended up winning, 6–4.

As we headed toward U.S. Cellular Field, I was a little disappointed, but the sky was clearing. We were hopeful that it would not affect the second game of our day. We parked the car and made our way into the stadium. We soon got back to feeling giddy about the adventure. To make the situation even better we were sitting five rows from the field and the guard looked the other way as we walked to the edge of the field, leaned over the wall, and touched the warning track! That was the first field we had actually touched! We were feeling even sillier by this point. We laughed at the fact that neither of us could think of anyone else that would have done that, save for the other one of us.

We were rooting for the home team, the White Sox. The game started, and we put the first part of the day behind us. Both pitchers were doing well through the top of the fifth inning. In the bottom of the fifth, at his second at-bat, Jermaine Dye doubled. The next batter hit a home run to give the White Sox a two-run lead. That lead didn't last long. Kansas City retaliated with a two-run home run to tie the game. The White Sox made two more pitching changes, and another run gave the Royals the lead.

In the bottom of the seventh, Danny Richar hit a home run to tie the score again. Chicago manufactured another run in that inning. The final score was White Sox 4, Royals 3, in front of over 35,000 fans in just over three hours. I was surprised that the Cubs drew a bigger crowd on a work day then the White Sox did for a night game—just an observation.

We made our way back to the car and headed home pleased with ourselves for having done it—two games in two ballparks in one day! When we got back to the house, there were several people sitting outside waiting for us to see how it went. We were still pretty excited about seeing two good games. I began to realize how excited the others were at what we had done. Kelly again said that he wished he had been able to come along.

After everyone else left or turned in for the night, we talked about what we had shared and realized that no one else would ever understand what we had experienced that day. It was a very good day, and it felt so good to have our special friendship back!

The next morning came way too soon. We said our goodbyes, discussing the possibility of another trip out in October to watch the playoffs together. Back at the airport it hit me that I was heading home. The flight flew over Navy Pier. I smiled, but my eyes watered at the same time. It had been a good trip.

NORTH OF THE BORDER

Cindy and I had our second Toronto trip planned for September 16–18. Eric had sent me tickets for a Monday night game, so my sister and I decided to drive up to Toronto the day before so we could go to the Ontario Science Center on Monday before baseball. The trip up went well and getting through customs wasn't bad.

On Sunday night we checked into the hotel, scouted around the area, ordered in and watched the ball game on TV. Unfortunately, we caught just the tail end of the Red Sox game. The bases were loaded in the bottom of the ninth when Big Papi came to the plate. But he struck out to end the series with the Yankees at Fenway with a loss. Not what I wanted to see last thing before going to sleep, but that was the way it was.

Because parking in downtown Toronto was nearly impossible, we again stayed about twenty miles outside of the city and made plans to take public transportation to downtown. But you know what they say about best laid plans. We arrived at the Science Center at 10 AM when they opened, to make sure we had enough time to see all we wanted to there and still have time to get to the game. All went well, and we headed out around 4:00 PM. Despite what we had been told, the subway parking lots were still full at that time. We had planned to get downtown in plenty of time to grab a bite to eat, window shop, and maybe even get to the game early enough to watch some batting practice. With our original plan not looking good, we returned to the hotel. There our concierge suggested catching the bus a block from the hotel, transferring to another bus, and then taking the subway to the ballpark. Not thinking we had any other choice, off we went. The bus ran every fifteen minutes. Wouldn't you know, just as we got within sight of the bus stop, a bus was pulling away. Okay, only fifteen more minutes to wait.

We both were sporting Red Sox caps and t-shirts and basically wearing red all over, so everyone knew of our baseball loyalties. One man already on the bus suggested that if we were going to the game that we stay on the bus all the way to the last stop and then take the GO train to Union Station, which was only a twelve-minute ride versus the twenty-eight minute ride on the subway not including the transfer time. The GO train cost only an extra seventy-five cents each. We decided that would be worth it to avoid the extra bus transfer and the whole subway part of the trip.

When we got off the bus at the last stop, the man kindly showed us where the GO Train ticket booth was. We proceeded to buy round-trip tickets, assuming we would retrace our steps on the return to the hotel. While waiting on the platform for the GO train that only came on the hour, we met an older couple who were also going to the game. They were Blue Jay fans, however. They teased us that they weren't going to let us on the train. We chatted for a while about baseball and other things when an announcement came over the loudspeaker that our train was cancelled as a result of a pedestrian fatality. Feeling shocked and sad, we faced a dilemma of what to do next. We had two choices: stay there and wait a whole hour, which would ensure our missing the first part of the game, or somehow get to the subway. Luckily, our forlorn faces prompted the nice older couple to offer us a ride to the subway, as that was what they had decided to do. While we were all getting our refunds, another threesome was attaching itself to our helpful couple, who led a convoy to the subway parking lot, which of course was now nearly empty. In gratitude we offered to buy their subway tickets, but they adamantly declined.

The subway ride was fairly uneventful as the group stayed together and chatted the whole way. Others joined in who were also heading to the game. Baseball fans are most always willing to get into a conversation about the game and the teams. One gentleman was informing us that he would be watching the game from one of the suites because his neighbor was somehow connected to the Blue Jays. Most of us were just happy to be going to the game and politely listened to his rambling.

When we finally got to the game, we thanked the kind folks for their help and made a beeline to our seats, as the game had already started. Our seats were in the second section up from the field, very near home plate on the first base line. The place was really crowded. Later we found out there were over 42,000 people in the stands, a lot of them wearing red like us.

The game was still in the top of the first with no score, so we didn't miss much. The third batter was David Ortiz, one of my sister's favorite players. She seemed to think he looked sad. He proceeded to strike out. It took a bit to get settled, and I can't really say I ever got totally focused on the game with getting back to the hotel on my mind.

The game was interesting. Cindy got to see Tim Wakefield pitch for Boston. Dustin McGowan tossed a complete game for the Blue Jays. We got to see Frank Thomas hit his 510th, 511th, *and* 512th career home runs, driving in five of the six Toronto runs. I am always pleased to be at a ballpark to see a part of history being made. It would have been a much closer game had it not been for those home runs. The Red Sox lost the game, and I believe they ended up losing that series. Losing a series in September *always* gives fans cause for concern. The Red Sox had led the division most all year, but the lead was disappearing fast and there was a fair amount of baseball left to play.

It took us longer to get to the game than it did for the Red Sox to lose it, and now it was time to figure out how to get back to the hotel. We had decided to take the GO train back and catch the bus, if we could get to the GO soon enough. Well, the train was scheduled to leave at 9:43 PM and we got there to get our tickets at 9:40. But there was a line! Off to the subway we went.

We were on the first leg of our journey when we started discussing how to get back to the subway stop we wanted. A nice threesome heard our conversation and offer to guide us, as that was the direction they were going also. One of the threesome was a youngster, a very neat boy. He was only nine years old but could tell you baseball statistics, playoff scenarios, and other facts that I had to really think about to know for sure. I believe his name was Nathan. Nathan and his father continued to chat with us after the third member of their party got off the subway. Cindy and I had been rehashing the bus stops and transfers to get back to the hotel, and

Nathan's father asked us where our final destination was. We told him, thinking he might be able to give us definitive directions. He said if we rode the subway to one stop beyond where we had planned, that was where was car was. He lived only a couple of blocks from the hotel, and he offered to take us back to our lodging. There were two of us, he had his son with him, and we were very tired, so we took this relative stranger on his offer. We chatted about baseball the whole way to our hotel, and Nathan continued to impress me.

If it hadn't been for the kindness of strangers at the right place at the right time, we never would have made it through that trip. So I say another big "Thank you" to all the wonderful people in this world who take the time to help others.

The next day we headed home. The wait at the border wasn't nearly as bad as our last trip. We talked on the way home about getting to a Mets game for the team's final season at Shea Stadium the following year, and maybe even planning a trip for Cindy and I to go to Boston and see the Red Sox at Fenway. I was feeling good that she was enjoying baseball and hoping we could maybe even watch games on TV together sometime.

The playoffs and World Series were extremely exciting that year. I was sad when the Mets fell apart late in the regular season and missed the postseason, but at least the Red Sox had a chance. Cindy and I watched as many of the games together as we could. Even when we watched separately, we would call each other to cheer the good plays. With Eric living in a different state, he and I also had to watch the games together long distance, but we all were together in spirit! I did make another trip to see him to watch some of the playoff games together. What a wonderful World Series it turned out to be. Another championship for the Red Sox, Mike Lowell the Series MVP, and just an awesome, awesome team! I was so proud of the team. What a wonderful time to be a Red Sox fan. I made another trip out to see Eric in early December, and we celebrated my birthday and the Red Sox victory together. He even took me to the Signature Room atop the Hancock Building for a fabulous surprise birthday dinner.

2008'S GONNA BE GREAT

It wasn't long afterward that the tentative schedules for 2008 came out, so I began plotting my trips to see the last remaining stadiums. I was spending many hours on the computer again, researching when teams were at home. With so many things to consider and so much anticipation welling up, I could hardly stand it.

The first tickets that went on sale were for the Red Sox. Cindy and I looked at getting tickets for the first weekend in June. Tickets went on sale on a Saturday morning at 10:00 AM. I stayed online until I got tickets to a game during the week of vacation Cindy had put in for at work. I ended up getting tickets to a Tuesday night game against the Orioles after almost eleven hours of waiting. The long wait didn't surprise me, because everyone wanted to see the 2007 champions, I scoped out hotels and parking, and mapped routes to each to find just the right scenario. By the time I was ready to book the hotel I'd picked, it was full, so I chose the next one on that same street within our price range. I found some neat activities to check out in the area to round out the trip.

The next target was Colorado. Eric was going to go with me to Coors Field, so we had both arranged to take a couple of extra days off so we could see some sights in Denver. Eric had never been there before. I had only been to Denver long enough to get off a plane and catch a shuttle to Vail. Planning things in Denver were exceedingly easy. There were interactive maps and so many wonderful things to do. The hardest part was deciding between all the options. Even getting the tickets to the game was extremely fast and easy, considering the Rockies were the 2007 NL champions. Even booking the flights went well. I guess this trip was meant to be.

The first trip of the 2008 season was to Shea Stadium. It was the last year the Mets would play at Shea. Cindy and her special friend, Ron (a Mets fan for many, many years) had said they wanted to see a game, so I got tickets for a matchup against the Braves. Tom Glavine had rejoined the Braves, so I thought it would be neat to see him pitch against his former team. Unfortunately, the week before the game, Glavine went on the disabled list for the first time in his career. Seeing him pitch to the Mets was not going to happen. The matchup was Tim Hudson for Atlanta against John Maine for New York, neither of whom I had seen before.

Cindy and Ron showed up on my doorstep at 6:45 AM. We wanted to get there early so we could tailgate and have time for both of them to look around, because neither of them had been there before. This was to be Ron's first visit to a major-league ballpark. So off we went in our Mets garb. My sister had made up a song about going to the game and sang it to us *many* times on the trip.

The trip down went off without a hitch. They were both a little nervous about driving in the city, but there were only a couple of spots that were congested. I was familiar with the route, so the drive went fine. We arrived early enough to get a prime tailgate spot with the sidewalk behind us. We proceeded to cook our hot dogs and veggie dogs (Cindy and Ron are vegetarians) before we wandered around the park.

I have been to many games. But it's always exciting, and even more special when I share the moment with someone who was experiencing it for the first time. It takes me back to my first ball game. It is just so neat to see their reactions. Sharing their joy makes a ball game a new experience for me again.

We walked around the outside of the park and went inside to our seats. Ron and I tried to get down to the field level seats to see if we could get some autographs, but they wouldn't let us go down, because we didn't have tickets for that section. It was really too bad, because Nelson Figueroa and Jose Reyes were out there signing autographs. Reyes came up through Binghamton, so it would have meant a lot to Ron to get his autograph. But that didn't happen. I felt bad. I went to one of the team shops and bought him a baseball with all the team autographs on it. The store-bought gift wasn't the same as an autograph you get yourself, but it was a souvenir from his trip to Shea at least.

Our seats were in right field, second level from the top section, only seven rows up on the aisle. Aisle seats are great for getting in and out without bothering anyone, but when people in the center of the row get up, you must get up too. Also, people coming up the aisle will sometimes block your view. All of this is part of the baseball game experience.

The group of guys that sat next to us had gone to college together and were there because they were groomsmen for one of their group's wedding. The game was a gift to them from the groom. Ron noticed that the bottles of beer they were drinking bore pictures of Shea Stadium. He asked them if he could have a couple of the bottles as souvenirs. They were happy to give him the empties, so we brought six of the bottles home. Later in the game we had ice cream served in replica helmet cups, even though it was a cooler day. We wanted the helmets as keepsakes. I have collected a mini-helmet for each team on my trips to their stadiums, so it seemed appropriate to get an extra Mets helmet bearing an image commemorating the team's years at Shea.

The game started, and in the first inning John Maine walked the third batter with Mark Teixeira on deck. I remembered Teixeira when he played for Texas. I didn't have a good feeling about facing him. Sure enough, he hit a double and the runner scored from first. Fortunately, that was it for that inning.

In the bottom of the first, David Wright got on after the third baseman bobbled a grounder, but the gift was wasted. Maine got out of the second in short order, but in the bottom of the second inning with two on base, Maine (in his turn at bat) struck out to negate another chance to score. In the top of the third, the Braves scored on a wild pitch. I was getting nervous because the Braves are not a team you want to give any kind of edge.

I was calmed in the bottom of that inning when both Chavez and Wright hit singles and Beltran doubled to bring them home and tie the score. Then Church hit a triple to score Beltran, and Ryan Church scored on a groundout by Delgado. Damion Easley hit a double with two out, but Gustavo Molina lined out to end the inning, but not before we took a

4–2 lead. I was a little bit relieved, but it was too early in the game to feel comfortable. Tim Hudson only made it through three innings, which was a surprise to me.

The next couple of innings went smoothly, with only a couple of hits and no damage from either team. We took that time to talk about the neat things you can see in person at a ball game that can't be seen when watching on TV. I asked Ron if he missed listening to the commentators. He said no, although when there was a home run, he did like to hear them get excited. I told him not to worry. If there was a home run, he would hear excitement, probably way more than he wanted to, from the person sitting to his right. Plus he would get to see the apple pop up! Unfortunately, that didn't happen that day.

It was a chilly day, and our seats were in what seemed like a wind tunnel. We bundled up as best we could, while admitting to ourselves that we really hadn't dressed properly for the weather.

In the top of the sixth, the Braves manufactured another run. A rookie making his first major league start, shortstop Brent Lillibridge, was up to bat. I was affectionately calling him a Baby Brave. He had struck out his first two at-bats. Fortunately, his luck didn't change and he grounded out to end the inning before any more runs could score. The Mets failed to get any insurance runs in their half of the inning, so we were on pins and needles. Billy Wagner entered the game, and the crowd went wild. All the excitement gave me confidence. Yes, he ended the game facing just three batters! High fives and cheering everywhere! Ron was so happy. We watched the team celebrate on the field and then made our way out of the stadium. It was good to be in the warm car!

The drive home was fairly uneventful, barring one minor glitch in the computer-generated directions. Cindy sang the after-the-game version of her song. We shared stories of other trips we had taken and talked about our next trip, toying with the possibility of even planning another visit to see the Mets that year, at Shea or maybe even in Philly. I laughed, because going to a game always makes me happy and want to go to more games! We arrived home toting all our treasures from the day, a bit worn out from the trip. I smiled at seeing another person become a believer in the joys of seeing a game in person.

MIDWEST AND MOUNTAIN TIME

Eric's birthday is in early May, and I wanted to do something special for him. So I planned a weekend trip out to Chicago. It just so happened that my trip fell on one of the weekends when tours of Wrigley Field are offered. I got us tickets to take a tour as part of his birthday present. Wrigley is the second oldest ballpark, and was celebrating its ninetieth anniversary. On the tour, we got to hear so many details about the history of the park, and visited the box seats where many famous people have sat, including American presidents. We got to visit the press box, sit in the bleachers, visit both clubhouses, tour the home dugout, sit on the bench, and stand on the on-deck circle. My feet didn't touch the foot rail when I sat on the bench, which only raised my childlike excitement. The weather wasn't ideal, but the tour was wonderful. The guides were very knowledgeable, and they even kept us updated on the game that was going on in St. Louis that afternoon. The Cubs won. My favorite part was walking into the Cubs clubhouse and seeing all the uniforms neatly hanging, waiting for their player, with name plates above the lockers proudly identifying its occupant. It was such an awesome sight!

Two weeks later, it was time to go to Denver, Colorado, to see the Mets play the Rockies. Coors Field was the one of the last stadiums I had yet to see, so I was pretty excited. Getting to see the Mets as well as meeting up with Eric again were pretty good things, too. On my way to work the morning we were to fly out to Denver, the lead story was tornadoes that had hit overnight just north of Denver. Great, I thought. That would most certainly cause delays at the various airports. I soon heard that dozens had lost their homes and there had been one fatality. I felt like a real heel regarding my prior thought. I stopped to pray for all of those affected directly by the tornadoes.

My flight left on time. I had a short layover in Detroit then would arrive about an hour ahead of Eric in Denver, so I brought some things to keep me busy while I waited. As it turned out, distraction wasn't necessary, because my flight was delayed getting out of Detroit. The delay resulted in a pleasant conversation. The woman sitting next to me on the plane on the first leg of my journey was a fellow quilter, and we had a grand time chatting. She had a long layover in Detroit also, so we hung out and got something to eat together while we waited for our respective flights. Another nice person I met along the way!

When I finally boarded my flight for Denver, a women behind me asked where I gotten my baseball tote. I had made it out of fabric squares, one for each team with their logo on it; I even made ones for the Expos and Blue Jays as those weren't available. I told her I had made it as an accessory on my quest to get to all the parks. She said her son was doing the same thing. She wanted to make a tote for him. Her seat was across the aisle and one back from mine. There was a joke made that she was going to find a way to take my bag when I wasn't looking. Thankfully that never happened. She did ask for my address, to send me something that she had gotten for her son that he already owned a copy of. It was a publication all about the old Yankee Stadium, still in the plastic. This gift certainly was a very sweet thing for a complete stranger to give me, and I appreciated it.

The family sitting across the aisle from me on the plane was also going to the game on Saturday. The father had been to several games but had never seen the Mets win. I told him I hoped this would be his first time. We compared notes on some of the stadiums we had both been to, which turned out to be a fair number.

The timing ended up working out really well, as Eric's flight and mine landed in Denver within five minutes of each other, so neither of us had to wait for the other. Eric and I collected our bags and went to pick up the rental car. We drove to the hotel. We hadn't made definite plans for Friday yet, so we talked about our options a little and then got some sleep.

Friday morning, after fighting with a temperamental shower and having breakfast at the hotel, we headed toward Pikes Peak. I had been to Vail, Colorado, several years before and had taken a ski lift to the top of a mountain. I figured this adventure would offer the same type of experience. It was similar in some ways but also quite different. Driving up the mountain, climbing 14,100 feet in nineteen miles, was very interesting. The temperature was fifty-seven degrees when we started out. By the time, we reached the top, it was twenty-three degrees. Snow flurries began a few miles (road miles, not elevation miles) from the top. We weren't surprised and kept right on going. We got to the top, where there was a sign saying "You Made It." There was a real excitement to having "made it," I assure you!

We walked around a bit and went into the gift shop, and saw where the cog train, the other means of getting to the top of the mountain, arrived and departed. There was a sign that made for a wonderful photo opportunity, so I had Eric stand next to it so I could take a picture. We had come prepared for the cold, but the wind was bothering me. We decided to take our leave. As we were heading for the car, the wind just whipped us. Mind you, at that elevation there is about half the oxygen in the air as there is at sea level. I had to remind myself to take slow, deep breaths. The bitter, cold wind was affecting me, so like a dimwit I ran the last few yards to the car. The exertion of running made it impossible to catch my breath. Tears were running down my face. Eric didn't know what to do for me, and was very concerned.

After a couple of minutes, I regained my composure. The experience scared me a bit. It was right then that we heard an announcement via bullhorn telling everyone to head down the mountain right away. We did just that. Going down, I kept the car in low gear. There were times that visibility was nil. We were going very slow and leaving plenty of room between us and the car in front of us, but the roads were icy and we did slide a bit. Luckily we didn't crash into anyone. I had never felt as alive as I did that that day on the mountain. Partway down, we saw cars headed up being turned around by officials. I believe I heard on the news later that they had gotten a foot of snow on the mountains that afternoon. Glad we missed that. Once off the mountain, we found a nice Mexican restaurant for lunch, accompanied by a well-deserved margarita.

That was about enough for one day. We gathered all the information I had printed out and the materials we had gleaned from the brochure rack at the hotel and sat down to decide what we were going to do before the game on Saturday. We went to turn the TV on. Lo and behold the remote wouldn't work. In the end the TV didn't get the channel airing the Mets-Rockies game. We ended up listening to the game on the clock radio while chatting about plans. The Mets lost the first game of the series, but Eric and I had a nice time catching up.

On Saturday, we decided to go downtown early and just scout things out. We ended up finding the perfect breakfast place on the way downtown. We found our way to the stadium, parked the car, and set out on foot to see Coors Field from every angle.

It was a very nice place. We wandered around downtown for a while looking for a place to buy some sunscreen. We didn't find any. It was time to move the car to the stadium parking lot. We loaded up the baseball tote with our rain gear, binoculars, and extra shirts in order to be prepared for whatever weather might come. With that done we made our way to the stadium.

We saw that people were lining up way early, well before the gates were to open, so we followed suit. It turns out they let people in to watch batting practice from the bleachers, which was an excellent way to get a home run ball. We weren't that lucky, but we did get to see some of the Mets pitchers in the outfield shagging fly balls and tossing them to kids in the bleachers. It was a great time, and it was also another thing I had not experienced before.

When batting practice was over, we made our way to our seats, right behind home plate about twenty rows up, directly under the press boxes. These were just about the best seats I have ever had. Eric, my hero once again, found some sunscreen at one of the shops. We didn't get burned, even though it turned out to be a mostly sunny day.

We were expecting to see John Maine pitch for the Mets, but it ended up being Claudio Vargas against Jeff Francis of the Rockies. The game started with a single from Jose Reyes. Luis Castillo walked, followed by a double steal. I loved to see that! It was a perfect example of teamwork. David Wright walked, and all three scored on a double by Carlos Beltran.

Eric and I just looked at each other. We couldn't believe what we were seeing. Fernando Tatis singled, advancing Beltran to third. Carlos Delgado struck out for the first out. I felt bad for him. I thought he was a very good player but was having a really tough start to the year. Eric disagreed about Delgado, believing he was at the end of his career. Ramon Castro singled, scoring Beltran and advancing Tatis. Nick Evans, just called up, came to bat. I had seen him play in Binghamton earlier that year. Evans hit a double to score Tatis and advance Castro to third. Okay, I needed to be pinched to be sure I was not dreaming. I didn't tell Eric that, because he would have pinched me, probably hard! The Mets brought up ten batters and scored five runs in the top of the first inning. Wow!

Vargas had only pitched two games that year and was the losing pitcher in both. We figured it was good to have run support right off the bat, pardon the pun. The first two batters flied out and grounded out in that order, but then Matt Holliday hit a home run. Okay, 5–1. Leading by four was nice, but balls seem to just fly out of Coors Field, so we weren't too comfy. Wright hit a home run in the top of the second. Like I said, balls just fly out of this park. In the top of the second inning, in his second at-bat in the majors, Evans got his second double, but unfortunately didn't score. I was happy for Evans and it was neat to see his batting average at 1.000. In the bottom of the third, Jeff Francis helped himself, getting a single with one out. He eventually scored, making it 6–2 Mets: not bad, but early yet.

The next few innings were fairly uneventful. There was a single hit here and there, a couple of walks. Evans grounded out in his third at-bat. In the top of the eighth, Ramon Castro hit a double. Evans hit his third double to knock him in and ended up scoring himself afterward, making it 8–2. We were feeling a lot more confident, but then it wasn't over until it was over. In the top of the ninth, Delgado hit a home run! I was happy to see him hit a home run. I keep rooting for him, even though it had been a tough year for him thus far. Mets won 9–2. That wonderful first inning would have been enough! The Mets really needed that win. I thought about the man who had sat across the aisle from me on the plane, and was glad that he finally saw the Mets win. That was the only game of the series the Mets won. It was a good game, especially for rookie Nick Evans.

We walked around downtown a little bit more and then headed back to the hotel to decide where to have dinner. There was a strip mall nearby, so we headed there to maximize our options. We ended up going to a BBQ chain that neither of us had ever eaten at before. It was mobbed, but we were willing to wait.

When we got back to the hotel we started discussing what we were going to do the next day. We had planned to go to Fort Collins, to the Anheuser-Busch brewery, to see the Clydesdale horses, but they didn't open until noon. We decided to drive up to Wyoming to see what that state was like. There was a computer with Internet access at the hotel, so we availed ourselves of that to map things out. We had reservations for dinner Sunday night, so we had to keep that in mind. We firmed up our plans and watched *SportsCenter* to see what had happened in the other games of the day before we turned in.

The next morning we grabbed breakfast at the hotel and set out to prove that Wyoming did indeed exist. We stopped at a visitor's center welcoming us Wyoming which was very nice. We took a few minutes to look around. We headed back to Colorado to see the Clydesdales at Anheuser-Busch. The facility there was a training facility, so they just had a few of the four-year-old geldings. They were beautiful. I had hoped to see some foals, but was happy to see any horses.

We then decided to take a less direct route back to the hotel, as we had plenty of time before our dinner reservations. We found a neat scenic route and happened upon a mountain diner. It was rustic and inviting. It was the kind of place where every head turned when you walked in. The waitress knew everyone in the place. It wasn't an uncomfortable feeling, though. The food was good. Eric had a buffalo burger, of which I had a bite. I thought it was pretty good.

We got back to the hotel with more than enough time to get ready for dinner at the Chart House. We always try to find a place, preferably with a good view, to have one really nice meal on every trip. I was a little disappointed with the view, but it was a very nice place and the food was good. We had a waitress that reminded me of Malibu Barbie. She was very bubbly and talked in a very high-pitched voice. I am all for friendliness, but her demeanor bordered on annoying. It was a nice meal and a very nice evening. I couldn't finish my meal and asked for a doggie bag, which I promptly left on the table when we departed. We went back to the hotel and spent the rest of our time relaxing. We toyed with the idea of going to a fair that was happening downtown. We could see the fair from the highway on our way back to the hotel. But we thought better of fair rides on such full stomachs.

Our flights didn't leave until Monday afternoon, so we had breakfast and hung out at the hotel until we had to check out. We dropped the rental car off and caught a shuttle back to the airport. We checked in at our respective airline, went through security, and found a place to have some lunch. The server was very personable and we all shared sports stories. It was a fun way to spend the time before our flights. It was hard to say goodbye to Eric, but we were going to see each other again in a couple of months, when I would head to Chicago for what I like to call the "Sox-Off," when the Red Sox played the White Sox in Chicago. Eric had gone to the Sox-Off the prior year with Kelly and his family. In 2008, Eric had gotten tickets for them and me to go a game in the Chicago-Boston series. I had another baseball trip coming up in just a couple of weeks, a jaunt to Boston with my sister.

BACK TO BEANTOWN

The weather had been extremely hot for June, with temperatures well into the nineties. As we got ready to head for Boston, it wasn't going to be any cooler. We began changing our thoughts of what to pack for the trip. I brought a long-sleeved shirt. I had been to enough night games to know that if you don't bring it, you will need it. We left early, excited at the prospect of seeing the Red Sox play at Fenway. I always enjoy going there. It was without a doubt my favorite ballpark. It wasn't the most glitzy or the most modern but it was by far the most exciting. The place has a life of its own. I was so excited for Cindy to see Fenway, even though her spirits were dampened because David Ortiz, her favorite player, was out with a wrist injury. I wasn't happy about that either, but there was still a good game to be seen.

The drive wasn't a bad one, only about five hours to the hotel. We got there early. The clerk at the hotel was nice enough to let us check in early and even gave us some advice as to the best way to get to the ballpark, which was, as we figured, the T.

We set out to find some lunch. Cindy was in the mood for Italian so we found an Uno's restaurant for lunch. The route we were on reminded me of the route we stayed on way back in 2002, my first trip to the Boston area. The road was a divided highway, and you had to go way out of your way to get turned around if your destination was on the other side of the street. The waitress at lunch asked if we were going to the game, as we already had our Red Sox shirts on. We were happy to say yes. Not long after that, the manager came over to chat with us about going to the game and our having traveled all the way from New York.

After driving around so much, we decided it might be best to take the train downtown. So I dug out the directions I had printed off the Internet on how to get to the station, and off we went. We made it to the station in time to get a train that would get us to the ballpark two hours before the game, so we could walk around and even do some shopping.

A group got on the train a couple of stops later all decked out in red, wearing Red Sox earrings, hats, and t-shirts. They asked us if we were going to the game. When I asked if they were all together, they joked that they just happened to meet at the train station. Actually, they shared the story the one daughter and her husband actually met at a Sox game, sitting next to each other in the bleachers. They had been married for nineteen years. The woman's mother and sister were going to the game with them. The sister shared the story of how she missed seeing Derek Lowe's no-hitter, even though she had tickets for it, because she had baby-sat for them to go out to celebrate their wedding anniversary. She didn't sound bitter though! Our new friends suggested getting off a stop before we had planned to. Even though it was a little farther of a walk, it was an easier, more level trek than the walk from next stop. We took their suggestion and walked with them to the stadium. Once again, we met a group of very nice, helpful people who were also baseball fans.

We walked around the outside of the stadium and I got to see the newest championship flag. Did I mention yet that I just love Fenway Park? It is so unique and holds so much history. We stopped in a couple of souvenir shops before going in to find our seats, which were near the top of the grandstand section, thankfully under a roof. It was ninety-eight degrees and humid at 6:00 PM when the game started. The time was moved up because of the Celtics game later that night. The family on the train had said something about Manny getting his award before the game, but I thought they were talking about the next night, when he was to turn his 500th home run ball over to the Hall of Fame, so I didn't give that another thought. They were correct, Manny was getting an award. Eddie Murray, the player who Manny was tied with (at 504 home runs) at the time, gave him a plaque and welcomed him to the 500 Club.

He was only the twenty-fourth player to hit 500 home runs in the history of the game. Manny's family went out on the field with him. It was great to see him presented with the award. His little son brought a bat with him and was swinging away while his father was getting the award—it was so cute! Manny then took a lap around the bases, which I thought was also neat.

A little girl threw out the ceremonial first pitch. Lo and behold who was to catch for her but David Ortiz, left wrist in a cast and all! Cindy was thrilled to see him. We were really touched to see him go out to the mound to give the little girl a hug. The game got under way. We were fortunate that the seats on either side of us stayed empty for most of the game. It was so hot that everyone wanted as much space around them as was possible. Wherever there was an empty seat in the row people spread out. There was a little breeze, but it was so hot and humid that it really didn't help much. Still, we were at Fenway watching our beloved Red Sox, so we were happy.

Josh Beckett was on the mound for Boston. He sat the Orioles down one-two-three with two fly outs and a strikeout. Daniel Cabrera was pitching for Baltimore. Jacoby Ellsbury hit a single, Pedroia hit a double, and Drew walked, loading the bases for Manny! I could hardly believe it! At the time Manny was tied with Lou Gehrig for career grand slams at twenty. Might we get to see another Manny milestone? Could the game have gotten off to a better start? Unfortunately, he hit into a double play. But Ellsbury scored and Drew was still on third. Lowell walked, but Youkilis grounded out to end the inning. We were up by one after an exciting inning.

The excitement didn't last long, as Kevin Millar, whom I still can't root against because of his connection to Boston back in 2004, hit a double. Beckett walked the next batter then hit the next with a pitch to load the bases with one out! Okay, Josh Beckett was one of the best pitchers, but even the best have off days. The next batters popped out and there was a collective "Phew" in the park. The next two batters each hit doubles, scoring four runs before the inning ended. Down by three runs in the bottom of the second wasn't an insurmountable deficit, I told myself.

In the next inning Jason Varitek hit a single to get things started. Coco Crisp drew a walk, and it looked like we were off to another good start until Alex Cora hit into a double play and Jacoby Ellsbury grounded out to end the inning, wasting another opportunity.

In the top of the third, the Sox were at it again. Dustin Pedroia hit a single and took second on a wild pitch. J. D. Drew walked and Manny singled to load the bases. Mike Lowell grounded to second and that got Ramirez out, but Pedroia scored. There were still two on with one out. The crowd went wild. Youkilis hit a ground ball. The throw to second erased Lowell but allowed Drew to score. Varitek struck out, leaving us still down one.

There was a young man sitting in front of us who knew all the songs that were played when each player came to the plate for the Red Sox, and did a little dance to each one. I thought that he must have had to go to a lot of games to know all the songs. It momentarily made me think of trying to gather that information also, but then I decided I would just enjoy the game.

In the bottom of the fifth inning, Pedroia was hit by a pitch. Then, with a full count, J. D. Drew hit a home run! We took the lead! The place went absolutely nuts! Ramirez came up to the plate and the place was still going wild.

Cindy said, "He is going to hit one too!"

I responded "Maybe."

Sure enough, he hit the second pitch over the Green Monster! We saw Manny Ramirez hit his 505th career home run. Sorry, Eddie Murray. The place continued to go nuts and high fives were everywhere. We were ahead by two, and still no outs. The next three batters went down though, two of them striking out. Speaking of strikeouts, I think it was neat the way they keep track of Beckett's strikeouts, of which there were three that night. They had his name spelled out, and each time he struck someone out they added a "k" (facing forward or backward depending on whether the punch-out was swinging or looking) to the middle of his name. Just one of those things you might not get to see if watching on TV.

In the top of the seventh, Hideki Okajima replaced Beckett. Okajima was another Boston pitcher I had not seen in person yet. He struck out the first batter, and then allowed a double. A walk followed! Uh oh! There was a silence in the ballpark as Aubrey Huff came to the plate. Huff hit a single to score two runs and tie the game. That was it for Okajima. The other Manny, Manny Delcarmen, came in to pitch. Kevin Millar came up to bat. I couldn't root against him, but at that point I couldn't watch either. He hit a sacrifice fly to score one more run before the next batter struck out. The Orioles had taken the lead again.

The next two innings we faced three more of their pitchers and couldn't get anything started. In the top of the ninth Craig Hansen took the mound for the Red Sox and gave up three more runs. The bottom of the inning was one-two-three for the Red Sox. The Orioles won. It was a good three-and-a-half-hour game and another sellout at Fenway. That was the only game of the series the Sox didn't win, in front of 37,858 loyal fans. I teased my sister that she was bad luck, as the Sox had lost all three games she had seen them play with me. She was having no part of that.

We made our way out of the stadium and back to the train. It was ninety-three degrees with a slight breeze, but it felt better to get out in the air. The line to get on the T was fairly long, and it took us until the fourth train to get on. Trains were running one every two minutes so it wasn't too bad.

We watched *SportsCenter* when we got back to the hotel and then turned in. The next morning we decided not to head back into Boston. But we wanted to see the water, so we drove through Rhode Island, grabbed some breakfast, and then drove the coast through Connecticut and stopped at Mystic. We stopped at DeBowis Beach for a little bit and continued our drive toward Gillette Castle. It was a beautiful place with amazing view and lots of history. We stopped for an early dinner at a unique restaurant, where everyone was a Boston fan happy to hear we had been to a game. Our waiter's father had a connection to get tickets to the suites, so he got to see the games in style when he went. I wondered if sitting the suites was all it was cracked up to be. I would probably never know.

QUICK TWO-STEP IN TEXAS

don't know what I was thinking when I made the final plans for my Texas trip. I booked a flight that left from the airport over an hour from my house at 5:44 AM. That meant getting up somewhere around 3:00 AM. At least I would arrive in Houston by 10:30 AM local time, giving me plenty of time to drive the four hours up to Arlington and get checked into the hotel. I would get to the game in plenty of time to walk around the stadium per my custom. I was also hoping to get to my seat early enough to see some batting practice.

The next morning would be another early one. My Astros tickets were for a 1:00 PM game, and I would need to make the four-hour trek back to Houston. My return flight left Houston at 6:20 AM the next day, so that meant yet another early morning. I had found out earlier that week that there would be fireworks after the game on Saturday night, so that would make it an even longer day! I made sure I got everything done early so I could get enough rest Friday night to start the trip off on the right foot. I did get everything packed and ready to go. I printed my boarding pass, and I had filled up the car with gas to be completely ready to roll in the morning.

Well, you know what they say about best-laid plans. Sleep was more than elusive.

I still managed to get up at 3:00 AM on Saturday, grab my bag, and head toward the airport. It was foggy, so I had to go slow, but I made my flight. Thank God for smaller airports. The flights were on time, and I was actually

196

able to nap on both legs, even with many people around me snoring. On the second leg of the flight there was a young woman on her first solo flight, so I did my best to reassure her when I could. She was meeting her aunt and wasn't sure if her aunt was going to be able to meet her at the gate. I told her I would make sure she got to baggage claim to meet her aunt. There have been more people than I can count who have helped me out, so this was the least I could do for the young lady.

The flight arrived ahead of time, at 10:00 AM. We headed off toward baggage claim where she successfully met her aunt. I headed toward the rental car shuttle. I was given another Chevy Cobalt, which I wasn't overly impressed with in Colorado. But it was good on gas, so I took it. Off I went toward Arlington. After a little u-turn here and merge left there, I was on my way.

Not too far out of Houston, I noticed a large, white, round shape ahead on the right. As I got closer, it became apparent it was a statue. As I passed, I saw it was a statue of Sam Houston. I thought it was neat and made a mental note to look him up on the Internet when I got home. I also made a mental note of where the statue was, so I could try to get a picture of it on my way back to Houston the next day. The second thing that caught my eye was a sign for a museum. It was the Texas Prison Museum. I knew I really was in Texas then.

The drive up went very well, and finding the hotel was fairly easy. I checked in with enough time for an hour nap before proceeding to the ballpark. I had done my homework, mapping out the parking lots in Arlington so I could pick the one with the easiest route back to the hotel. Fortunately, the Rangers Web site was very detailed. The information it provided proved invaluable in my planning.

I arrived at the ballpark parking lot amazed at how light the traffic was. I pulled into the parking lot and stopped to pay, but the attendant waved me by. I thought maybe there was a special going on, like in Miami. I parked the car, making note of the markers so I could find the little red Cobalt later on. There was a shuttle that ran from the parking lot to the ballpark just across the street from the lot, so I headed that way only to miss it by a little bit. There was another woman, an employee of the ballpark, walking that way also so we commiserated about missing the shuttle. She said they run every few minutes. I could see the park, which was really only a couple of blocks away, so I said I thought I would walk. She said she would walk with me. I mentioned to her about the free parking. She explained that it was likely because I was so early and had a blue shirt on. The attendant must have thought I was an employee. I wanted to go back and pay the $10, but my walking partner said to just buy a little something extra inside, which I did.

I have to admit, I was awestruck by the stadium. One of my favorite baseball movies is *The Rookie*, part of which was filmed in Arlington. The place was *big*. I walked around the outside snapping pictures and taking in some of the sights. Seeing the large black wrought-iron gates I recalled from the movie gave me chills! Not far away the Dallas Cowboys' new stadium was being built, which was neat to see, not that I am a Cowboys fan, mind you.

I went in to walk around the inside. I made my purchases on my way to my seat. I went down toward the field, to seat five in the eighth row. I was eating my hot dog and watching batting practice perfectly content, finally really happy to be there. After batting practice I took my garbage up to the concourse to throw it away. Looking at my ticket again, I realized that it said row five, seat five not row eight! I was thrilled to be sitting even closer to the field.

I called Eric and he was glad, saying that I sounded happy to be there. Before the game there were a couple of neat events. Some air force recruits took the field, lined up along the first and third baselines, and took their oaths in front of the whole crowd. The officers drove onto the field in little airplanes. It was neat to see.

Between the teams playing—the Phillies and the Rangers—I would normally be inclined to root for the Phillies. But because the Phils were ahead of the Mets in the division, I was hoping that the Rangers would win. Even though it was early in the season, I didn't want to see the Mets get far behind in the standings.

This was only the third time I had seen the Rangers, so I wasn't as familiar with their players as I was with the Phillies. From my seat, right about even with first base, it was easy to recognize the players I knew.

The first inning was a quick one-two-three inning, so I was thinking the game might go well for Texas. I should have known better than to be thinking like that in the top of the first inning. I was encouraged in my thinking when Michael Young of the Rangers hit a two-run home run to take an early lead. That didn't last, as the Phillies soon hit a two-run home run of their own to tie the game. Darn it!

The couple in the seats next to me were discussing the game in a way that made it clear that the woman didn't know much about the game. Prior to the start of the game we had shared some stories, and the man had indicated he was definitely a serious fan. She mentioned halftime and other things that aren't a part of baseball. Guys, I must request that you give your gals a chance. The only reason I was able to learn the game at all was that my friends, Eric especially, were very patient and explained things to me when I got confused. No one was born knowing everything about anything, including baseball. Gals, it helps to pay attention when actually at a game, instead of talking on a cell phone or chatting about everything else under the sun. I tried to stay focused on the game and not get drawn further into their discussion.

In the top of the third inning, the situation got worse with two more home runs, making it Phillies 6, Rangers 2. I got fairly discouraged when it began to rain. I decided it was raining too hard to stay out in the open, so I headed for cover. Just as I reached the seats that were covered, a woman moved over from the aisle seat and told me I could sit there because it was an empty seat. I thought that was very nice of her, and I took her up on the offer, not wanting to miss the game. That was just another example of the kindness of strangers that I am so grateful for. The next two innings went quickly and the nice woman and I chatted between innings. It turns out her son played baseball in college and was actually a twenty-sixth-round draft pick for Cincinnati (or so I recall). But her son had already accepted another job, so he turned it down the chance at a baseball career. How cool was that! I actually got to meet him, as he was sitting in the row behind us. It rained really hard at times, and there was a lot of lightning. An announcement was made that the team asked fans to come down from the top deck of the stadium. I was so glad I was not sitting in my original seat out in the open.

In the bottom of the fifth, there was some hope when the Rangers scored two runs. But in the top of the seventh, the Phillies got another run, making the score 8–4. The bottom of the eighth was, I started to think, our chance. Ian Kinsler singled but then got picked off first! Josh Hamilton hit a single with two outs—here we go. Milton Bradley got to first on catcher interference, the first time I had seen that happen. Marlon Byrd hit a single to load the bases. The tying run was at the plate. Yeah! I had seen it happen before: just one swing could tie the game. Well, Max Ramirez hit a single for one run, leaving the bases still loaded. The tying run was on first. On came new pitcher J. C. Romero, who proceeded to walk in a run! Okay, two outs and bases still loaded. I felt myself getting really hopeful, but then Saltalamacchia struck out, darn it! We still had the bottom of the ninth, I reminded myself. Two more pitching changes and three more hits followed, but no more runs scored for either team. The Phillies won 8–6. To make matters worse, the Mets and Red Sox both lost their games. It is not a good baseball day for me when that happens.

After the game there was a wonderful fireworks show. Apparently, the Rangers usually do the fireworks on the Fourth of July, but the club was on the road that weekend. So they celebrated it early. That was probably one of the best fireworks shows I have ever seen.

I was extremely tired after the fireworks, so I didn't pay any attention to what exit I went out and found myself on the wrong side of the stadium. I asked one of the people directing traffic which street I needed to follow back to my parking lot, eager to make my way back to the car. I was so pleased that I had done my homework, because the directions I had brought helped me get back to the hotel quickly once I got to the car. It was already late and I had to be up at 6:00 AM in order to make it back to Houston in time for my pregame routine.

The early drive back to Houston proved to be an easy one. There was little traffic, it being Sunday. I was even able to get a picture of the Sam Houston statue while I was driving. Traffic was sparse at that point and I could safely slow down enough to take aim and get the picture.

All was well as I headed into Houston. I could see the stadium from a fair distance away and found myself getting giddy–so giddy that I had to remind myself to pay attention to my driving. This was the last of the new baseball cities. In addition, Minute Maid Park was one of the stadiums I had really liked seeing on TV, making me eager to see it in person. I was going to see the Red Sox for the second time that month. Manny Ramirez had hit his 505th home run the last game I was at. Even though Manny had been in a little bit of a slump, I could hardly wait to see what he would do that afternoon.

I got downtown and parked in the first lot I found. I could see up ahead that the price of parking went up about $5 per block. It was a nice day so I didn't mind walking, as it would give me a chance to see the sights along the way. I made a mental note of the intersection of the parking lot and headed in the general direction of Minute Maid Park. I took a walk around the stadium, which also looked so big. I am not sure why, but both stadiums on that trip looked big. There were some really neat things on the building and on the sidewalk, so I took several pictures. I soon became so enchanted with the stadium that I didn't notice which stadium entrance was the best one to use as an exit, which would come back to haunt me later on.

I went into the stadium and looked around. I then found my seat in the second section from the top, eight rows up from the railing. Wow, what a view. The Red Sox were still taking batting practice so I sat to watch for a while. I also walked around the stands and took some more pictures. I always enjoy seeing the players interact during batting practice. They seem so approachable and human.

I wandered around the seats at the level I was sitting in—the roof was closed that day because of the heat, plus thunderstorms were forecast. I happened upon an usher who asked if I needed help. I told him that I was just taking some pictures and admiring the stadium. He asked if it was my first time there, and I confessed it was. He started to point out some of the features like the CITGO sign in the outfield. I asked if that was a tribute to Fenway. Chuckling, he said yes. He asked if I had been to Fenway. I nodded. I shared that I had been to all of the stadiums with the exception of the new Nationals park, just opened that year and the new Busch Stadium. He had to shake my hand. He had never met anyone who had done that. It felt really neat to have someone so close to baseball think that I had done something cool.

I grabbed some lunch and made my way back to my seat. I watched the grounds crew work their magic. There was an announcement about Jim Lovell throwing out the ceremonial first pitch. Wait a minute, I should know that name. They announced that he was the man who coined the phrase "Houston, we have a problem." Wow, that was so neat!

As the game began the gentleman sitting next to me—his name was Edward—and I started chatting. He was obviously a big baseball fan. He told me he was from Houston. He had many neat stories to share about games he had attended. My favorite of his stories was about the time when he decided last minute to see if he could get a ticket to a game. He drove down the crowded street just as a car was pulling out to find a great parking spot right outside the stadium. He got to the ticket window just as some of the player tickets were released, providing him with a wonderful seat on the third base line right above the visitor's dugout. Edward also told me why the CITGO sign was positioned where it was. Apparently, there was a gap between the buildings to the west of the stadium, so at the most common start time for a game, when the sun was setting, its rays would blind everyone on the first base side. The CITGO sign was positioned to block out the sun at that time of day. Pretty smart idea, eh?

Josh Beckett was pitching for Boston again. I was looking to see Boston win even more than usual, since the last time I had seen them had been a Red Sox loss. The first inning looked promising, with a single by Dustin Pedroia and a couple of walks to load the bases, but no one scored. The first score wasn't until the bottom of the second, when Geoff Blum hit a homer off Josh Beckett with two outs. Ty Wigginton was the next batter. Even though the Astros were ahead, I still couldn't root against him. I still have a sense of pride in the guys I saw play in the minors on their way to the majors. He popped out to end the inning.

Pedroia lead off the next inning with a home run to tie the game. The score held until the bottom of the fifth, even though both teams had hits in each inning. Lance Berkman drove in a run to take the lead. Drats! In the top of the sixth it looked like the Red Sox were going to come right back. They loaded the bases but couldn't score. Beckett got through the next inning with just one hit, a double by Ty Wigginton—I said a little cheer for him. After the first batter came up for the Sox in the top of the next inning, there was another pitching change for the Astros with Ramirez coming to the plate. Manny jacked one out to tie the game again. I had seen him hit his last home run eighteen days ago. What a game! I was a little surprised at how quiet the stadium was during most of the game, especially with a sellout crowd of over 42,000 present.

The Red Sox brought on a new pitcher. During the time it took for the new hurler to warm up, it was neat to see Pedroia, Julio Lugo, Ramirez, and Mike Lowell gather for a chat. That is just one of many things you miss when watching the game on TV. I maintain that there is nothing like being at a game!

David Aardsma pitched the bottom of the eighth for Boston. I was pleased, as he was one of their pitchers I hadn't seen in person before. He got one out and gave up a single before Hideki Okajima came in. I had a sense of dread, as Okajima was not having a very good year.

I said aloud, "Oh no!"

Edward, the gentleman sitting next to me, asked me why I didn't want to see Okajima pitch.

I explained that last year Okajima had been very tough to hit, but that this year either the batters had become accustomed to his pitching or he just didn't have very good command of the ball. Edward, being an Astros fan, was happy with the situation, especially with a man on base. Miguel Tejada moved to second on a wild pitch. I could barely watch. Mark Loretta came to the plate with two outs. The night before, Loretta had won the game for the Astros, so I was actually holding my breath. I had seen Loretta play for Boston and knew he was a good player. He did it again. Houston took the lead again on Loretta's single, going ahead 3–2. That was the final score.

In the three and a half hours it had taken to play the game, it had clouded up. I was thinking I would have to pass on my plans to drive down to Galveston and see the Gulf of Mexico. I had discussed with Edward the best way to get back to my car.. He offered to walk out with me to point me in the correct direction. I took him up on his offer. As we walked out of the stadium he said he had parked at his work, which was about eight blocks in the other direction. We had made our way to the correct side of the stadium when it started to sprinkle. When I say sprinkle, I mean quarter-sized raindrops. But the drops were far apart. I offered to drive Edward to his car, because it looked like any minute a downpour would commence. I was about half a block from the car when the sky opened up, totally drenching us. Edward hesitantly took me up on my offer. We got in the car and he directed me toward where he was parked.

En route, he pointed out some of the interesting sights of downtown Houston. He updated me on how to get on the highway that would take me back to the hotel from there. We said goodbye. It was another instance of the right person being there at the right time during my travels. I am grateful to Edward.

When I reached the hotel, I was drenched. All I wanted to do was check in and then get something to eat. I asked the desk clerk if there was a restaurant close to the hotel. Of course there was, but even though it was only about a block away with all the one way streets and service road it was not as quick and easy as I had hoped. It was still raining. I took my stuff to the room, got back in the car, and set out to get something to eat. The restaurant was a Wendy's at a truck-stop-type place. Eric had called while I was almost up to the drive-through window. I told him I would have to call him back. The young man at the window had a really fun personality. He got me laughing when he cautioned me to never eat at McDonald's.

I humored him by saying "Oh, I wouldn't dream of it."

I finally got back to the room. I was ready to relax, shower, and watch the Sunday night game of the week. The game happened to be the Cubs-White Sox cross-town rivalry, which I knew Eric would be watching. I ate, called Eric back, and then hit the shower. I pulled the shower curtain back and laughed. The shower had one of those puny shower heads. When Eric found one of those at a hotel, he always said we should have brought one of our own to change out just for our stay, so we could actually get wet in the shower. What else would you expect from a plumber?

When the alarm went off at 3:00 AM I thought it was a cruel joke at first. But I had no one to blame but myself. I got up, got dressed, and checked out. I had made sure I had enough change for the toll booth, the one I knew about at least, because I had noticed that the toll booths at the exits didn't open until 5:30 AM. One needed to have exact change before that time. I made my way toward the airport and started to see signs for a toll ahead. Uh oh, that was one I hadn't known about! I was starting to worry, as I knew I only had bigger bills left. I arrived at the toll booth at 4:00 AM to see a couple of police cars and a white van sitting there. Uh oh! Fortunately, it was just the toll booth clerk opening up. The escort must have been normal procedure. The clerk was a very pleasant person. I apologized for only having a $10 for a $1 toll that early, but she assured me it happened all the time. Phew! Another time the big guy was looking out for me.

I made it to the rental car return and waited only a few seconds for the shuttle to arrive. I knew the airport would be very busy on a Monday morning but I was a little shocked at how long the lines were. I looked at the time, and reminded myself there was nothing to do but get in line and get through as fast as I could. I noticed that everyone was going to an agent instead of the kiosk. When I got closer, with maybe three people ahead of me, all towing luggage, I asked the agent if I couldn't just go to the next available kiosk, as I wasn't checking a bag.

She said "Please do," with strong relief in her voice.

I jumped right in there and voilà, I had my boarding pass. I made my way through security and to the gate.

I sat down and noticed a couple sitting across from me wearing Boston gear. I asked if they had been to a game. They had been at the whole the series. We got to talking and he asked if I had been to Fenway, to which of course I was proud to say it was my favorite stadium of them all. We chatted some more and were discussing all the ballparks we had been to. It was getting to be time to board so I excused myself to visit the restroom. When I returned, there was a gentleman sitting in the seat I had been in, so I sat in the one next to him.

The Boston couple and I continued talking. Something was said about how I had been to all the parks after that weekend, which was when the gentleman next to me joined in the conversation.

He commented that it was quite a feat to have been able to see every stadium. I told him that I had had a lot of help from my family and friends. They encouraged me, took care of things on the home front, chatted with me on the long drives, and sometimes even went with me. I also told him that I felt God also put the right people in my path at the right time. I felt blessed to have been able to work a second job to be able to afford my adventures, as well as being able to afford the time off my full-time job that they necessitated. He was smiling. I couldn't tell if it was a I-wish-she-would-stop-talking-smile or what. I realized I was giving a testimony that might have been more than this poor man bargained for. I wrapped up by asking him about the purpose of his trip. He had been in Houston to attend an annual conference. As it turned out, he was a minister. He had a wonderful story to tell about his journey as well. I was so glad he happened to take my seat in the airport.

I was able to take a nap on the plane. When I got to Philly, I knew I had a longish layover so I went to get something to eat. As I made my way to what seemed like the only open table, a woman reached it at the same time. Because we were both alone, we decided it would be fine to share it. We sat and chatted for a long time. She told me all about her family, her home, and her marriage. It is funny how open we can be with total strangers sometimes.

I was able to get another little nap on the plane. I knew once I landed I faced an hour drive from the airport directly to work. When I landed, I let my family know I was back and drove to work.

The next morning, it all seemed like a dream. I got a call from Eric to make sure I made it back, and even got an e-mail from Edward in Houston confirming that I had made it back safely to New York. I thought that was a nice thing for Edward to do.

CHICAGOLAND CENTRAL

I was planning to get back to St. Louis to see the new Busch Stadium. As long as I was that close, I thought I would go back to Kansas City to see another game because the last time I was there, the game was called after the fifth inning because of a tornado approaching. I wanted Eric to come with me, but the scheduling was tough. Eric had tickets for the Sox-Off on August 9. I decided to just take a week of vacation to be in Chicago for both Eric's housemate's birthday on August 1 and the Sox-Off. It worked out well. The Red Sox were playing in Kansas City earlier in the week, and I could see the new Busch Stadium while in Missouri. I would make those trips while Eric was working. We would still have most of our evenings to do stuff together.

The Dodgers, the team that Manny Ramirez had just been traded to, were playing the Cardinals that week, so in the interest of being economical I thought I would catch the day game on Thursday, August 7. I could make it back up to Eric's that night. In the Royals–Red Sox series, I wanted to see Jon Lester, who had already pitched a no-hitter in his young career with Boston. In order to see Lester, I would have to go down on Monday, see the game, stay overnight, and drive back on Tuesday. I would then make a second trip down to St. Louis on Thursday. So that was what I planned to do. Eric was not going to be able to go with me, so I ordered just one ticket to each of the games.

I drove out to Eric's on August 1, with his housemate's parent along for the ride. Having company in the car made the eleven-hour drive much more enjoyable. We were very fortunate to have great weather and light traffic the whole way. The birthday party was already starting when we arrived, so we hit the ground running. Needless to say it was a long day. Eric and I took our leave from the party early, giving us a chance to chat deep into the night. The next couple of days we just puttered around the house, did some sightseeing, and tried some restaurants that Eric had been wanting to eat at.

On Monday I had breakfast with Eric and then headed to Kansas City when he left for work. During breakfast, it got really dark out and started to storm. His housemate was so concerned about it, that he followed me out to my car telling me I probably shouldn't go. I had to admit, the heavy rain was not what I needed to start my long trip. But once I got a few miles away the sky lightened up and the rain stopped altogether within the hour. As luck would have it one of the highways along the way, Route 36, had major construction. The four-lane highway was reduced to one lane in each direction. I was planning on seeing my cousin Dougie for a little while before the game, so these delays were very frustrating. I finally got to the hotel well over an hour later than I had planned. To make matters worse, as I was in line waiting to check in, the clerk was telling many people that the hotel was filled up. Apparently *American Idol* was in Kansas City scouting for the next season. I had a reservation, so I was fine, but it still took more time to check in than I wanted. I got directions to Dougie's house from the hotel and took off for a quick visit. It was only about fifteen minutes away. I arrived to find him sitting on his car waiting for me when I got there. He was anxious for me to finally get there. He is such a good cousin! After a nice visit, I left armed with his directions to the park. I made it without any problems.

I pulled into the first parking lot I saw and headed into the ballpark. I was in my seat about fifteen minutes before the first pitch. My seat was in the first section from the field, only eleven rows up. I was lucky enough to be sitting next to some other Red Sox fans. We got acquainted. As it turned out, my neighbors were a family. They had lived in Boston until Ben, the son, was a teenager, at which time they had moved to Kansas City. Ben went to college in Chicago and had a good friend who lived in the same town as Eric, which we both thought was funny. His girlfriend, Laura, lived in Kansas City and was a Royals fan even though we all kept trying to convert her.

They were all very nice people whose presence enhanced my experience at the game.

That night, I was lucky enough to see Clay Buchholz, another young pitcher who has thrown a no-hitter, instead of Jon Lester, whom I was expecting. It was the week right after the trade deadline, and also the year that the Red Sox finally traded Manny Ramirez. I was heartsick, but there was nothing I could do. I admit I don't understand all the ins and outs of the business side of baseball, but I really hated to see Manny go. He was a beloved player for the Red Sox. I know I will always cherish the times I was able to see him in the Red Sox uniform. As luck would have it, he was traded to the Dodgers in a three-way trade with the Pirates that landed Jason Bay in Boston. The Dodgers were playing in St. Louis on Thursday, so I at least had the hopes of seeing Manny then. Ben and his family were really disappointed as well. Ben admitted he was a bit envious that I was going to see Manny in a couple of days and he wasn't.

Kauffman Stadium was one of my favorite parks because of the beautiful fountains. Next to the fountains was a new scoreboard. It was really nice. They were also doing some renovations to add suites in left field. It saddened me to see the stands so empty on my last visit, so I was glad to see lots of people in attendance for this game, almost 25,000.

My seat was so close to the field. I was looking forward to getting some great pictures. It wasn't until later on that I remembered that when sitting behind the foul ball screen it is best to use manual focus. Oops. I did end up with some good pictures, but some didn't come out very clear.

The game started and Gil Meche took the mound for the Royals. I had seen him pitch for the Royals the year before. Laura told me he was their best pitcher. Okay, I prepared for whatever might happen. The first batter was J. D. Drew. He walked. Dustin Pedroia hit a double. Cool, two on, no outs. David Ortiz grounded out to first, but Drew scored. Yeah, we are on the board with Pedroia still on third and only one out. Kevin Youkilis hit a double, and Pedroia scored! Way to start the game! The next batter was Jason Bay. I wasn't sure how to feel about him. After all, he was replacing Manny Ramirez. One of the Royals fans sitting a few rows behind us started saying "Where's Manny?" and continued to say it every time Jason Bay would come to the plate. It stung to hear that. Ben later said the joke wasn't funny the first three times he heard it. Ben said it broke his heart too. He had really hoped to see Manny at that game, as he thought it might be his last chance to see Manny play for the Red Sox before he was a free agent.

Jason Varitek and Sean Casey struck out to end the inning, but we were ahead. Buchholz gave up a hit but no runs in the next inning. Meche only faced four batters, walking one, in the top of the second. In the bottom of the second, Buchholz gave up a home run but still only faced four batters. I wasn't too worried yet. Meche had it all together now, so Buchholz just had to do the same. It didn't work out that way, as two runs scored in the third, helped out by a wild pitch, a couple of walks, and a hit batsman. Ugh! Laura wasn't upset, but the rest of us in the row were.

The next several innings were much less stressful, with each side getting just one hit. In the sixth, Varitek got a hit. He had been in a wicked slump, so I was happy to see him get a hit at least. Ramon Ramirez, who came to play for Boston in 2009, came in to pitch for Kansas City against the top of the Boston order. Justin Masterson pitched the bottom of the seventh, which was good for me, because he was another of the Boston pitchers I hadn't seen. He gave up a hit, but no runs scored.

In the top of the ninth, Joakim Soria came in to pitch for the Royals. Coco Crisp hit a single, and Pedroia hit a single—okay, here we go! Big Papi grounded out for the second out but advanced the runners! The speedy Ellsbury pinch ran for Pedroia with Kevin Youkilis at the plate. They intentionally walked Youk to load the bases. We were all on our feet! Jason Bay was coming up. We all knew that one swing of the bat could give the Sox the lead. Bay hit a single and Crisp scored. The bases were still loaded. The place went wild, with high fives flying everywhere! Sean Casey flied out to end the inning and the game. We lost by one. Laura said that this was probably the only game Kansas City would win in the series, because the rest of their pitching wasn't very good. It was little consolation for me, but I appreciated her effort and sentiment. They were very nice people and I was glad to have shared the game with them. They asked me to take a picture of them in front of the field, which I was happy to do for such nice people. Ben and I exchanged business cards so I could send him some pictures I had taken at the game. We said our goodbyes.

After the game, I made my way back to the hotel with just a little bit of trouble. After a quick phone call to Eric, I got ready for bed, looking to get a good night sleep before the seven-hour-plus drive back to Eric's place the next day. I had decided to take a different route because of all the construction on Route 36 on my way down. Before heading out the next morning I reviewed the atlas I carry in my car. The trip back went really smoothly. I arrived back earlier than I expected, which turned out to be a good thing. Eric had been grumpy and his phone calls showed it. But he seemed to cheer up considerably once I got back, evidenced by him meeting me in the driveway with a big hug, ready to make our plans for the evening as soon as I pulled in the driveway. He even admitted that he was less grumpy just at the sight of me. He could be so sweet sometimes.

Over the next couple of days, we just hung around the house, watched baseball on TV, and enjoyed each other's company. We also spent time with the neighbors, Eric's housemate, and his housemate's parents. During the visit, Kelly (Eric's next-door neighbor) asked us if it was ever inappropriate to wear the gear of our favorite teams to games where they weren't playing, as fans at those parks might take offense. I had never considered the possibility. As a habit, we wore Mets gear to NL games and Red Sox gear to AL games, regardless of who was playing. Because the game I was about to attend was the Dodgers versus the Cardinals, neither a rival of the Mets, I figured I would be fine.

Thursday came around and I headed out early to get to St. Louis to see the next game. I knew what to expect en route as it was the same way I had come back from Kansas City Everything went as planned. I made my way to the parking lot where I wanted to park. I had been careful to choose the lot that would make it easiest to get back on the highway to minimize my travel time.

Once I got to the stadium I took my usual walk around outside. I couldn't get around one side, so I had to turn around and go back the way I had come to see the other side of the stadium. While I was walking, I heard someone yelling something about my Mets gear. Moments later, a man was right up in my face, asking me was I kidding with my support for the Mets. I kept right on walking, and politely assured him I was serious.

After I finished my walk around the stadium, I made my way inside. My seat was in the upper deck, but in the first row, so it was an awesome view. I had a great view of the Arch from there. The whole park was beautiful. After admiring the view for a bit and taking some pictures I decided to go get something to eat. As I made my way up the stairs to the concourse, I saw the gentleman who had commented about my Mets shirt sitting in the same section. *Great*, I thought to myself. He pointed me out to his buddy. I just smiled.

The first pitch was thrown by Billy Bob Thornton, which was another one of those special touches that enhance the baseball game experience. I didn't think I would know that much about many of the players for either the Dodgers or the Cardinals, with the exceptions of Derek Lowe (who was listed as starting that day but didn't), Manny Ramirez, and Albert Pujols. It did look like the Cardinals had a very good pitcher on the mound for the game. At the start of the game, I was just happy to see Manny and thought I would be rooting for the Dodgers if for no other reason than his presence. Perhaps it was also that going-for-the-underdog thing. In the top of the first inning, the first two batters grounded out and fouled out respectively, not a great start. Jeff Kent, whom I had seen play four other times, hit a double. Okay, maybe we can get something started here with Manny coming up. The Cardinal fans booed Manny, which was a new experience for me. I was used to the place cheering like crazy for Manny. Well, Manny drew a walk. James Loney, who I had also seen before, hit a single to score Kent. Wahoo! The Dodgers scored first! It was neat to see how well received Manny was by his new team. They were tapping the top of his head and laughing with him all day.

Clayton Kershaw took the mound for the Dodgers. I knew nothing about him. The first two batters lined out and struck out, in that order. Not bad, not bad. But then Kershaw walked the next two, Albert Pujols being the first, which I didn't think was a bad thing. Luckily the next batter fouled out to end the inning. Phew! In the second inning, there was only one hit by either team. In the top of the third inning, Kent hit a one-out single, always a good thing in front of Manny. And then it happened—Manny hit a home run! He hit a home run in front of over 40,000 mostly St. Louis fans. Perhaps that will teach them to boo him. That was the third game that year in which I had seen Manny Ramirez hit a home run! Wahoo! Soon the inning was over, but the Dodgers led 3–0. I was excited!

That took a lot out of me, so I decided to go for something to drink. As I went up to the concourse, the fan who was so concerned with my Mets shirt commented that at least I filled it out well. Again, I just smiled and kept walking.

I just got back to my seat for the top of the fourth, in which the Dodgers manufactured another run. Thank you very much, a 4–0 lead. The game seemed to be going fast, but I had been to enough games to know that could change in later innings with all the pitching changes. There were no more hits by either team until the bottom of the fifth. Kershaw gave the Cardinals fans hope with a wild pitch that scored one run. But the Cardinals rally only produced that lone run, causing a collective groan from the stands.

Once again I headed up to get out of the sun for a minute and get another drink. On this trip, the Mets-shirt-obsessed man made a rude comment, grabbing at the waistband of his pants as he said that he had something that would make me forget about the Mets. I smiled and shot back something to the effect that that unless it was Jason Varitek in there he could forget about it. His friend laughed at him.

The rude guy noted that I was a Red Sox fan as well, and asked whether I remembered the 2004 World Series, when the Red Sox had thumped the Cardinals.

I confirmed that I did, and kept on walking. Needless to say, that ended all exchanges between the two of us. I am not out to tick anyone off. If we all like the same team or same players, baseball wouldn't be very interesting to watch. I made a mental note to mind my wardrobe depending on who was playing at future games.

The next innings went fast and yielded no hits for either team. In the top of the eighth, Jason Isringhausen came in to pitch for St. Louis. I had seen him pitch in Chicago almost exactly one year earlier. He had gotten the save in Chicago. I was even happier at that point that the Dodgers were up by three. Kent got a single again. With Ramirez up next, they brought in a pinch runner for Kent, but the opportunity was lost.

Albert Pujols struck out for the final out of the eighth inning. Would three runs be enough? It was only a couple of hours into the game, and it was already the bottom of the ninth. A quick inning would have made it the fastest game I had ever been to. Jonathon Broxton came on to pitch for the Dodgers. The first batter singled. Uh oh. The runner then advanced on a wild pitch! Uh oh, I had a bad feeling. A groundout advanced the runner to third. I could barely watch. The next batter walked! Are you kidding me? A pinch-hitter, and then a stolen base! A strikeout was the second out. I was able to take a breath. Finally, a pitch-hitter for Isringhausen struck out! The Dodgers won, thanks in large part to Manny Ramirez's two-run homer in the third. The game didn't end up being the shortest full game I had been to, but was close at just about two and a half hours long. I was happy with that, as well as with the outcome of the game. Upon arrival back at Eric's, I was very happy not to have to drive for any distance for a few days. We went out to get some dinner.

The next game, the Sox-Off, was Saturday. Kelly's family we would be going with were fans of the White Sox. Kelly and I had predicted that the two teams would split the four-game series, but each chose a different configuration of how the split would happen. He thought it would go win-lose-win-lose for the White Sox. I thought it would be lose-win-win-lose for the Red Sox. Eric, to be different, thought the Red Sox would take the series after losing the first game. So far, we were all correct. The White Sox had won the first game Friday night.

I was especially excited to see the White Sox, because Ken Griffey, Jr. had just been traded to the White Sox from Cincinnati. He was one of the star players I had never seen. Both times I had seen Cincinnati play, Griffey hadn't been in the line up. Unfortunately, he wasn't in the lineup for this game either. I would eventually get to see him play when he was with the Mariners in 2009.

Just as important as the game was preparations for the tailgating we planned to do. Eric was going to make some hot wings, and the neighbors were going to cook some brats and hamburgers. Both groups would bring other goodies, like sweet corn. When Saturday came, Eric had to work. I went shopping and things started to come together. After Eric got home from work, we loaded the cars, plural. Yes, we had to take two cars to fit all of us and the supplies necessary to tailgate. We got to the parking lot and began setting up when a big black cloud opened up. We had brought our rain suits plus a couple of umbrellas, so we managed to keep the coals and food dry during a very hard and cold rain. We ate and made it to our seats by the bottom of the first inning.

Daisuke Matsuzaka was pitching for Boston. He had a great record but was a frustrating pitcher to watch, because he walked too many batters for my taste. That game was no exception. He started off the bottom of the first with a walk. Eric and I looked at each other knowingly. Fortunately, Matsuzaka got the next three batters out, so the walk didn't come back to hurt us. I had been told that Jose Contreras was one of Chicago's best pitchers, so I was a little bit concerned about the matchup (even though I picked Boston to win that night). Early in the game, Contreras went to cover first on a play. He took a wrong step and hurt his ankle. We eventually found out that he had ruptured his left Achilles tendon. I hate to see anyone hurt, especially seriously. D. J. Carrasco came in to pitch for Chicago and got the final out of that inning.

It wasn't until the bottom of the fifth that Dice-K gave up a walk that hurt us. He walked the first batter. We knew it was going to happen: they were able to convert that to a run. Grr. He did get out of the inning without further damage.

It was Boston's turn in the sixth inning. David Ortiz led off with a single and came around to tie the game. Boone Logan came in to pitch for Chicago. A couple of singles, one by Varitek (still in a slump, so I was very pleased to see him get a hit), and a walk loaded the bases. Okay, let's see what we can do with that, boys! Pedroia hit an RBI single, and a run scored! The Red Sox were up by one with the bases loaded, no one out, and Big Papi at the plate. My heart was just racing! Ortiz hit a double to clear the bases! All of a sudden the Red Sox were up by four. Ozzie Guillen made another pitching change. The new pitcher got out of the inning.

Our companions at the game were not very happy with how the game was going, but seemed to be having an okay time anyway. Kelly kept saying that five was not enough. I understood. Only time would tell. Dice-K pitched a one-two-three seventh and eighth, which were beautiful to see. Adam Russell gave up a solo home run to Jacoby Ellsbury to extend the Red Sox lead to 6–1 in the top of the eighth. At that point, there was a concession that maybe six was enough. In the top of the ninth, Youkilis and Lowell both got singles but didn't score any more runs. Mike Timlin came in to pitch the ninth. I have mentioned before that I have come to have faith in Timlin. He was a then-forty-two-year-old veteran, a smart pitcher. He got the first two White Sox out, but then gave up a home run to Jim Thome. I have become so familiar with Jim Thome. He sure was a clutch hitter. I really didn't mind the homer because the kids (okay, and the adults, too) had wanted to see the fireworks go off when a White Sox hit a home run. It cheered our companions up. The Red Sox won the game 6–2. Oh, five runs would have been enough.

We waited until things cleared out in that parking lot, chatting a while before we headed back to the house. We shared the events of the game with the rest of the gang. As it turned out, we *all* had correctly predicted the first two games of the series. The neighbor predicted the other two games correctly, but I was also right that they would split the series. Eric, who professes to be a pessimist, was incorrect about the Red Sox taking the series.

Monday came all too soon. The drive back home went well, but I was a bit sad knowing that I only had one more game to see that year and no definite plans to see Eric. I was also feeling amazed at how fast the season seemed to be going. I had plans to make for the September game in Washington when the Mets would be playing, which helped to occupy my mind some. I also began thinking that because the only new stadiums scheduled to open in 2009 were both in New York, I might want to get back to Cleveland to see Progressive Field, formerly known as Jacobs Field. That became a goal after I drove past that stadium on my way home.

ALL DONE

The following weekend I began looking into hotels, parking, and transportation in Washington DC. I would soon see the new Nationals Park. I started looking at what the pitching matchup was likely to be, barring any major changes. I decided I would shoot for the Monday night game on September 15 with he hope of seeing Johan Santana. But I hadn't seen any of the Mets' then-current starting rotation except Pedro Martinez, whom I wouldn't mind seeing again. So it really didn't matter which starter I got to see, as it would either be someone new to me, or one of my favorites.

I finalized my plans, ordered the tickets, booked the hotel and was even able to incorporate dinner plans for before the game with a friend of mine who worked in DC. I had seen a game in DC before at RFK Stadium, but Nationals Park was the last existing big-league ball park I had yet to see. After this game, I would have seen all thirty parks, until the new ones opened the next year.

My sister had contacted the local paper to tell them what I had accomplished, and they actually sent the sports writer to interview me. I really enjoyed sharing my stories with him and looked forward to seeing his write-up in the paper. The only thing he lacked was pictures of me at the stadiums. Believe it or not, I didn't have any pictures of myself at a game. So I had to make sure I got one in DC.

I left early on Monday morning so I could take my time. Little did I know that there was major construction on the main route I was to drive along. There were times the highway was down to one lane and it was very slow going. It took almost an hour longer than expected to get to the hotel, but I arrived in plenty of time. I got my stuff organized in the room and headed to the Metro station, which was only two miles away. Each subway system was a little different, but I figured I had had enough experience with different ones that I could figure DC's Metro out. On the Internet I read that I would have to buy a Smarttrip card to get out of the parking ramp, but that card would also work for the Metro fare. I had planned to just buy that card and skip the fare ticket altogether.

One of my concerns about parking at the Metro station was coming back there after the game, late at night, all by my self. As it turned out, there was a parking spot just two in from the door on the first level, directly under a light. Once again I felt blessed and gave thanks to all my friends and family who were praying for me as I traveled. I made my way to the lobby only to find out that the Smarttrip card machine was out of order. I asked the attendant what to do. He indicated that I could purchase a fare card and it would be accepted at the parking ramp instead of the Smarttrip card. I calculated the amount I would need for a round trip and parking and bought the fare card. Traveling before 3:00 PM and returning after 7:00 PM meant that I got a reduced rate.

I caught the Metro and headed to the stop where I was to meet my friend for dinner. I exited the Metro station and looked around for someplace to kill some time until she got out of work. Shortly after I began looking around, she sent me a text message giving a new location to meet her at, which of course was in the exact opposite direction. I turned around and headed that way. I found the place and decided to head inside to wait.

When I walked inside, a gentleman greeted me and asked if I wanted a booth or a table. I asked if I could sit at the bar until my friend got there. He pointed the way and asked if I wanted something to drink. I was wearing my Mets t-shirt, Mets headband, Mets earrings, and carrying my baseball tote. There was really not much doubt where I was going. When the bartender came out, he started talking to me about baseball, which was a wonderful way to pass my wait. When my friend showed up, the bartender came over to wait on us at our table. He had been afraid I was I was being stood up. It made us both laugh.

We had a nice visit and meal, and then we parted company. I headed to the park, just a couple more Metro stops away. As I was getting on the escalator to exit the Metro station, there was a young man with a Johan Santana t-shirt on. I struck up a conversation with him, telling him that I had been hoping we would be seeing Johan pitch. We were both very happy with seeing Pedro pitch, and hopeful that he could get us a win. He said it would be a good birthday present for him. I wished him a happy birthday, adding my hope he got his birthday wish. We walked to the park together. He took a picture of me outside the stadium holding up my sign proclaiming my success for visiting every major league ballpark. When other people saw the sign, they took pictures too. Even the photographers outside the stadium who take pictures of the fans for the team Web site even got in on the picture-taking.

Once I got inside, I wanted to take my walk around before finding my seat, in hopes of getting more pictures as requested for the local paper at home. Trading high fives and yelling "Let's Go Mets!" I wished him a happy birthday and moved on.

I got to my seat and asked an usher to take my picture down by the top of the dugout, which he was happy to do. I took pictures of the stadium. This was going to be my last game of the season. As I was looking around the stadium, it seemed to me that the turnout was very small. I hoped that it would fill in as the game went on. I was disappointed. The total attendance ended up being around 22,000 that night. It made me almost as sad as the first game I saw at Kauffman Stadium in Kansas City. The stadium was new and pristine, but there really wasn't anything outstanding about it, other than the building outside the park that was outlined in blue lights, which looked really neat after dark. Along the side of the subway station on the other side of the stadium there were some interesting banners.

I prayed for the Pedro of old to show up. No such luck, as the Nationals scored the first run early. *Only down by one*, I kept telling myself. During lulls in the game, I was holding up my sign after asking the man behind me if it would bother him. He said he didn't care as long as I didn't block his view when the game was going on. I thanked him and we chatted more throughout the game.

In the top of the third, we tied the game partly because of Pedro's sacrifice to advance the runner. Yahoo! The score held until the bottom of the next inning when the Nationals scored again to take back the lead. Darn it! The next couple of innings both sides made the pitchers look good. In the sixth, the Nats scored two more runs, extending their lead to 4–1. Ugh! The seventh inning was more of the same "Ugh!" feeling, as Duaner Sanchez gave up a three-run home run. This was not the way I wanted the last game of the season at the last new stadium to go.

The Mets got one more run, but that was all. The final score was Nationals 7, Mets 2. I was very disappointed. I made my way back to the Metro station, bound for my hotel.

I wound up standing on a Metro platform waiting for a connecting train. I was a little nervous about the situation until the three guys standing nearby noticed my shirt and asked if I had been to the game. When I said yes, they included me in their conversation. I was a little relieved thinking, I could stand near them on the platform and no one would realize I wasn't with them. As we continued to talk, all waiting for the same train, we were sharing baseball stories. It turned out one of the men was a New York State Police trooper. Again, I really felt like all the prayers of my friends and family were protecting me.

Our train came and off we went. I was getting tired and anxious to get back to the hotel. I thanked the guys for their company, wished them luck, and got off at my stop. When I got back to the lobby, I had enough on my fare card to get out of the parking lot. But I was informed by the attendant that because the Smarttrip card machine was now fixed, I had to buy one of those cards to get out of the garage. I was a little bit miffed because that wasn't what I was told earlier. What should have cost me $4.25 would now cost me almost $15.00, but I just spent the money and went on my way.

When I got out of the subway, I saw that Eric had called. So I called him back when I got back to the hotel. He congratulated me on completing my goal, and we reminisced for a while about some of our trips. I tried to get some sleep but seemed to just toss and turn most of the night. I was even up before the alarm went off. I packed up and grabbed some breakfast before checking out of the hotel. I knew what I was in for on the route back, but it was still irritating to be at a complete standstill on the highway.

I got home and sent a few pictures to the local paper, eager to hear when the story was going to appear. The season was a tight one for my favorite teams, so I was glued to the TV or radio for every game. The Red Sox clinched the AL wild card the last week of the season, and the Mets were tied for the NL wild card going into the last game of the season. Talk about being on the edge of your seat!

It wasn't long afterward that the 2009 tentative schedules came out, so I distracted myself some with plans for next year. I also went back out to Eric's for New Year's, partly to help him get a résumé together, as his company had recently downsized, and partly because we hadn't seen each other in several months.

AGAIN ONLINE IN 2009

I was planning to attend spring training games in 2009, but I couldn't target any dates definitely until the spring training schedules were finalized. I looked at the Mets and Yankees schedules to get some dates in mind for the next year's trips. Over the years since my divorce I have stayed close to my ex-husbands family, especially his parents. I still consider them family and still refer to them as my in-laws. My mother-in-law was interested in accompanying me on those trips. I was looking forward to them. I also knew they would be hard tickets to get, so I wanted to be ready to make a purchase as soon as the tickets went on sale.

The spring training schedules came out, so I could finally make plans to get tickets. I scoped out some games that were close to my in-law's house in Florida. She was a big Yankees fan, but we decided to go to two games at one of the nearby spring training stadiums instead of trying to travel to the Yankees, Mets, or Red Sox spring facilities. It worked out that both the Mets and Yankees would be in Lakeland, at the Detroit Tigers camp, in the same week in March. We made plans to go there. I would spend a few extra days with the in-laws to do some other things as well.

My sister and Ron were planning to accompany me to Citi Field. Cindy and I were planning a trip to Boston at some point as well. My mother-in-law and I were planning to get to the new Yankee Stadium early that year too. There were a lot of plans to be made.

With the economy the way that it was, my sister, Ron, and I made a compromise and decided to go to the final exhibition game at Citi Field, between the Mets and Red Sox. That was a good scenario. Cindy and I would get to see the Red Sox play, Ron and I would get to see the Mets, and we all would get to see Citi Field. Tickets went on sale at 10:00 AM on a Friday. Within twenty minutes I had tickets! I was so excited. The year was starting to take shape. I was still waiting for Yankee regular season tickets to go on sale so that I could get tickets for a game with my mother-in-law, but at least some of my plans were taking shape. I still had to figure out how I was going to see Ken Griffey Jr. play. He had been picked up by the Mariners, and I really wanted to see him play. He had eluded me both times I saw Cincinnati and again in 2008 in Chicago when he was playing for the White Sox.

Early in March, I was off to Florida to see my in-laws. I had gotten the tickets to attend a couple of spring training games for me and my mother-in-law. All my flights were on time and all went well with the traveling after we were de-iced in Binghamton.

The next day, Mom and I headed off to Joker Marchant Stadium to see a game, not knowing what to expect for sure. We got in line to enter the parking lot, but the man who was directing traffic walked up to the car to tell us there was another entrance at the next light. Using that entrance helped us get a really good parking spot. We walked toward the park, and I snapped a few pictures. We made our way to our seats to watch the players warm up and take batting practice. It seemed weird to be so close to the players. We enjoyed seeing them, and I snapped a few more pictures. While the grounds crew prepared the field, we decided to get our lunch before the game started. I wanted to stay with tradition and got a hot dog. It was very good, albeit fairly expensive.

We settled in for the game with more than 9,600 other fans. When everyone was seated out on the outfield berm, there was hardly any grass showing. The place was packed. The couple seated next to us were from Boston and big Red Sox fans. I had a nice time chatting with them. With the World Baseball Classic going on, we knew we wouldn't get to see all of the players. But it was going to be a good game, because the pitching matchup was the Yankees' newly acquired pitcher C. C. Sabathia against Justin Verlander of the Tigers.

The Yankees took an early two-run lead in the first frame. In the second inning, the Yankees added two more runs. But Sabathia gave up six hits and five runs, including a two-run home run by Gary Sheffield.with two outs in the second innings to drive Sabathia out of the game.

It was fun to watch the grounds crew fix up the field partway through the game. During their work, they stopped at second base and danced to the song "YMCA."

The Yankees couldn't score any more runs. The Tigers, however, added on two more runs, one on a solo home run by Sheffield and another on a solo shot by Wilkin Ramirez. The final score was Tigers 7, Yankees 4. We got to see a few of the regulars, and Mom was satisfied with that, even though she would have preferred to see the Yankees win. It was a warm, sunny day in Florida. What better time could there be for my first baseball game of the season?

Two days later, we were back, along with a much smaller crowd of about 7,700. We decided to get there even earlier to see if we could catch more practice. Thankfully, our seats were not directly in the sun that time, and it was not as sunny as the previous game.

When the grounds crew came out to prepare the field, we went to get some lunch. This time we opted for strawberry shortcake with a scoop of vanilla ice cream on top instead of sandwiches, hot dogs, or other ballpark food on offer.

The Mets were playing the Tigers. We were sitting next to some real Tigers fans that day, and we enjoyed teasing back and forth. For the first couple of innings I was on the receiving end of the taunting, but as the tide changed, our roles reversed. It was all in good fun of course.

Very few regular Mets players were in the lineup that day. I was pleased to see Jose Valentin playing second base, even though he was a non-roster invitee. I was so excited to see him in a Mets uniform even under those circumstances. Edwin Jackson for the Tigers was going up against Freddy Garcia, another non-roster invitee, for the Mets. He had previously played for the Tigers.

The Tigers scored first in the bottom of the second, and in the third they added another run on a solo homer, which drove Garcia out of the game. The Mets retaliated in the top of the fourth when Cory Sullivan and

Valentin went deep back-to-back to tie the score. I was ecstatic! I am very fond of Valentin and to see him hit a home run after not playing in the majors the previous year was just so cool! The Mets got four more runs to jump ahead 6–2.

When the grounds crew came out to freshen up the field partway through the game, they did the dance at second base again. But they weren't as good as on our previous visit. It was still entertaining to watch.

The Tigers got another run in the fifth, making it Mets 6, Tigers 3. In the seventh inning, the Mets tacked on one more with an unearned run on two hits. They sealed the deal in the eighth when Rene Rivera hit a two-run home run, making the final score Mets 9, Tigers 3. I was rather pleased to see the "baby" Mets and a bunch of non-roster invitees beat the Tigers.

Dad had made dinner for us while Mom and I were at the game. It was ready when we got back home. We had planned to watch the space shuttle take off but it was postponed. Eric called to check in and we had a short conversation. He had been a little distant at that time, but we were still in touch fairly often. I was lucky enough to see the shuttle take off on Sunday night. We were about sixty miles away, but we still saw it fairly well. It was just another special part of my Florida visit that year. The next morning I flew home.

Before I left Florida, it was announced that because of such high demand, the Yankees were having a drawing to purchase tickets a day early. So I entered with my work e-mail address, home e-mail address, Mom and Dad's e-mail address, and my sister's home e-mail address, in order to maximize our chances. No luck. We had to wait until the general public could buy tickets.

The on-sale day came, and I got permission to bring my laptop to work to get tickets when they went on sale at 10 AM. I had decided to aim for tickets later in the year because it would be cooler. Also my father-in-law was to have hip surgery in May, so we wanted to make sure he was recovered before we left him for a coupe of days to go to the game. I signed on and the wait was minimal. But the ticket choices were slim. I was able to get tickets, but they weren't where we wanted to sit. Still, we were going to see to the new Yankee Stadium! I booked a hotel, pre-purchased parking, and then locked in reservations for a stadium tour as soon as those tickets went on sale.

Plans were set for the two new stadiums, but I still had a couple of other desires to fulfill. I wanted to see Ken Griffey, Jr. I wanted to get to Fenway. I also wanted to see Oakland to watch Nomar Garciaparra one more time before he retired. My mind kept working as to how I could accomplish all that. I had offered to fly Eric home to go to Citi Field with us, but he declined. I was getting the impression I would not be seeing him again. I even offered to go out to see him in May for his birthday, but he said it wouldn't work out. He was working a new job, and I guess I just didn't fit into his life anymore.

April 4 was the date of our trip to Citi Field to see the Red Sox play the Mets in the last exhibition game of the spring. I kept telling myself that I wouldn't care who won because it didn't count anyway. I was going to see the new stadium with my sister and Ron, so all would be good. I bought new Red Sox shirts for both Cindy and myself, so we were set to go.

All week long it looked like April 4 was going to be a nice day in Flushing. The temperature was supposed to be in the mid-sixties, with sunny skies, a bit windy but still nice. On Friday the forecast changed, predicting cooler temperatures and rain. Drats! We had planned to go early in order to tailgate, but that part was up in the air. The morning of the game, we decided to go for it. We packed up all the cookout stuff but also brought our winter jackets. I even brought an extra winter jacket just in case, which was good because Ron ended up wearing it. I always carry a couple of blankets in the car, which we vowed to take into the park to be as prepared as we could be for the weather.

It was sprinkling when we left but we really didn't run into any heavy rain the whole trip. We made our first stop to top off the gas and get something to eat. We were making good time. We were about an hour from getting there when we noticed the traffic ahead of us was slowing down, completely stopped on the other side. I thought it was probably just Looking Lous on our side, but as we got closer we could see what the problem was. A horrible accident had just occurred. A car had flipped over and landed on its roof. Part of the car's bumper was on our side while the rest of the car was blocking all four westbound lanes. Both my sister and I saw a person stuck in the car. There were some people stopped trying to help, but no emergency vehicles were even there yet. Cindy was very shook up. I am not sure if Ron, who was in the back seat, saw as much as we did, but he tried to calm her down. All I could do was pray for the people in the car, the people trying to help, the emergency squads that hopefully would arrive soon and even myself, so I could keep it together enough to get us to our destination safely. The sight haunted us for days afterward. On our way back, I felt myself tense up as we passed the spot. A few miles later Cindy asked if we had passed the spot. It was helpful to me that she didn't ask at the actual spot, as it gave me time to regain my composure.

After that unpleasantness, we made it to the stadium. We got the parking spot that we had hoped to get, partly because the parking staff was very nice to us. We were able to back in next to a wide walkway. We had plenty of room to cook our veggie burgers and veggie dogs. We were all anxious to see the stadium, so we didn't waste a lot of time sitting around after we ate. We had driven most of the way around the stadium trying to get to the parking lot we wanted, so we knew where we wanted to go to get pictures.

I absolutely love the way they blended the past and the present at Citi Field. The Jackie Robinson Rotunda was especially amazing! I had watched the previous night's exhibition game on TV the night before so I already had an idea of where I wanted to go once we got to the new park. When we got inside, we walked around a bit on the way to our seats. They were way better than we had hoped! It was windy, so we were really glad that we brought the blankets in. We watched batting practice for the Red Sox and my heart was just pounding to finally see them after a winter of not knowing whether Jason Varitek was coming back, along with all the other trades that had happened in the offseason. I can't put into words how happy I was that Varitek was back! I very much hope that he will finish his career in Boston.

I did take a minute to send Eric a text message from Citi Field. He called and we talked, but he was working so the chat was brief. After that I set about mentally preparing myself for the game, reassuring myself that it didn't matter who won. The Mets had won a close game the night before in their first game (albeit exhibition) in their new home. If the Red Sox won today, they would split the series, which would be about perfect for a split personality (that's what I call myself as a fan). Big Papi hit two out of the park in batting practice and my eyes filled with tears when I saw Jason Varitek in the uniform again. There was Mike Lowell, and Dustin Pedroia, Jason Bay, Kevin Youkilis, J. D. Drew, Jed Lowrie, and our new centerfielder, Rocco Baldelli. They were all there, and I was psyched! Oh, and Daisuke Matsuzaka was scheduled to pitch! Cindy was so excited. She had never seen the Red Sox win in person. She felt that Dice-K on the mound meant this was to be the time. I was more skeptical, but time would tell.

On the other side, I was looking forward to seeing the regular Mets players that had been at the World Baseball Classic the prior month in Florida. While the grounds crew was getting the field ready, the players came out for their warm-up sprints. I was so giddy, I was like a kid in a candy store, or, as I prefer to say, like a Candy in a baseball stadium! Just the week before, the Mets had announced that they signed Gary Sheffield, pending his passing the physical exam he was taking that very day! Adding Sheffield was a good thing, but also meant that a couple of the players were in jeopardy of losing their spots on the team. It was always tough to see young guys have to go back to the minors. I tried to put that out of my head and just enjoy seeing them all play. The other plus was that Oliver Perez was going to start. This was the first time I would see Perez in person. The Mets were also planning on having John Maine pitch. Before the game started, we got some snacks. I knew I wasn't going to want to leave my seat once the game started.

Some of the greatest things during that game didn't actually have to do with the baseball being played, but I'll get into that later. Oliver Perez had an awful start. He walked four, gave up two hits, and allowed six runs, four of those coming on a grand slam by Jed Lowrie with two outs. That was the first home run hit in Citi Field, even though it wasn't in the regular season. I was there for the first homer in stadium history! Lowrie was the last batter Perez faced. Nelson Figueroa came in for the Mets to finish off the first inning. Daisuke Matsuzaka pitched in his usual frustrating way. We have a little saying for when he pitches: "Do a little dance, throw a little strike, and strike them all out tonight." He still walks too many guys for my tastes, but he seems to work himself out of trouble most of the time. That day was no different. He walked four, gave up one hit, and only struck out one in four innings, all without allowing a run—so I really couldn't complain.

Some of the fun of that day was just watching the players interact. David Ortiz and Carlos Delgado had just played together in the World Baseball Classic, and it was fun to see them fooling around on first base. Ortiz was walked and seemed to be teasing Delgado that he was going to steal. Delgado was blocking him like a linebacker, pushing him back, smiles on both of their faces. David Wright and Kevin Youkilis also played together in the WBC. When Wright was walked, he and Youkilis high-fived each other. It was neat to see. It was a windy day, so the players were constantly picking up garbage and putting it in their pockets during play. The grounds crew came out between innings to clean up the field.

Figueroa pitched the second, giving up two hits, walking one, and striking out one. John Maine pitched the third and fourth innings, walking two and giving up just one hit. I was concerned that Jerry Manuel wasn't giving the starters enough work that far into spring training, but what do I know?

Ramon Ramirez pitched the fifth inning for the Red Sox. He gave up one run. The RBI went to Daniel Murphy, one of the young players I had seen play in Binghamton. Murphy made me proud, especially when he also stole third base after his hit. Ramirez walked two and struck out two.

Dillon Gee pitched the fifth inning for the Mets, striking out the side. Justin Masterson pitched well in the sixth for the Red Sox, giving up one hit and striking out two. Gee had a harder time in the sixth. He gave up three hits, one of which was a solo home by Jason Varitek. My eyes filled with tears of joy and pride. I think I just about lost my voice cheering! Cindy and Ron missed the home run, as they had gone to get something to drink. The guy behind me was teasing me that I cheered for everyone. I explained that I was watching my two favorite teams. As I turned around, I saw he had a Boston hat and a David Wright t-shirt on. When I saw that, we both just laughed. We were in the same boat.

At that point, many of the starters were out of the game and the non-roster invitees were on the field. As luck would have it, Alex Cora was playing third base for the Mets at the same time David Ortiz was on third base. Throughout the game, the players had been picking up the garbage blowing around the field and putting it in their back pockets. Well, Ortiz started picking up some garbage and stuffing it in Cora's backpocket. The whole place started laughing. It was so great to see!

In the bottom of the ninth, the Mets scored two more runs, but the Red Sox won 9–3 in just under three and a half hours, in front of almost 39,000 fans. Cindy was very happy to finally see the Red Sox win. Ron was okay with the result because the game didn't count. He had gotten to see Citi Field for the first time. On our way out, we took a stroll through the Rotunda, and it was so worth it. It was a beautiful tribute to Jackie Robinson.

We loaded up the car, took a couple more pictures, and headed home. Getting out of the parking lot was so easy. Granted, it was cold and many people had left early, but it seemed to me that getting to the highway was easier than it had been at Shea. The Yankees had played a game that afternoon also, so I expected really heavy traffic getting by Yankee Stadium. But because the Yankees finished earlier than the Mets, the congestion wasn't too bad.

Once we were about halfway home, we decided to stop for a sit-down dinner to get something warm in us after sitting in the cold for so long. We got home a little after 9:00 PM. We discussed the possibility of going down for another game that season, which I totally encouraged. The only other plans I had for 2009 was a trip to the new Yankee Stadium in mid-September.

It wasn't looking like Cindy, Ron, and I were going to be able to coordinate our schedules to get to Boston or back to Citi Field. I had to decide what I wanted to do. I was looking into going to Boston at the beginning of July to see Seattle and Oakland, to see Junior Griffey and the former Red Sox great Nomar Garciaparra, now on the Athletics. It would be Nomar's first time back to Fenway in five years. It wasn't to be, though. One of my oldest friends was going to be in town that Sunday, and I wanted to see her and her kids. I decided to make a trip to Cleveland the following weekend to see Seattle and take a couple of days off to go to Boston at the end of the month to see Oakland. Because I wasn't going to go to many games that year, I decided to spend the extra money to stay at hotels close to the parks. I ordered my tickets and then made the hotel reservations. I decided I would try to take a tour of Fenway before heading back home. I was really excited about the tour.

The weekend prior to my trip was a class reunion. My oldest friend, whom I met when I was three and she was two, came home and we went together. We had a great time, and it was good to see everyone.

It had been a busy month to that point, and I was looking forward to getting away for the weekend. Two days before I left, one of my cats passed away. Getting away would hopefully take my mind off her passing.

I tried to sleep in the day of the trip, but I found that I was awake early. I headed out around 8:00 AM. It was a five- to six-hour drive to Cleveland, depending on traffic. That gave me plenty of time to get there, check in, and get something to eat before the game.

The drive went well. Because I travel alone so often, I am in the habit of bringing an audio book so that I don't have to keep finding a new radio station to listen to. My mother had gotten me a few for Christmas, so I was all set. Once I was out of range of the local station, I put the tape in. It really helps to pass the time. I was there before I knew it.

The hotel was directly across the street from the ballpark, so I was thrilled. I checked in and then headed out for some lunch at a restaurant a friend had recommended. It was a very good meal. I made it back to the hotel in plenty of time to get ready. Getting to the park was easy: It was just across the street. I had lots of time to take a walk around the stadium. I had been to Jacobs Field three other times, but now it was called Progressive Field. I took many pictures of the new logos. I got in line and chatted with some of the people around me. It was a giveaway night—Surfin' Sizemore bobblehead, specifically. It was also "Beach Weekend," which I was confused about, as Cleveland is in the middle of the country. But I rolled with it.

I had a great seat, albeit in the dead center of a row, only a couple dozen rows up behind home plate. There were a couple of gentlemen sitting behind me chatting when I made my way to my seat. They were talking about the stadium, comparing it to others. Of course that drew my interest, so I turned around and said hello. They were very pleasant. As it turned out, they were from Fresno, California. They had tickets to all four games of the series, something I'd still never done. We continued to talk and compared thoughts on some of the stadiums. They told me about a minor-league stadium that I needed to see. I also learned that the deal for Oakland to move to Fremont had been squashed. I was disappointed, because I was planning to make another trip to California in 2011 for the new A's park. I told myself I could still make a trip if I wanted to, in an attempt to distract myself from the disruption of my future plans.

The game started. It was a beautiful night for a baseball game. It was about seventy degrees and cloudy with a slight breeze. The forecast called for a possibility of rain, which was why I thought the stadium was fairly empty, including many of the seats in my row. The attendance was about 25,000 fans.

My goal for this game was to see Ken Griffey, Jr. play in person. But I was rooting for the Indians for no particular reason, perhaps because I was used to them winning when Eric was with me. Cleveland was almost exactly halfway between where Eric lived and where I lived. We had flirted with the idea of meeting there to see a game together. That never happened. As a matter of fact, the last time I heard from Eric was the end of that May.

Jarrod Washburn was pitching again for Seattle, and Tomo Ohka was pitching for Cleveland. The most exciting thing in the first four innings came in the second, when Griffey hit a ball hard but right at the outfielder for an out. At the start of the third inning, a couple took the seats next to me. The man sat down and asked me where I was from. They were season-ticket holders, so they knew I wasn't a regular. We chatted through out the game.

Ohka walked Griffey to start off the fourth. The next batter, Franklin Gutierrez, hit a two-run home run on the second pitch. The game felt like it was going quick. In the top of the fifth, Ronny Cedeno started off with a double. Cedeno scored after sacrifices by Suzuki and Russell Branyan. The threat continued when Jose Lopez singled, but Grady Sizemore, leaping at the wall, grabbed a long fly ball to center by Griffey to end the inning. That was certainly something to see, and the crowd went wild! Seattle's runs went unanswered until the bottom of the seventh when the Indians finally manufactured themselves a run, their one and only tally of the game. Kerry Wood, who I had seen pitch for the Cubs in 2008, pitched the ninth for the Indians. David Aardsma, who I had seen pitch for the Red Sox in 2008, got the save. The final score was Seattle 3, Cleveland 1 in just about two and a half hours.

I said goodbye to the couple next to me and wished the gentlemen behind me safe travels. I took a few minutes to enjoy the park, snapping a few more pictures before heading back across the street to the hotel. I was very pleased with myself for selecting that hotel. I took some pictures of the outside of the stadium and even snapped some from my room window.

I didn't set an alarm for the next morning. I had a hard time sleeping in, so I grabbed breakfast at the hotel and headed home. I was pleased with my trip. While making my way out of Cleveland, I was thinking about what the next week would hold. I had just a few more days before I headed to Boston for a Red Sox game against Nomar Garciaparra and the Oakland A's. I put in an audio tape and drove on home.

The following weekend was my family reunion, which brought my cousins from New England to town. They stayed with me, which gave us the opportunity to visit well into the night. We had a great time but it left me a bit tired as I started my trip on Monday morning. The time with them was so worth it, however! I was determined to get to Fenway early enough to get in line with other Red Sox Nation members for a chance to sit on the Green Monster during batting practice. After getting out of range of local radio, in went an audio book to keep me company. Traffic was light and I made it to the hotel around 1:00 PM. I was pleased at how close the hotel was to Fenway.

I grabbed lunch at the Bleacher Bar under the Green Monster then got in line, confident I would be one of the 120 allowed in for Red Sox batting practice. I chatted with a couple from New Hampshire who had seats on the Budweiser Porch for the game. We got in around 4:30 PM and watched about forty minutes of batting practice, which was so awesome! Sitting there so far above the field watching baseballs fly overhead was almost indescribable. When the gates opened, we were scooted out of those seats. But I was free to wander around inside Fenway until game time.

I decided to find my seat and watch Oakland take batting practice. Nomar Garciaparra took batting practice, so I was hopeful that he would play. But he wasn't in the lineup. I still had hope that he would at least pinch-hit. I was able to take some nice pictures of him before the game, even though that was the last time I saw him on the field.

The matchup was interesting, Josh Beckett for Boston going against Trevor Cahill, whom I had not seen nor did I know much about, for Oakland. I had a good seat, just past third base about a dozen rows up after the first walkway in the lowest section. That was my first time sitting on that side of the field and I liked it, as I had a nice view into the Boston dugout! The only problem with the seat was that it was in the corner with a railing behind and beside my seat. Many people were crossing over into the next section by climbing over the railing beside me, which was distracting. Still, I was at Fenway watching most of my favorite players in baseball.

Beckett took the mound and struck out Adam Kennedy. Orlando Cabrera hit the ball back to the mound, but Beckett missed it, making the only error of the game. He settled down and got out of the inning without any harm done. Cahill took the mound for Oakland. Dustin Pedroia hit the first pitch for a home run! Fenway went wild. I couldn't help but cheer as loudly as I could while jumping up and down! We led by one after the first inning! I love it when that happens!

In the bottom of the third Pedroia drove in the second run of the game on a sacrifice fly after Ellsbury started the at-bat off with a triple. Boston 2, Oakland 0. Beckett was on that night, and I could tell his name was going to get long with all his Ks. The bottom of the next inning started off with a walk to Jason Bay, a single by J. D. Drew. Adam LaRoche hit a double to score Bay, moving Drew to third. Here we go! Jason Varitek hit a single to score Drew, moving LaRoche to third! I could hardly contain myself! With two on and no outs, Jed Lowrie flied out. Ah, drat. But Ellsbury hit a single. LaRoche scored and Varitek moved to second! Boston led 5–0 with two on, one out, and Pedi on deck! The excitement was short-lived, as Pedroia grounded into a rare double play. In the fifth, Beckett faced just three, posting another strikeout. Cahill was still pitching for Oakland in the fifth. He gave up a single to Youkilis, followed by a single to Ortiz, moving Youk to third. A single by Bay scored Youk and moved Ortiz to second. Well, here we go again! Drew struck out, and LaRoche grounded into a double play to end the inning, but we were up 6–0!

Beckett ran into some trouble in the sixth. In his last game he had pitched a complete game, and with a low pitch count. The lady behind me and I were discussing the possibility of him tossing another complete game. Beckett loaded the bases in the sixth but Oakland only scored one run. Phew! Okay, the Sox led by five runs, but I didn't want the momentum to change.

Beckett came back out for the seventh. His pitch count was low, but I wasn't sure it was necessary to keep him out there with a five-run edge. But they didn't ask me. The first batter drove a deep double. A fly out for the first out advanced the runner to third. Uh oh! A sacrifice scored a run. The

A's knocked another single, but it was wasted as Beckett struck out Cabrera to end the threat. Phew again.

Edgar Gonzalez took the mound for Oakland. Ortiz grounded out, darn it. Bay drew a walk and was advanced to third on a double by Drew. Varitek was intentionally walked, which made me feel good to see that opponents still respect him. Lowrie hit a ground-rule double to score both Bay and Drew, putting Varitek on third! Wahoo! The place was going wild! Ellsbury grounded out to end the inning.

Beckett started the eighth by surrendering a triple to Scott Hairston which ended his day. The hard-throwing rookie Daniel Bard took the mound. He was truly amazing to see. The look on the batter's faces when Bard threw pitches at 100 miles per hour, which he did consistently, was priceless. Bard struck out the first batter, but allowed a run to score. The only other hit in the game was by Pedroia. Manny Delcarmen closed it out; the final score was Red Sox 8, A's 3. Nomar didn't play. But other than that, it was a great game in front of another sellout crowd of almost 38,000 fans, lasting about three hours.

I was really excited after this wonderful day in Boston. I had been playing phone tag with a friend from high school who had mentioned maybe meeting for breakfast on Tuesday. We never made contact until the next morning. She was caught in traffic at 7:00 AM so we knew it wasn't going to work out that trip. At least we had gotten back in touch and could try again in the future. I grabbed breakfast in the hotel and checked out before I made my way back to Fenway for the tour. I took a walk around and couldn't help grinning thinking of all the wonderful memories I had experienced there. I was a little sad that Eric wasn't around anymore, but I was focusing on the future.

I was chatting with some of the others in line. A father and son from Chicago, both Cubs fans, asked if I had been on a Fenway tour before. I said no but that I had toured Wrigley. They had toured the Friendly Confines as well, but they had done it when the team was in town, as they hadn't seen the clubhouse, dugouts, or the field. That made me think we weren't going to be allowed in those places at Fenway either, but that was okay.

After getting our tickets the tour guide gathered us to go inside. We went up to the Budweiser Porch, the State Street Pavilion, and then up on the Green Monster, hearing history and interesting information the entire way. As we made our way toward the Green Monster there were workmen doing some repairs on the brickwork. There were brick pieces lying on the ground. A couple of us asked if we could take a piece of brick. The guides said sure, so I grabbed a small piece and put it in my pocket. I brought home a piece of Fenway!

We sat on the Green Monster and then made our way down to the area I had sat in the night before, learning more about Fenway as we went. After the tour I made my way back to the parking garage. I got in the car and pulled up to where the attendant was standing. He had asked questions about my visit the day before when I parked my car, so he waved for me to stop. He asked if I was able to accomplish everything I had planned and if I enjoyed my visit. I assured him I had, thanking him again for his assistance. I made my way to the Massachusetts Turnpike and headed home. I put a tape in to keep me company.

I found myself more tired than I had thought I would be. I had to stop more often then usual. I wasn't on any deadline, so that was fine. I arrived home safely, exhausted but very happy for having made the trip. My next planned trip wasn't for almost two months, but the excitement from this one would surely carry me that long.

NEW YANKEE STADIUM

The week before the next trip, my voyage to the new Yankee Stadium with my mother-in-law, things were extremely busy. But I was looking forward to the trip. We had gotten our tickets to the game, reserved tickets for the stadium tour, prepaid for parking, and booked our hotel in March. I had printed out all the maps and directions already, so I felt ready for the trip. The weekend before, I checked the trip folder and made sure everything was there, because I had plenty of other stuff to do to get ready to be gone from work for two days. I also had evening meetings to attend. I was also keeping an eye on the probable pitcher for the Yankees would be. It was looking like the starter would be Andy Pettitte, who was one of mom's favorite players along with Derek Jeter. I had never seen Pettitte pitch in person, so that would have been the icing on the cake.

We weren't planning on leaving until mid-morning the day of the game. When a board meeting ran late on Tuesday night, I figured it was no big deal. On the way home I was listening to the Red Sox game on the radio, so I decided to not take the highway because sometimes the station fades out more on that route. I had been underway for about ten minutes when a nice sheriff pulled up behind me with his lights going. I pulled over feeling pretty confident that I hadn't done anything wrong, thinking maybe a tail light was out or something like that. For a brief moment, I thought perhaps something had happened to a family member. But I put that out of my head because my cell phone had no messages at last check.

I was right; both of my license plate lights were out. Those lights were not something I had thought to check, I was actually grateful that he had stopped me. I could get them fixed before I left town the next morning. He asked for the usual forms of identification and asked the usual questions before sending me on my way. I did thank him for letting me know the lights were out. He probably could have given me a ticket but was nice enough not to. Okay, I thought, one more thing to do in the morning. I drove by the auto parts store on my way home to see when they opened. Fortunately the shop opened earlier than we were going to leave, so I was all set.

When I got home, I checked the computer one last time before the trip. The Yankees were giving Pettitte extra time off due to a sore shoulder. Darn it! I shut the computer down and got ready for bed. I was letting my mind, as if I could really stop it, run over everything I had left to do. I remembered that I had some light bulbs in a box of supplies I kept in the trunk of the car. I hoped there was one for the license-plate lamp. I made a mental note to check in the morning and tried to get some sleep.

First thing the next morning I dug through the box in the trunk. Sure enough, there was one bulb for the license plate lamp. I put it in before I headed to the auto parts store to get the other one. Thankfully, those are some of the easier bulbs to change on my car. I ran back home to finish up the last-minute details for the trip before I went to pick up Mom.

She was ready and excited to be going. She has always been a big Yankees fan, so it was exciting for me to be going to the new stadium with her. I had told her I might not be able to root for the Yankees, depending on how the Red Sox were doing, but I promised her I would not outwardly root against them, for her sake. She was going to wear a hat we had specially made for her. The hat had the team name, names and numbers of her favorite players, Pettitte and Jeter. Everyone kept warning her not to wear it because someone might take it. I assured her and Dad that if someone took her hat (well, someone bigger than me), I would buy her another one. We weren't going to be wandering too far outside the stadium, so I really didn't think there was much danger of hat theft. I wanted her to be able to wear her hat without worrying.

We said our goodbyes to Dad and headed out. We had packed plenty of snacks and planned to stop for lunch en route. I had allowed plenty of time to get there, check into the hotel, and get to the stadium to watch batting practice, or so we thought.

We made a note that at one spot on the highway where traffic was backed up for miles going the opposite direction. We discussed the possibility of coming home a different way to avoid that delay on the way home. We found a place to eat and continued on our way, making good time. We crossed the George Washington Bridge and took the appropriate exit, feeling confident we were in great shape. Oops! The next turn was blocked off, so we had to take a detour. Uh oh! We thought we knew where we were, but we were wrong. Mom has a problem with motion sickness, so I was concerned that all of this city driving might be a problem for her. She was looking at the directions I had printed out, but they really didn't give us enough information to get us there. I found a gas station to pull into and looked at the atlas. That didn't help much, but between the map we had for getting from the hotel to the stadium and the other map to the hotel, we were able to figure it out. But between that delay and there being several people in front of us to check in to the hotel, we had lost the time we had allotted to relax before heading to the stadium.

We basically put our suitcases down and headed right back out. We found our way to the stadium without a hitch, except for the rude person who honked behind us when we stopped for a school bus. I guess he was telepathic, because he passed me just as the bus driver closed the door and pulled in the stop sign on the side of the bus. *Oh well*, I told myself.

We found the parking area and crossed the street to Gate 8 of Yankee Stadium. We were there! The man just inside the entrance was directing people to Monument Park. I asked if that was part of the tour. It was part of the tour that we would be taking the next day, so we went ahead and watching batting practice from the first level in the outfield, not far from where our seats for the game were. I was thinking we would just go up a couple of levels when it was time to go to our seats. It wasn't exactly that easy, but the seats in that section were really comfy. Several batting-practice home runs were hit into that section. Most were caught in front of us, but one bounced off the seat two to my right. I ducked out of the way of the mob of people who were diving for the souvenir.

We did get to see Andy Pettitte on the field during batting practice, even though he pretty much just stood chatting with his arms crossed. I am sure he was not supposed to do much more so as not to aggravate his sore shoulder. We both noticed how many more players were on the field with the late-season expanded roster. After batting practice, we made our way to our seats, which meant going all the way to the other side of the field to get the only escalator to the third level and then making our way back to the side we started on. We passed an amazing food court on the main level—it felt like we were in a mall or something, there were so many choices. We still had plenty of time, but I wanted to get to the proper lever before we decided what we would eat before the game started. Even with all the choices available in the new stadium, we still ended up with hot dogs.

A guy took the seat next to me, and we began chatting. He asked if we were Yankees fans and I said that Mom was. He asked which team I was a fan of. I told him I wouldn't tell him for fear that he might toss me over the edge of the stands. Our seats were only about four rows from the edge. He assured me he wouldn't, so I told him.

We had another nice surprise before the game when they presented Derek Jeter with the Roberto Clemente Award. I mentioned to Mom that I hadn't voted for Derek, because of all the good Kevin Youkilis and Mike Lowell had done for the community that year also. The guy next to me said that not voting for Jeter was enough to get me tossed over the edge! I was pleased to be there to see the award presented. I have a great deal of respect for Jeter, and do believe he is a classy player. I know seeing him get the Clemente Award meant a lot to Mom.

Before the game started, I went to scope out the exits that would get us to the gate we wanted to exit from. That exit was just across the street from the parking garage we parked in. I asked a female usher who was near the elevators about the best way to get out. She offered to take us down on the elevator later, but only if we left in the eighth inning. The only other options were to go around to the other side of the stadium to use the escalator or use the stairs at the top of our section to descend the three levels. I left it up to Mom to decide which way we were going to go. She thought the stairs were best if we could take our time, even if it meant waiting out the majority of the crowd.

The lineup was announced, and it was confirmed that Chad Gaudin was going to be the starter for New York. Brian Tallet was the starter for Toronto. It had been two years since I had seen the Blue Jays play in person, but I was still familiar with some of their players. The expanded rosters did add a new wrinkle to September games though.

Just before the American national anthem, they play the Canadian national anthem when the Blue Jays play in the United States, and visa versa in Toronto. I was familiarizing myself with where things were in the new stadium. I searched on the various scoreboards and display for things like pitch speed, strikes and balls, and of course the out-of-town scoreboard, the last being the most important. I needed to keep an eye on how the Red Sox were doing, because the Red Sox were leading in the wild card but only by a few games.

The inside of the park was very nice. They had done a really nice job on the new stadium. There was a section behind the bleachers that displayed all the team's many championship flags and retired numbers. It looked to me like the Yankees have the most retired numbers of any place I had been. The scoreboard was pretty neat, especially with the big "Yankee Stadium" logo across the top. We would have time to see more around the outside the next day before the tour.

The game got underway. Chad Gaudin had a one-two-three inning. Brian Tallet had a more difficult inning. The crowd went completely wild again when Jeter was introduced. The veteran shortstop looked a little bit embarrassed by all the attention. Tallet started off with a walk to Jeter. Jerry Hairston, Jr. flied out, but Mark Teixeira hit a deep double and Jeter scored the first run of the game. Well, then. Mom was happy. Hideki Matsui hit a single and Teixeira scored the second run, with Matsui landing on second on the throw home.

In the second inning Gaudin gave up a double to Vernon Wells but Lyle Overbay lined out, Edwin Encarnacion struck out, and Rod Barajas, who came to the Mets in 2010, flied out to end the inning. In the top of the third, the first batter hit a home run. I sat still but was clapping inside. Sorry, Mom. The Angels had taken a 1–0 lead over Boston in the third inning. Uh oh. The next Toronto batter hit a single. The next hitter, Marco Scutaro, who came to play in Boston in 2010, hit a single as well. Both runners then advanced on a wild pitch. There were two on with no outs. Two groundouts scored a run to tie it up.

In Boston, the Angels had tacked on another run, so I was happy that the score was tied in New York, at least for the moment. In the top of the fifth, Aaron Hill made it safely to first on a rare error by Jeter. As soon as the error happened, Jeter covered his face with his glove as if to say oops! The runner advanced to second on a wild pitch but was unable to score. In the top of the sixth, Toronto scored the go-ahead run. That prompted a pitching change for New York.

The Angels added another run in the top of the sixth, which the guy next to me was kind enough to point out. I didn't feel too bad, as the Yankees were behind by one at the moment and Texas was also down 3–0. The worst case, if all the scores held, was the Red Sox not losing or gaining any ground.

Brian Bruney came in for the Yankees in the seventh. Mom said "Uh oh." She was right. Bruney gave up a double to Scutaro and a single to Hill before the Yanks brought in Phil Coke to replace him. Adam Lind hit a sacrifice to score Scutaro, making the score Blue Jays 4, Yankees 2.

The Red Sox had a five-run bottom of the sixth to take the lead, which I was happy to point out to the guy next to me. But the excitement was short-lived because the Angels came back with four runs in the top of the seventh. Ugh!

I took a moment to find a team employee to see if they could tell me where to go for the tour the next day, because our tickets for the tour didn't say where to go. This errand gave me a chance to stretch my legs a bit.

In the top of the eighth, Nick Swisher flied out, and Robinson Cano was the next batter. I explained to Mom that I called him "Uh Oh Cano," because it seems he was always making something happen. Right then he hit a double. Melky Cabrera was safe at first on an error by Encarnacion, which brought up Johnny Damon to pinch-hit for Jose Molina. That was enough for a pitching change for the Blue Jays. A good move, as the new guy struck Damon out. But then he walked Jeter to load the bases. Fortunately, Hairston grounded into a fielder's choice to end the inning. Phil Hughes took over on the mound for the Yankees. Francisco Cervelli came in to catch, Cabrera moved to left field, and Brett Gardner took over in center. Hughes made easy work of the Jays in that inning.

In the bottom of the eighth Matsui hit a no-doubter to right field with A-Rod on base to tie the score. Much of the crowd was already heading out, a phenomenon that always amazed me. People pay all that money to watch a game, how could they leave before it is over? Especially when it's a close, ahem, *tied*, game. I will never understand it. The guy next to me left as well. He told us to enjoy the game. I said goodbye to him and told Mom he was going to miss the good stuff.

In the top of the ninth we had another surprise when Mariano Rivera came in for the Yankees. I had never seen him pitch in person before, so that was another one of today's greats I got to see. I was especially happy that Mom got to see Rivera in person. Rivera gave up a bunt single to Travis Snider and a fielder's choice to Scutaro to erase Snider at second. Scutaro, "the pest" as Mom called him, stole second base before Lind grounded out to end the inning. Rivera got rousing applause when he left the field. I clapped too, because I was glad to see him. He really did do well.

Mom said she was hoping the game wouldn't go into extra innings. Part of me wasn't sure I would mind that as much, because the Angels and Red Sox were still playing in Boston and I wanted to keep an eye on that score. But the seats were getting hard and we had been there for over six hours already, so I knew what she meant. I was prepared to offer to leave early if extra innings happened. Fortunately, that wasn't the case. Brett Gardner hit a single then stole second. Jeter grounded out but advanced Gardner to third. Oh boy! Cervelli hit a single to score the winning run. Yankees won! Mom was happy and I guess I was too, if only on Mom's account. We were relieved that there would be no extra innings.

The Boston game was going to the bottom of the eighth with the Red Sox down by two. I resigned myself to the possibility we would lose ground in the division race. The Rangers had lost so the wild card race would stay the same. There were two more at-bats for Boston, but I would just have to wait until we got back to the hotel to see what happened.

The crowd was thin enough that we could make our way down the stairs, all three levels of them. We both commented that we didn't think we were ever going to reach ground. We crossed the street, climbed the two sets of stairs to the car, and reviewed the directions I had scribbled down on how to get back to the hotel. That part went very well once we cleared the first block of traffic. We had decided to take the back streets instead of the Major Deegan, which was always congested after a game.

We got back to the hotel and climbed the last flight of stairs for the day up to our floor. I kicked off my shoes and searched the TV for the final score in Boston. I was ecstatic to see the Sox had tied it in the bottom of the eighth. The Angels retook the lead again in the ninth, but my team had come back to win on a two-out, two-strike, two-on single by Alex Gonzalez that scored two. We gained ground in the wild card race and didn't lose any ground in the division race. Not bad at all.

We were so tired that we just about fell into bed after a brief discussion about what time to get up. The clock in the room didn't seem to be working, so I set the alarm on my cell phone to get us up in the morning.

As luck would have it, my phone shut off in the night so the alarm didn't go off the next morning. Fortunately we both woke up around the time we had planned to get up anyway. We went down for the breakfast offered by the hotel and then spent some time in the room just chatting and gathering our things, trying to wait until we had to check out before we left because we really didn't know of anywhere else we could go until the tour at the ballpark. Once we got there, we would still have a half hour to kill before the tour started. We found a parking place in the same place we used the night before. We walked across the street to the stadium, planning on taking some pictures as we made our way around it.

All along one side of the stadium, they have player banners, which were really neat. I took pictures of a few of Mom's favorites for her. Outside of the main entrance was a large gold NY logo. The Yankee Stadium lettering on the top was also gold, which looked really nice.

We read some signs full of facts about Babe Ruth, and then spent some time in the gift shop until it was time to get in line. The tours run every twenty minutes. We weren't able get in line too early for our assigned tour. Mom was able to find a couple of souvenirs that she wanted in the gift shop, which also made me happy. We also saw people working on top of the old stadium, presumably doing some disassembly work, which in a way was sad to see. I took a picture of them.

On the tour we went into the team museum, which was so neat, even for a non-Yankee fan like me. There was a wall of signed baseballs from every player that played for the Yankees, even if it was for just one game! It is an amazing sight. They also have a model of the new stadium, a display of all the World Series championship trophies (including a ball signed by all the players that played for the team for each title), and so much more.

We went to the new Monument Park. I had visited Monument Park in the old stadium, but it was arranged very nicely in the new stadium as well. One of the most touching things for me is the plaque in memory of 9/11. It brought tears to my eyes and chokes me up even to talk about it. The wreath placed there on the eighth anniversary was still there, although the flowers were fading at that point.

Lastly we were allowed into the Yankee dugout. The team was still in town. We had assumed they would be flying to Seattle for their next game that day but we were wrong. Even though it was an off day, some players were using the clubhouse, so we weren't allowed in there, much to our disappointment. The view from the dugout was neat. I took a picture of our seats to see how we looked to the players if they had looked in our direction.

We said our goodbyes to the stadium and headed to the car. We reviewed the way we were going to go, after deciding we were taking the slightly longer route home to avoid getting caught in the construction delays we had seen on our way onto the city. That turned out to be a great decision. We made it home without any problems. Even after stopping for a late lunch, it only took us about a half hour longer than it would have the other way.

As exhausted as I was when I got home, I listened to the Red Sox game in bed, hoping we would gain some more ground. The following day the announcement was made that the preliminary schedules for 2010 were out, so I had to start my plans for heading to Target Field in Minnesota, the Twins' new outdoor stadium opening in 2010! I was planning on seeing the Red Sox there, as that was one of just five states where I hadn't seen the Red Sox play (not counting the states without baseball teams, obviously). I marked my calendar to keep those dates available and waited until Twins tickets went on sale.

OFF AGAIN IN 2010

In the meantime, plans were made for another spring training trip to Florida. I wanted to get down to City of Palms Park in Fort Myers, the Red Sox spring training stadium, to see a game. I checked out flight availability against the games I could get tickets for. It didn't work out that I could get tickets to the game when the Mets were playing the Red Sox, so I got tickets for a weekend game against the Pirates. My mother-in-law and I talked about her going with me, but we concluded that she probably wouldn't like to go, as it was a long drive from her Florida home, plus it wasn't her team playing. So I got my ticket and booked my flight. After giving it some thought, Mom decided that she would like to go after all. But the game was sold out at that point. I went through a third-party seller to get two tickets together. I was able to sell my original ticket through the same third party and everything was set.

I arrived in Florida on a beautiful Wednesday afternoon, very happy to see Mom and Dad. We caught up while planning out my visit. The next couple of days, the forecast called for rain. We were okay with that as long as it was nice on Saturday for the game. Fort Myers was almost a three-hour drive away, so it would be a bad situation to go all that way and have the game cancelled. Fortunately, that didn't happen.

On Thursday, there were tornado warnings and one twister did touch down about sixteen miles from where we were. When the alarm went off, we headed for a concrete building nearby. I had never seen rain fall almost horizontally before that day, an eerie sight for certain. By Friday we were both getting a bit excited about the game. I had brought the books written by two of my favorite players, along with a Sharpie. I was hoping to get some autographs, so we made sure we got there plenty early.

We made our way to the park and were directed to a good place to park just a block away from the stadium. I was so excited! I knew that this was probably the closest I would ever get to some of my favorite players! This was to be the final year of the contracts for Jason Varitek, David Ortiz, and Mike Lowell so I didn't want to miss my chance to see them. I had on my Jason Varitek t-shirt. Have I mentioned that he is my favorite player? Okay, okay, I have mentioned it, but only a few dozen times. If I were lucky enough to get his autograph, it was going to go on the t-shirt. Any other signatures could go on the plain red visor I was wearing, or in the case of Ortiz or Lowell, in their books.

We made our way into the park and found what we thought were our seats. Our tickets said "row B," so we took our seats in the second row from the field. I made my way down to the gully near the field, just behind the fence on the edge of the warning track. I was grinning from ear to ear! Mom kept our seats warm while I was zooming around taking pictures and standing down in the gully watching the players. We kept a close eye on each other. At one point when I looked back at her, she was standing up and talking to the usher. It turned out we were in the wrong seats. The real row B was right in the gully where I was! We brought our stuff down and took our seats. We were in the section right next to the Red Sox dugout, in the second row back from the fence on the edge of the warning track!

I took my place by the fence again and was standing there when Mike Lowell walked by. He was about ten feet from me! Someone a few feet to my right said something to him, causing him to look in our direction.

So I said "Hi, Mikey."

He waved and said hello! The young couple next to me looked at me with their jaws dropped. I wish I had been holding his book at that point. Maybe I could have gotten his autograph! Who knows if he would have signed it anyway. Only a couple of the non-roster invitees signed any autographs that day, as far as I saw.

We grabbed some lunch while the Pirates took batting practice. It was a nice day to be at a ball game! There was an announcement that the players would be coming back out on the field to warm up in a little bit. I dug both books out of my bag and jumped back into my place by the fence. I wasn't going to miss another opportunity. Several of the players were introduced, and they commenced their sprints and stretching. David Ortiz was swinging a bat around when he looked in my direction. I yelled "Papi" and held up his book! He did a double take, and then smiled and pointed in my direction. He then did something that I will never forget as long as I live. He put his forefinger and thumb together, making the okay sign, touched it to his chest and pointed back at me! You could have pushed me over with a feather! The people around me were just as blown away. The young couple next to me said they were sure that was for me, and that they were going to go get books to bring with them next time, as they had never thought of that. The gentleman to my left commented that at least he was standing next to me when Papi did that. I didn't get any autographs that day, but I came away with a couple of very special memories.

When we took our seats for the game, the usher said we could go to the fence at the edge of the dugout to get pictures between innings as long as we got back to our seats when the action began again, so as not to block anyone's view. I did that a few times and did get some nice pictures of players, along with shots of other people's heads and elbows as they were trying to do the same thing.

The game started out slow and stayed that way through the first five scoreless innings. The bright spot was seeing Clay Buchholz pitch for only the second time. He did well in the three innings he pitched. The second pitcher for the Red Sox was their closer Jonathan Papelbon, who came in for the fourth inning. I have seen him several times before, and that day he pitched a perfect inning. The first run scored was a Pirate home run in the top of the sixth. The Red Sox didn't retaliate until the bottom of the seventh, when they posted three runs. Pittsburgh managed one more run in the top of the eighth. It was a nerve-wracking ninth, as the Pirates had two on and no outs. I said to Mom that it was time for a double play. The gentleman in front of me looked back and sort of rolled his eyes. But the next batter hit a pop fly to Mike Cameron, who was playing center field for the Sox for one out. Cameron threw it to second base in time to get the runner. Two outs! The second baseman, Tug Hurlett, fired to first base, but the throw was wide and Aaron Bates couldn't get it. So the runner headed to second. But Bates got to the ball quickly and fired it back to second, nailing the runner. Voilà, game-ending triple play!

The gentleman in front of me turned and said "Well, you got your double play and then some."

I smiled. The Red Sox won!

We made our way back to the car, my face hurting from grinning so much. It was great to have been to a ball game. Mom said she enjoyed it too, which I was really glad to hear. She was such a trooper while I stood at the fence and took pictures. Traffic cleared out quickly and we were on our way back home. We stopped for a little dinner and arrived home just after dark, very tired after our long day but in a good way.

On Sunday, Dad and I washed the car to get all the "Southern Florida" bugs off. On Monday, we went up to Silver Springs for the day, which was very interesting and enjoyable. We took glass-bottomed-boat rides, saw many animals (including bears), and took a tram ride through the wildlife part of the park. I flew home on Tuesday, grateful for a wonderful trip and time spent with two of my most favorite people.

HITTING THE TARGET

T wins tickets had gone on sale while I was in Florida, so I needed to see what I could get, as I was late to the party. The home opener was the day I wanted to go, but tickets were extremely expensive and only available through a third-party seller. I had to rethink the trip. As it turned out I could only get a couple of days off, I ended up getting tickets to the Wednesday game, which meant I would have to fly out after work on Tuesday, see the game on Wednesday, and head back early Thursday in order to work a half-day that day. I would be fine because the only other thing I really wanted to do on that trip was get to the Science Museum in St. Paul. That museum had five of the Dead Sea Scrolls on display. Going to see the exhibit was the plan for after the game on Wednesday.

As the calendar got closer to the trip to Minnesota, I kept an eye on the weather, which was looking iffy. But what could I do but go and hope for the best? Tuesday came, and off I went with only minor delays at the various airports. My schedule wasn't tight. I was just getting my rental car and heading directly to the hotel.

When I got in line to pick up the car I had reserved, the people ahead of me in both lines took what felt like forever, asking many questions, making phone calls, and digging out identification or other paperwork. I was trying not to get cranky, but I was tired after working a full day and traveling another several hours. Finally, I got up to the counter and then went to get the car. When I got to the booth, there was a nice young lady there who noticed my Red Sox jacket. She was a fan and told her story of going to opening day at Target Field just the day before! I was so excited for her and told her how that had been my goal, but at least I was going to the second game at the new stadium. We chatted a little while longer, and then I headed to the hotel in a better mood.

It was a very reasonably priced hotel that had a hot tub, spa, and a business center, which meant I could print out my boarding pass for the return trip to save me time at the airport. All of these things were a big plus.

The next morning, I had breakfast at the hotel and headed into Minneapolis. I found my parking spot easily thanks to my GPS, which I had brought along. I took a walk around the stadium. I have to say that the things they did in tribute to the Twins' history and players were very tasteful. They have a walk on one side of the stadium with many of their old players' posters on a fence. There are four statues along another side, and the gates are numbered in tribute to four of their greatest players, which I think is neat. The park certainly was a tribute to the town and its baseball history.

I got in line behind a nice young couple about 9:30 AM and asked if they knew when the gates opened. The woman said she thought the park would open an hour and a half before game time. That meant I had a fairly long wait facing me, because it was a 12:20 PM game. When the gentleman with her noticed that I was a Red Sox fan—my earrings, t-shirt and jacket gave it away—he said that he thought the gates opened at 2:30 PM for Red Sox fans. We chatted for a while. As it turned out, she went to college in Boston, so she wasn't completely against the Red Sox, which was nice. The gentleman behind me was busting on me and quoting facts about the two teams. He asked if I was old enough to remember when the Red Sox were bad. I told him I became a fan in 2002. He asked if I had been to Fenway. I confirmed I had, and he went on to tell me that his dream was to get to all the ballparks. I encouraged him and told him of my adventure. He said that he wanted to do it in one season, and that he could in a few years when he retired. Traveling to ballgames after retirement was certainly a goal that he and I shared.

When the gates opened, I walked around and made my way down to the lowest level to watch the Red Sox batting practice. I was pleased to be able to get so close. My seat, although three levels up, was right behind the dugout, looking directly down the first base line. Another Red Sox fan began chatting with me. Her boyfriend was a Twins fan, so we ribbed each other a bit. An usher overheard us commenting on the stadium, so he joined in. He was very nice. After I related many stories, he considered me a true fan. He offered to let me sit in that section if there were any empty seats after the game started. I thanked him and told him I would go get something to eat and wait an inning or two to be sure most everyone was there before I did that. But I was definitely interested and would stop back to check for empty seats.

After getting a hot dog (which was really good) and a drink, I watched the first inning from my ticketed seat. Sitting behind me was a nice man and his son. They were almost giddy to be at the new stadium, outside at a ball game in the middle of the day. I echoed their feelings and told them about the completion of my adventure. They began asking questions about it all. I was happy to be sharing baseball stories with more fellow fans! I did confess that I was happy the Twins won the season opener at their new stadium, even if it was against the Red Sox. But I didn't want to see them win again that day.

Pitching for the Red Sox was John Lackey. That would be the first time I had seen him pitch in person. I was squirming in my seat from excitement. Soon the touching pregame ceremony started. There was a serviceman there to raise the flag during the national anthem. There will be a similar ritual observed at every Twins home game in the 2010 season. The whole place erupted in applause, expressing much gratitude to our military. I was deeply touched and was soon fighting back tears.

The game got underway with a single from leadoff man Marco Scutaro, an acquisition the Sox made that offseason. Dustin Pedroia then hit a deep double, allowing the Red Sox to score the first run of the game. I was excited! Not knowing what to expect from Lackey, I got nervous when he walked the first batter he faced. Fortunately, a double play erased the walk, and a groundout ended the inning with the Red Sox still ahead.

I had been keeping an eye on the right field gate. I decided it was safe to go see if my usher buddy had an empty seat. Luck was on my side, and he pointed to a seat in the eighth row behind the Red Sox dugout! In front of me were a man and his young son, both Red Sox fans. Next to me was another man, also with his young son, both Twins fans. It was a great place to be!

The second inning had started by the time I made it there, so I quickly sat down and watched quietly. The man next to me began talking to me. It was the standard conversation, where we each were from, how we came to be at that game. Turns out he was an architect for the company that had built the stadium! I told him how impressed I was with it. It was his son's birthday. What a nice way for them to be celebrating. The score stayed the same until the bottom of the third inning, which was also when it started to rain. They had been announcing that a storm was coming. The architect pulled up the radar on his cell and showed me that the storm was headed directly for us. Most people got up and took cover, but I had a visor and a jacket on. I was going to stick it out as long as they were playing.

In the third inning, Big Papi drew a walk with two outs. It gave me hope that he was seeing the ball better. Unfortunately, he was thrown out trying to steal second to end the inning. In the bottom of the inning it started to rain, and Lackey had some trouble. He gave up two runs to tie the score. The man next to me had brought a large umbrella for himself and his son, so they stayed put too. That was good, because the son's favorite player, Joe Mauer, soon drove in the tying run. The Boston fans in front of me had an umbrella also, but the seats were raised enough that it didn't interfere with the line of sight of those behind, which was really cool. The man beside me had a poncho for his son and an extra one he offered to the kid in front of us, which I thought was very nice. He had come prepared with an extra umbrella and offered it to me—I gratefully accepted it. It continued to rain for more than three innings.

In the top of the fifth inning, Pedroia hit a home run to put Boston on top again. I was careful not to cheer too loudly and risk having my umbrella loan revoked. Some people came and went as the rain let up and then came down harder again.

In the top of the eighth inning, the Red Sox still up by one, with Youkilis on and no outs, Ortiz struck out for the second time. You could see the frustration on his face as he walked directly toward us to the dugout. The man next to me asked if I thought Ortiz was struggling because of Manny's departure. I told him I really didn't know. They were close friends, and in my opinion, one of the greatest one-two combos in baseball. Certainly it was harder to pitch around Ortiz with a big bat like Ramirez behind him. All I knew was that I felt really bad that David Ortiz was struggling, not just for the team, but for him. He was always an upbeat guy, but you could tell he was frustrated. The Red Sox added three more runs on a double, a walk, and another deep double. The scoring ended the conversation about Papi.

In the bottom of the inning I was excited to see young phenom Daniel Bard come in. He throws really hard. Control was something of an issue, but in Boston the year before, I had seen him leave batters wondering what happened, whizzing fastballs by them at 100 miles per hour. Unfortunately, the first Twin he faced, Michael Cuddyer, wasn't fooled. He hit a home run. Oops! The Red Sox were still up by three.

In the top of the ninth, Ortiz was up with two outs. I felt so bad for him. After two strikes, a foul ball, and one ball, he stepped out of the batter's box. I couldn't help myself.

I yelled, "We are behind you, Papi! We believe you can do it!" I have no idea if he heard me, but it made me feel better. And oh yeah, on the next pitch, Ortiz hit a double. One of the men sitting next to me on the other side said that was enough out of me! Tee hee! The Red Sox won 6–3.

After the game, I thanked the man for the umbrella loan and wished his son a happy rest of his birthday. I made sure to thank the nice usher again also. I took a long last look around the park before making my way back to the car. I programmed the address of the science museum into the GPS and slowly made my way through the heavy traffic to St. Paul.

Luck was with me still, because I found a parking spot right out in front. The spot was at a meter, but it was almost 5:00 PM, and the meters didn't have to be fed after 4:30. When I went to buy my ticket to get into the museum, the clerk noticed my Red Sox shirt and asked if I had been to the game.

I told him yes, but I added that I was also a Vikings fan, prompting him to comment what an odd combination that was. He confessed that he was a Red Sox fan and gave me a discount on admission. How cool is that?

The exhibit was wonderful. The museum did a great job on every aspect of it. Seeing the Dead Sea Scrolls was such a meaningful experience. Things continued to go according to plan. I headed back to the airport, dropped the car off, and was set to take the shuttle back to the hotel to eliminate having to deal with the rental in the morning, as my flight was quite early. The young lady that I had chatted with the day before was there again and asked how things went. I recapped the day with her, and we said our goodbyes wishing each other luck. The shuttle pulled in shortly after I made it to the pickup area. Once back at the hotel, I walked over to a nearby restaurant for some dinner and then changed into my bathing suit for some relaxation in the hot tub before turning in for a little sleep. At 4:00 AM, I was on the shuttle back to the airport, ready to make my way back home.

I had done it! In eight years, I made it to every major-league ballpark. What an adventure it had been. The different parks, the players, the games, the people, and the opportunity to see so much of this country have all been such wonderful blessings. I couldn't have done it without my family and friends who were there with me, either literally, via phone, or in thought and prayer during it all.

I am not done going to games, however. I have plans to go to Fenway in August, and there's also talk of a game or two at Citi Field. I would like to see an all-star game, a playoff game, maybe even an entire playoff series at some point, and of course a World Series game. There will be more new stadiums too, and there are a couple of states I haven't seen the Red Sox play in yet. When I retire I just might do it all over again—all in one season! Baseball, America's favorite pastime! See you at the game!